A HELLUVA LIFE IN

HOCKEY

A HELLUVA LIFE IN
HOCKEY

BRIAN McFARLANE

— A MEMOIR —

Published by ECW Press
665 Gerrard Street East
Toronto, Ontario, Canada M4M 1Y2
416-694-3348 / info@ecwpress.com

Editor for the Press: Michael Holmes
Cover design: David Drummond
Cover image: Brian McFarlane

LIBRARY AND ARCHIVES CANADA CATALOGUING IN PUBLICATION

Title: A helluva life in hockey : a memoir / Brian McFarlane.

Other titles: Hell of a life in hockey

Names: McFarlane, Brian, author.

Identifiers: Canadiana (print) 20210219017 | Canadiana (ebook) 20210219025

ISBN 978-1-77041-544-7 (softcover)
ISBN 978-1-77305-678-4 (ePub)
ISBN 978-1-77305-679-1 (PDF)
ISBN 978-1-77305-680-7 (Kindle)

Subjects: LCSH: McFarlane, Brian. | LCSH: Sportscasters—Canada—Biography. | LCSH: Hockey—Canada—Biography. | LCGFT: Autobiographies.

Classification: LCC GV742.42.M34 A3 2021 | DDC 070.4/49796962092—dc23

This book is funded in part by the Government of Canada. *Ce livre est financé en partie par le gouvernement du Canada.* We also acknowledge the support of the Government of Ontario through the Ontario Book Publishing Tax Credit, and through Ontario Creates.

PRINTED AND BOUND IN CANADA   PRINTING: FRIESENS   5   4   3   2   1

To Joan, my partner in this long parade:

Seventy years after we met, 65 since we married, she still has boundless energy. Seven years ago, at 81, she joined our daughter Brenda and her husband Kevin at Burning Man in the Nevada desert, where 60,000 people gather each year for a monster festival. She braved frigid nights and fierce dust storms, sleeping in a pup tent. But she rose each morning to teach fitness classes to "kids" in their 30s, 40s, and 50s. Not bad for a great-grandmother of three, one who can still drive a golf ball, has popped a hole-in-one, has garden plants taller than Jack who grows beanstalks, and who plans to live until she's at least 116.

In memoriam—Ted Lindsay:

Like millions of others, I miss you, Ted. We worked together on the NBC telecasts with Tim Ryan for three seasons in the '70s, and they were the best years of my career. Tim's, too. Such an honour for both of us to be in your company. You had a million friends, and you chose to become special friends to us. Lifelong friends. You led us on the ice, too, as captain of our NBC hockey team, which played media clubs all around the NHL before our *Game of the Week*. What a thrill it was to be your linemate and watch you toy with some of the eager media wannabes who scrambled over the boards to face you, desperately hoping to stop you—and failing. But they are able to brag, "I played against Ted Lindsay!"

Ted, you had all the class of a Jean Beliveau—a man you greatly admired. And for the kindness and generosity you displayed to one and all throughout your life, you are revered. Sometimes the path you followed to achieve hockey greatness was daunting, but you never faltered. You stood up to the vilification of greedy, self-interested managers and owners, because the game you loved needed change. You moved the game forward—at great personal cost. You are my hero and my friend. You are the only former NHLer I know who still had a locker in the Detroit dressing room when you were 90. It may be difficult for a restless rebel like yourself to grant my wish, but please: if you are in hockey heaven somewhere, be friends with old opponents, be forgiving of referees, managers, and owners who made you bristle. Ted, my friend, please rest in well-earned peace.

Table of Contents

INTRODUCTION

When I joined *Hockey Night in Canada* as a colour commentator in the mid-1960s—beginning a 25-year association with the famous telecast—the National Hockey League (NHL) was a six-team league. Everywhere across the land, Saturday night was reserved for watching hockey. The *Hockey Night in Canada* theme song was as familiar to most of us as the national anthem.

When I started working high up in the famous gondola at Maple Leaf Gardens, with legendary play-by-play men Foster and Bill Hewitt, colour television was a highly anticipated marvel a year or two in the future. Each NHL club carried just one goalie on its roster, which meant the seventh-best goalie in the world toiled in some minor league. A Hall of Famer like Johnny Bower spent 10 years away from the show. If a regular goalie was injured or ill, the team trainer or a junior netminder was hurriedly recruited to take his place. I found it farcical. A porous substitute in a single game could mean the difference between a team making the playoffs and losing out. It could bring a player a scoring title he didn't really deserve, because he'd collected four or five points against a floundering amateur. But nobody seemed to care. The team owners were frugal. Why hire a full-time backup if nobody complained, if nobody ordered them to? The Chicago Blackhawks once put a stuffed dummy in goal for practice sessions. How would the fans have reacted if they'd propped him up in goal in a real game? Or called for volunteers from the stands to don the pads in an emergency? That's an ideal segue to Moe Roberts's story. Roberts was a Blackhawks trainer in the early '50s, following a long pro career as a goalie, mostly in the American Hockey League (AHL), but with a handful of NHL starts.

Then on November 25, 1951, Roberts had to finish an NHL game for the injured Harry Lumley, the Blackhawks' starter. Although Roberts didn't yield a goal, his Hawks still fell to Detroit by a 5–2 score. At 45, Roberts, in his final game, became the oldest player ever to play in an NHL game, a record he held until broken by Gordie Howe in 1979 and also passed by Chris Chelios. He remains the oldest goaltender— and perhaps the most obscure goalie—to ply his trade in an NHL tilt. Johnny Bower, at 45, a few months younger than Roberts, is the oldest full-time goalie to play in the NHL.

No goalie masks, one or two helmets back then. Well, maybe one or two. No names on jerseys. No player agents. No million-dollar salaries. No Europeans or college players. I recall only one American, Tommy Williams from the U. S Olympic champs at Squaw Valley, California, in 1960. Olympians were all lowly amateurs—hardly worth a scout's time.

There was talk of NHL expansion, but it was mostly talk.

A proposal to start a new league, one to rival the NHL? Laughable. Who would dare? President Clarence Campbell pooh-poohed that idea. "It'll never happen," he stated.

The Russians? Forget the Russians.

Saturday night was hockey night. It was a tradition that began with Foster Hewitt on radio in the '30s. Then, from 1952 on, all across Canada families gathered in their living rooms to watch the games on television—on the CBC. But not all of the game. They were deprived of most—if not all—of the first period. Showing the full game might hurt ticket sales, the big shots wrongly figured.

Youngsters were seldom allowed to watch a complete game before being ushered off to bed. Many would sneak to the head of the stairwell and listen to Foster Hewitt's voice from there. Wives made trips to the kitchen, where they gossiped with other wives and prepared snacks for the male fans, who smoked their cigars and cigarettes—and drank their beer or their rye and gingers close to their black-and-white TV sets. Small sets, many with rabbit ears. You don't know about rabbit ears? Ask Grampa. No, better not. He's a kidder. He'll tell you they were real rabbit ears.

Most of my telecast teammates—Foster and Bill Hewitt, Jack Dennett, Ward Cornell, and Danny Gallivan—were already household names, as familiar as the powder-blue jackets we all began to wear on TV. Foster's three-star selections were as eagerly awaited as the national news.

Some viewers thought Murray Westgate, the actor who pitched commercials for Imperial Oil while wearing a cap and an Esso patch on his uniform, actually owned a service station.

Westgate and I were there when the NHL doubled in size in 1967, the year the Leafs won their last Stanley Cup. My wife and I crashed the victory party at Stafford Smythe's house. Drank from the Stanley Cup for the first and only time. I wonder how many others who were at the game that night are still around? Not many, I'll bet. If my wife and I live long enough, we may be the only two people who actually saw the Leafs win the Cup. Bill Hewitt and I called that game, not thinking for a second it would be the Leafs' final Cup win in the century. And they haven't come close in this century.

I was among a group of broadcasting pioneers in a televised world of skill on skates, bench-clearing brawls, one-man coaching staffs, iron-fisted owners, and a mere two playoff rounds to decide the Stanley Cup champions.

And if we thought ourselves to be the luckiest broadcasters in the world, to be part of the season-long frenzy and the exhilarating playoff action, it's because we were. We brought the drama, the excitement, the crunch of body contact, culminating in a rousing spectacle of skill on ice to a huge audience on the most popular show in the nation—*Hockey Night in Canada*.

CHAPTER 1

NOW AND THEN

In writing this rambling memoir, I came to one conclusion: Today's generation of NHLers are bigger, faster, and certainly far wealthier than those I knew in the past. They all appear to be well-dressed, well-behaved, and well-mannered. Awesomely rich and handsome. They have stunning girlfriends and/or wives. Did they all come out of some giant hockey cookie cutter? Looks like it.

Where are the characters, and I'll name a few: Tiger Williams, Derek Sanderson, Phil Esposito, Gump Worsley, Jim Dorey, Jim McKenny, Mike Walton, Pete Stemkowski, George Morrison, Pierre Larouche, goofy Eddie Shack, and so many others—all pranksters, good story-tellers, and in-demand by guys like me—for interviews? Sanderson became the highest paid athlete in the world, Morrison munched on a hot dog during an NHL game, Charlie Simmer married a *Playboy* centrefold. When I asked him where she was one day, he actually said, "Oh, she's out somewhere, probably taking her clothes off." Perhaps that's why the marriage didn't last.

I miss the guys who acted out, broke curfews, played hungover, got in scraps, jumped to the WHA, gave us memorable stories.

I miss Peter Puck, who's been a part of my life for almost 50 years. There may not be room in this book for Peter's story, even though it's a good one. In my NBC days, I became known as "Peter Puck's father."

The game officials? They are barely noticed today. Draw scant attention until they scramble to get out of a puck carrier's way. Get their mug on camera only when they announce a "goal" or "no-goal" situation. Today's fans should have seen Red Storey in his prime. Or Bill Friday, George Hayes, Kerry Fraser, Vern Buffey, or Paul Stewart. When linesman George Hayes was ordered to take an eye test, he said, "I don't need one. I can read the labels on the whiskey bottles from across the bar, no problem." They were colourful men, often as prominent in a game as the biggest stars. I was annoyed when the league stripped the names off their backs to lower their profiles.

In the broadcast booth or the studio, there was Howie "Golly Gee" Meeker and Dick "Bedclothes" Beddoes, Red Fisher in Montreal, all so opinionated and controversial they kept producers and sponsors in a state of nervous fits. A few of us got fired—Scott Young was one, and I was another—for making comments that caused owners or sponsors to snarl in anger and reach for the phone. "Get rid of that dickhead." Even popular host Dave Hodge got the heave-ho after a flip of a pencil.

Don Cherry came along, and people said he'd get the axe, too. And he almost did before he even settled in. I worked an early *Coach's Corner* with him, and he talked of how, with Colorado, he almost throttled his defenceman Mike McEwen. "Yeah, I grabbed him by the throat. Gave him a shake. The guy wouldn't listen. I said, 'Listen, you little SOB. You're a selfish guy and you're costing us points.' I pushed him down on the bench."

Nobody ever talked like that on the intermission interviews. I said later, "Grapes, isn't what you did to McEwen close to common assault?"

He said, "I dunno. Maybe. Anyway, Rene Robert, my captain, came up to me after and said, 'You know, Don, when you had him by the throat, why didn't you squeeze a little harder?'"

Back then, the CBC people complained that Cherry didn't speak proper English. "Better let him go."

Hockey Night in Canada's Ralph Mellanby fired back. "If Cherry goes, I go." And Grapes stayed.

When he was still going strong into his 80s, I thought he might retire. His voice was going. The hockey world was no longer a "Rock 'em Sock 'em" society. It was changing, and I'd heard his bosses at Sportsnet were waiting to find an excuse to push Grapes aside. They'd dumped a number of high-salaried guys, and Grapes was in the million-a-year bracket. Then, on November 12, 2019—he was gone.

Turfed after his "you people" rant on *Coach's Corner*, gone for singling out new immigrants for not wearing poppies to honour Canada's veterans and dead soldiers.

Ron MacLean, sitting next to him, didn't catch the words "you people" or he might have asked Cherry to rephrase his rant and say "everybody" instead of "you people."

While the complaints started pouring in, MacLean nodded and gave his partner a thumbs-up. MacLean apologized on air soon after. Cherry did not. He said he meant every word.

Cherry was widely criticized, but one finger pointer, coach Bill Peters of the Calgary Flames, soon regretted it. He approved of Grapes's dismissal and talked about hockey standing for diversity. "I saw Cherry," Peters said. "Our country is based on inclusion. We have a very diverse country. I know, in the hockey community, we talk about 'hockey is for everybody.' And that's how we are in the country of Canada, too."

Hockey for everybody, Bill? Black players, too? Really? You really want to take the high road?

A few days after Cherry was sidelined, so was Peters. And for a better reason.

Player Akim Aliu says Peters used racial slurs while addressing the then-20-year-old rookie winger in the locker room of an AHL club a decade ago. Aliu turned up the music in the room, and Peters heard an earful. "Coach walked in before a morning skate and said, 'Hey, Akim. I'm sick of you playing that n— s—.'"

Former Hurricanes forward Michal Jordan described playing for Peters as "an experience with the worst coach ever by far." He went on to describe how Peters would kick and punch him and other players in the head during a game.

Current Canes head coach Rod Brind'Amour corroborated those claims. Brind'Amour said both of the incidents alleged by Jordan "for sure happened."

Peters found another coaching job rather quickly—but in Russia.

Peters essentially admitted that Aliu's allegations were true when he resigned as head coach of the Flames and apologized for the "offensive language [he] used in a professional setting a decade ago." He said the racial slurs he used were "made in a moment of frustration and do not reflect [his] personal values."

Maybe not. But Aliu had every right to out him. Grapes uttered a few words that would cost him a million-dollar income. He'd created a hockey world all his own, moving from coach of the year in Boston to a Colorado castoff to *Coach's Corner* and to Canada's Top 10 list. Even he must look in the mirror from time to time and say, "Can you believe this friggin' life I've led? The guys I worked jackhammer jobs with in Rochester, New York, must be stunned with my success, wondering how in the hell that ever happened." I can say this about Grapes: he was always good to me. He gets a full chapter later.

Then there are the team owners. They were always in the news back then. Some of them powerful, greedy men who kept players fearful of unemployment, who made certain the league president knew his place, that he worked for them. They treated Ted Lindsay and his supporters like lepers. With expansion came a few owners who broke the rules and served jail time. The NHL can't be proud of the fact that it leads all pro sports leagues in owners who became convicted felons.

And the players of the era must admit they weren't paying attention when Al Eagleson, the union leader they fully trusted and supported, stole from them and landed behind bars for a few months. Bobby Clarke and Bob Pulford support him still. Lindsay told me, "The guy should have served 18 years."

I'm sure I lived through—and somehow survived—the most turbulent era in the history of the NHL.

I have been involved in hockey for most of my 90 years and have been a player, coach, referee, chronicler, and broadcaster of the game as it evolved over most of the past century. The NHL itself, which began with three of four teams finishing the 1917–18 season, is only slightly older than I am.

Permit me to make this a casual walk back in time, and I'll begin on a pleasant morning outdoors in Naples, Florida, my winter home for the past 20 years.

An early morning riser, I am sitting outside my favourite coffee shop in Naples—the oddly named Fit and Fuel—and where the word "favorite" is Americanized—the vowel "u" a healthy scratch.

As dawn breaks, the cyclists straggle in for coffee and a pee. They are in for a surprise. Renovations are underway in the coffee shop, and both restrooms are closed. Good luck to the bloated bladder bunch.

They ignore me as they pass, their clacky shoes and skin-tight garb and odd head gear so unlike the hockey uniforms I'm familiar with. Uniforms I miss—even the odour—Oops! I mean "odor"—since I quit playing for the Snowbirds Old-timers in nearby Fort Myers six years ago. Then 84, old knee injuries and half a dozen concussions convinced me to stagger away. I often played on a line with two wealthy guys. One sold his company for $56 million, the other for a reported $400 million. I never told those two my net worth. Was afraid it would make them jealous. All of the Snowbirds—a mix of Canadians, Americans, and a couple of Europeans—are over 65. A few are in their 80s. I was the senior member, and when I ordered my Snowbirds jersey a dozen years ago, it came with the *C* stitched on the front—a symbol of respect from my mates. I was proud to wear the *C* and proud that I could still match my age with points over a season of 40 games. What you do— well, what I did—was keep track of goals and assists in my head—no cheating—and jot the number down when you get home. It may sound silly, especially at 84, but it provides incentive—even for an old fart on his last legs, walking pretty well. My hockey gear is still in my bag . . .

Then one day when I pulled my skates from my bag, they pleaded with me, "Why not put us back, old fellow. Let's go home."

I miss the old guys. I gave some of them their nicknames. Winnipeg Danny, the fittest of the group, walked out of the dressing room one day and dropped dead in the corridor. Luckily, two Fort Myers firemen were playing with us that morning and rushed out to bring Danny back to life. He was back skating with us after a few months of recovery—but no longer the fleetest on the ice.

There was jokester Danny Madgett from Calgary. Dead now, but well remembered. When a player was knocked down and tried to stagger to his feet, Madgett shouted from the bench, "Don't answer that phone!"

And Danny Sandford, who played with Bobby Orr in junior hockey in Oshawa, Ontario. Still slick with a stick. Sandford and I are in the Whitby Hall of Fame together.

And Rolf Nilsen from Norway, a multi-millionaire in the ship doors business. He bought the Zamboni for the rink we play in. And bought orange cones, which he placed on the ice for us to skate around.

One old-timer snorted, "You kidding, Rolf? Get rid of those friggin' cones. We're too old for that shit."

Nilsen desperately wanted his teenaged son Hakon to be an NHLer—even hiring a member of the pro Everblades of the ECHL to tutor him. The two spent hours together on ice time Nilsen rented—for his kid. Then, in a sudden move, he bought the Junior A Flint, Michigan, franchise—the Firebirds—and the Flint arena, spending millions and moving north, so Hakon could play at a higher level.

But in his first season, after a win over Oshawa—yeah, after a win!—Nilsen axed his coaching staff. Hakon was not getting enough ice time.

The players didn't take it well.

Neither did Hakon.

The morning after coaches John Gruden and Dave Karpa were fired, the entire Firebirds roster (including Hakon) turned in their jerseys and quit the team.

The following day, after the story received international attention, Nilsen rehired the coaches, handing each one a new three-year contract.

In Florida, we chuckled. Someone said, "I wonder if Rolf handed them his traffic cones as well."

I said, "If not, I know some cyclists who might enjoy riding around them."

But, later still, another surprise. Nilsen fired his coaches a second time, and the players were forced to run their own practices.

That's when Dave Branch, head of the Ontario Hockey League (OHL), stepped in and said, "Enough of this bull."

Branch suspended Nilsen for five years and placed his team under the direction of a man he trusted—Joe Birch. How appropriate. Birch and Branch, working together.

But that's not all.

In addition to the five-year suspension, the Firebirds forfeited a first-round draft pick, and Nilsen was fined $250,000 by the OHL.

Poor Rolf. He should have stuck with the Snowbirds, even though we'd labelled him "a fast skater who has no idea where he's going."

I can always say I skated with a guy who tried to buy his son an NHL career and failed miserably in the attempt.

He fit in with us. Sort of. And he couldn't fire us.

When I see Nilsen again, I'll ask him: "Was it worth the millions of dollars to buy the team in the first place? Only to be denied running it? Was it worth all the bad press? Then again, when you are Rolf Nilsen, and money is not an issue, do you even care?"

And Hakon? His NHL hopes have been crushed. Last I heard, he was playing in Norway. He should have taken the college hockey route. He was a bright kid.

CHAPTER 2

SKATING WITH SNOWBIRDS

From time to time, we Snowbirds were joined by former NHLers. Former Bruin Don Awrey was one of our best players, but clutch and grab is still one of his fortes. The guy played in close to one thousand NHL games and was a member of Team Canada '72. I liked Awrey, but I didn't like dressing next to him. "Why you using that coloured tape?" he'd ask. "Why no shoulder pads? Is that a wooden stick?" I always felt I was under close scrutiny. Besides, and he won't remember this, a dozen years ago, playing in a Sunday night league of hockey nobodies in the five-thousand-seat Florida Everblades arena down the road, he cross-checked me into our goalie during a game. Really smashed into me. The guys on our bench howled in outrage. "Dirty hit, Awrey!"

I was shaken up, but not hurt. I saw Awrey skate over to our bench, drop his gloves, and challenge any or all of my mates to a fight.

Fight? In an old men's league? They all started laughing at him. Then Awrey began to laugh. I didn't see him again until he joined our group in Fort Myers years later.

We got along. He gave me a good interview one day at lunch. All about the Bruins and Bobby Orr. And about his own career. How he felt cheated—justifiably, I thought—because he had his name on two Stanley Cups, but not three. He played all of the regular season games with Montreal in 1975–76, but was injured and missed the playoffs. Hence, no Stanley Cup recognition.

"Lots of players have two rings, but not many have three," he told me. "I've been trying for years to get credit for a third."

And, finally, he did.

I was one of several who wrote to the NHL supporting Awrey's case. His name was finally added to the Canadiens' '76 Cup roster. "They couldn't affix my name to the Cup," he told me, "But it's there in the records."

In his NHL days, according to one source, he was a mean and miserable SOB, not afraid to take on John Ferguson in some on-ice scraps. You take on Fergie and you risk hearing bells in your head for the rest of your life.

Awrey was often paired with the legendary Bobby Orr. How lucky is that? As a "stay-at-homer," he allowed Orr to soar into the offensive zone and give goalies fits. Which he did, better than anybody. Stay-at-homers like Awrey seldom got the recognition they deserve. But, hey, if you get selected for Team Canada '72, you must have a lot on the ball.

Early in 2020, I went to a Florida Everblades game with some old-timers. We were guests of team owner Craig Brush, who played at Cornell. And Awrey did something very touching. He saw that I was limping and using a cane. So, he took me by the arm and led me to the elevator. Guided me into the area where the old-timers were gathered. Found a place for me to watch the game. I felt old but grateful and decided Awrey was a fine, considerate fellow after all. I was deeply touched. One old hockey guy helping another.

Steve Jensen, a former Minnesota North Star who scored 113 goals in 438 NHL games, was a force when he showed up. No age restrictions back then. Jensen was born in 1955, the year I graduated from university. He was a big man who would bowl you over if you got in his way. Doug Gammie's adult daughter played with us one day, and Jensen came at her like a Sherman tank. Knocked her flat. But she was game. Got up and laughed at him. A lot of grit there. "You go, girl," as they say. Bob Murdoch, a former Hab, was a popular addition. He told me about his first training camp with the Canadiens, and how the team scrimmaged right off the bat. How, on his first shift, he nudged John Ferguson. The ending to that story appears later in this book. And it caused Murdoch to seriously consider a teaching career over a high-paying hockey job.

But Murdoch stuck it out, played 12 seasons in the NHL and coached another 10 years, winning coach of the year honours with Winnipeg one season. He was fun to play with. A newcomer—an amateur—joined us one year, a guy from Toronto named Paul. He dressed across from me, and I said, "Paul, welcome to the Snowbirds."

He walked across the room and said, "I used to hate you on TV."

His comment surprised me. Rookies—even in their 60s or 70s—are not usually that outspoken. What's more, I knew many viewers didn't like me much on TV. But hate me? I didn't think anybody ever hated me. So, I was upset.

On the ice, he played on my wing. One pass from him was 10 feet behind me. Another was 20 feet ahead of me. I skated over to him and said, "Paul, those were the two worst fucking passes I've ever seen."

Tit for tat. In time, we got to be friends.

He said, "I was surprised you used the F-bomb."

"It's my only character flaw," I told him.

I think of these men as my coffee grows cold at the Fit and Fuel. Unlike my Snowbird pals, these cyclists puzzle me. They are a snooty bunch. Getting a "good morning" out of any of them is like getting the Sphinx to burp or break wind.

One morning I vow to show up wearing a star-spangled, logo-covered shirt and tight black shorts and the clacky shoes. I'll pedal up to them on my old Schwinn Hornet with the huge worn tires and the basket in front. Yeah, and maybe with hockey cards stuck in the spokes— a Canadian tradition when I was young. Tell them I want to join them on their daily 10-mile ride. But I'd stipulate we go past Costco, so I can fill my basket and take time for lunch. "Guys, you gotta try Costco's $1.50 hot dog and drink deal." See how they react.

Maybe I won't want to hear what they have to say. But "good morning" would be nice.

I could have regaled them with Harold Ballard and Don Cherry stories. But why even dwell on it? They wouldn't know those names. They wouldn't know a hockey puck from a peanut.

Besides, with global warming coming on fast, they'll soon be trading in their fancy bikes for rowboats. We'll all be fleeing this beautiful place when the ocean waters rise six feet. But that's a few years away, I hope. Still, I'm thinking I should buy some rubber boots. Maybe a canoe.

It's then my memory—still functioning, for the most part—is jogged. In fact, I'm often startled at my solid memory. And startled by the loss of it, too. Names like Mosienko and Bodnar cross my mind.

Anyone remember those names?

Minutes later, I'm joined by my close pal Bob Posch, the former popular cruise ship entertainer, and I tell him about Bill Mosienko's three fastest goals in 21 seconds in the NHL in 1952—a long-standing record. Posch is a Snowbird—a hockey guy from Michigan—and he says he likes my hockey monologues, even though he yawns a lot when I tell them.

"Bob, I was at an event in Nova Scotia 40 or 45 years ago, and a well-known provincial politician was there, a hockey fan. I was standing next to Gus Bodnar, my old-timer teammate, when the politician says, 'Gus, I'll never forget the game when you set a record for scoring the three fastest goals. It was against the Rangers. You were with the Hawks.'"

"Sir," I say, "Gus didn't score the three fastest goals. But he assisted on all three."

"Oh, that's right." he says.

I carry on (knowing he doesn't recognize me or know my name), "I wonder if you recall the goalie Mosienko scored those goals against."

"Well, it had to be Charlie Rayner," he says. "The Rangers used Charlie in every game back then." He gives me a look. *Who the hell is this guy?*

"Not that day, sir," I tell him. "Rayner was injured, so a 20-year-old rookie, Lorne Anderson, was in goal. Anderson was from Renfrew, Ontario. It was his last of three NHL starts."

"No wonder I don't recall," the man said, "It was such a long time ago."

"Yep. It was March 23, 1952. Final game of the season."

Now he gives me a longer look. It said, *Why doesn't this smartass shut up and bugger off?*

But I'm having fun. The details of that game were fresh in my mind.

"Sir, do you remember the third member of that big line Gus centred?"

He struggles for an answer. "Uh, no, you've got me there."

"It was George Gee. Shortest name in hockey back then. What a shame that so few people saw Mosey and Gus set that record."

"Oh, why was that?"

"Sir, the fans stayed away. The Rangers and the Hawks were the NHL doormats. Only about 2,500 showed up at Madison Square Garden."

Gus Bodnar gets a word in: "Geez, Brian, I don't remember any of that."

Bob Posch laughs. "How come you knew all the facts about that game back then—decades ago?"

"Because I'd met Mosienko in Winnipeg a few days earlier, I'd researched that game. I even knew why Mosienko was able to have his photo taken holding all three pucks he scored with. He was hoping to have a 30-goal season and he had 28 or 29. When he scored the first of his three, he jumped in the Ranger net and snared the puck. He did the same thing after the other two goals."

"Wait a minute," says Posch. "You're telling me you and this politician guy talked 40 or 45 years ago. You knew all those facts then. How come you still recall them today—in 2018?"

"That's a great question, but I have no answer. It baffles me. I have memory lapses now. My nephew Pat Perez, the musician, tours with Neil Sedaka, but I can't seem to remember Neil Sedaka's name from one day to the next. Or Stevie Wonder's. But I can tell you a lot about Mosienko's record—even the name of the Ranger defenceman he went around three times in 21 seconds—Hy Buller. I'm a dummy with music names, but I can name the player who scored a Stanley Cup goal in a game in Winnipeg in 1902—Chummy Hill of the Toronto Wellingtons. The puck split in two and when Chummy scored with half of it, the referee—whose name was McFarlane—awarded him the goal."

"But you can't remember names like Neil Sedaka?"

"True. But, Bob, let's not venture too far down Memory Lane. There are too many potholes along the way. Besides, you're an entertainer, and I haven't forgotten *your* name—not yet."

"I'll ask you tomorrow," he answers. "By the way, did you have any other questions that stumped the guy in Nova Scotia?"

"Well, I was tempted to ask him if Mosienko scored his three goals in 21 seconds, then how many seconds did it take for Bodnar to earn the three fastest assists?"

"That might have stumped him," Posch says, laughing. "Anything else you wanted to ask him?"

"Yeah—if it were 20 years later. In 1998, he faced trial on eight charges including rape, attempted rape, and forcible confinement, for crimes allegedly committed in 1956 and 1969 against victims aged 14 and 18 at the time. A few days before Christmas in 1998, he was acquitted on all eight charges by a jury."

"Wow!" says Posch. "He must have taken a lot of deep breaths that day."

How and why, I wonder, *did all this happen? How did I come to be here in this place—beautiful, balmy Naples in my 87th year—a slight pain in my groin that I suspect may be cancer, two stents, a pacemaker, a few concussions, three knee operations, another hip replacement completed, four shots of insulin daily, and now this diagnosis of spinal stenosis and a tremor in my left hand which influences my new career—painting in acrylics (I'm a lefty)?*

This book follows my path and my passion for the game of hockey from the beginning to the present, with candid observations on the people who have sparkled and sputtered on the ice, in the front offices and in the broadcast booth. And if I tell a story or two I've told before in other books, I'll claim I simply don't remember that.

And if big-name ex-players like Phil Esposito, Bobby Hull, and Bob Pulford want to kick me in the ass after reading what I write about them, I suggest they kick hard, because I may have my Depends on. And I'm betting they can't kick hard, because now they're all old crocks like me, just trying to get through each day without someone shouting, "Put the toilet seat down!" I'm calling this book, which has a few F-bombs sprinkled through it, *A Helluva Life in Hockey*. Because that's what it's been for me.

CHAPTER 3

GONE FROM THE GONDOLA

It's been more than 30 years since I was bounced from *Hockey Night in Canada*. I believe "bounced" is the right word. "Ousted," "canned," "dismissed," and "rejected" are others. I wasn't fired, just not rehired, which is pretty much the same thing. All because some greenhorn 29-year-old sports director at the CBC decided anyone over 40 should be tossed from the broadcast booth, particularly one who occasionally said things on air that annoyed and sometimes antagonized viewers—especially the crusty owner of the Leafs at the time—Harold Ballard. Or, in earlier days, may have exasperated Leafs manager-coach Punch Imlach. May even have annoyed Punch's wife, Dodo Imlach, who admitted she wanted to throw a shoe through her TV set one night after hearing something she felt reflected negatively on her husband. Was the shoe aimed at me? Don't know. Don't care. But probably.

For the past three decades, only bombastic Don Cherry got away with saying things on *Coach's Corner* that others would be banished for—to a Gulag, perhaps. Or, because Canada has no Gulags, plopped down on a melting Arctic ice floe (due to global warming)—with no life jacket or even a paddle. I don't recall ever meeting the CBC whiz kid who wanted me gone. But he was so young there were wet spots behind his ears.

Recommending my dismissal in 1990 may have been his sole contribution to televised hockey because six months later he, too, was gone. He resigned his post to go work for Dick Clark in Hollywood. Was never heard of again. Guess I was in the wrong place at the wrong time.

I like ambition in young people, but only the CBC would hire a pup to manage such a huge operation as TV network sports.

"His name was Smith and he was ambitious, all right," one of his associates told me recently. "All for himself. You were either with him or against him. No in-between."

I wasn't with him or against him. I never knew him.

Smith wasn't the only CBC sports director who found me annoying. In Montreal, at the Forum one Saturday night, my boss, Ted Hough, head of *Hockey Night in Canada*, came wandering into the studio with Smith's predecessor, the head of CBC sports, in tow. Another guy I never got to know. It was obvious they'd been drinking and their invasion of the studio was not appreciated. They had no business in there.

It was a few seconds before air time, and as I took my place for my on-camera opening, the CBC guy lurched toward me. "McFarlane," he barked. "Don't fuck up here like you did in Toronto!"

I glared at him. Wanted to shout, "Get this dickhead out of here!"

Who was this drunk to embarrass me in front of the crew just seconds before I went on camera to greet a nationwide audience? His slurred comment was inexcusable.

This was the guy who once said of me, "McFarlane? I suppose he's a good utility announcer."

I wanted to tell the CBC guy he was a good utility sports director, that he was being a dickhead, but worried a mic might be open. Instead, I took a deep breath, collected myself, and flashed a welcoming smile when the red light flashed.

"From the Montreal Forum, it's *Hockey Night in Canada*."

And another hockey telecast was underway. One of hundreds.

See how easy it is to be on TV? With millions watching.

For more than 25 years, I had the pleasure and privilege of witnessing and helping describe to millions of viewers hundreds of NHL games, most of them played in two of the most famous buildings in the nation: Maple Leaf Gardens and the Montreal Forum. In my era, games from the Forum were often breathtaking. Games from the Gardens were often dreary by comparison, most of them after '67—those dreadful Ballard years. And when the home team loses, nobody is happy but the visitors.

I had the opportunity to interview all of the great stars and builders of the game—from 90-year-old Cyclone Taylor (the oldest skater ever on a hockey telecast), who skated with me on a memorable NBC telecast, to Aurel Joliat, Joe Malone, Ace Bailey, Conn Smythe, Leo Dandurand, Frank Selke Sr., the Conachers, the Patricks (Muzz and Lynn), to 12-year-old Wayne Gretzky, 12-year-old Glen Hanlon, and 17-year-olds like Bryan Trottier and Steve Yzerman. And all those Sutter kids.

I joined *Hockey Night in Canada* in 1965, on the eve of NHL expansion and an end to the Original Six era. It was black-and-white TV back then—colour would come a year later. As well as so many other innovations. It was a turbulent but fascinating time. The Leafs would soon be en route to another Stanley Cup (their fourth in the decade), before plummeting toward the cellar, and Bobby Orr, at the end of a dazzling junior career in Oshawa, was about to turn pro with the tail end Boston Bruins. Orr, with a yappy young lawyer named Eagleson as his agent, shamelessly screwing him all the way, would soon turn the NHL on its ear.

When I meet fans today who witnessed games between those original half-dozen teams—Toronto, Montreal, Detroit, Chicago, Boston, and New York—most of them insist that those rivalries were the most bitter and most thrilling they ever saw. Old friend Ted Lindsay, who passed away in March 2019 at 93, as a former player, coach, manager, broadcaster, and fan, felt that way. "Oh, they were fierce rivalries," he told me. "There's nothing like them today. When I was with the Red Wings, we hated teams like the Leafs and the Canadiens. And they hated us."

Lindsay was one of my idols. At 93, there was still a small locker in a corner of the Red Wings' dressing room with his name on it. Many fans (outside Detroit) cursed him when he played. But he had the guts—along with Doug Harvey—to start a player's association (not a union) seeking a few perks for the players, knowing the owners would react like he'd dumped hot oil on them. Jack Adams, Lindsay's boss, was scorched. He railed against Lindsay, went through the Wings' dressing room, asking each player what he thought—intimidating most. Gordie Howe hesitated, sat on the fence. "I just want to play hockey, Mr. Adams." Not much support there, Ted. But that was Howe—non-confrontational.

Then Adams pulled a sneaky one. Showed reporters a fake contract that indicated Lindsay was earning 25 grand per season. His actual salary was $13,000.

"See how greedy the man is," sneered Adams. "All for himself."

Adams's personal vendetta against two of the best players in the game—Lindsay and goalie Glenn Hall—cost Detroit fans dearly. The Red Wings—a great team—started a downward slide.

I don't like the name Jack Adams on the NHL coach of the year trophy. Perhaps they should change it to the Scotty Bowman Award.

Lindsay and goalie Glenn Hall were traded to bottom-place Chicago. Chicago couldn't believe their good fortune. Both newcomers at the peak of their game, both future Hall of Famers—for three or four so-so players. I call it the worst trade in NHL history.

The first time Lindsay played back in Detroit, he cracked Gordie Howe, his long-time linemate, over the head. Howe said, "I was mad. I laid him out with a check, and when he got to his feet, I snarled, 'Is that the way you want to play?' He smiled and said, 'No, not if it means breaking up a friendship.'"

Lindsay had helped the Red Wings win seven consecutive NHL championships and four Stanley Cups. A Hall of Famer in 1966, who voiced his displeasure when his family was not invited to the induction. Surely, his wife was invited. Not so, not then.

He was the first NHL player to play one thousand games, a First Team All-Star eight times, and a participant in 11 All-Star Games.

On second thought, Detroit's trade with Chicago wasn't the worst ever. The Blackhawks trading Phil Esposito, Ken Hodge, and Fred

Stanfield to Boston for Gilles Marotte, Pit Martin, and goalie Jack Norris left a mess of egg yolk over the faces of Hawks' management. It was the absolute worst deal I can remember.

The trade took place a few weeks before six new teams joined the NHL in June 1967. The Hawks wanted to get rid of some of their "floaters" and chuckled when Bruins GM Milt Schmidt showed interest.

The Bruins had missed the playoffs since the 1958–59 season, a total of eight years. Six times during that span they finished last. They were the Basement Bruins.

Before the May 15 deadline in 1967, the Bruins acquired Fast Eddie Shack from the Leafs for centreman Murray Oliver, a replacement for Red Kelly who was done. The Leafs got a Dave Keon look-alike in Oliver—sort of. They sent the Bruins a colourful clown.

Shack wasn't in Boston long before he critiqued the owner's hats. "They're real crappy, you know. I'll sell you some better ones. Biltmores from Guelph. I sold Imlach some."

The owner was pissed. Shack soon found himself traded to Los Angeles—as far away from Boston as possible.

The Bruins followed up with the blockbuster deal that would bring raw talent to the moribund franchise. The Bruins reluctantly surrendered 22-year-old defenceman Gilles Marotte—a so-called hard rock who'd been playing with rookie sensation Bobby Orr. But Marotte, who looked tough, was only five-foot-eight—maybe five-foot-nine—and would be no more than a decent defender on any of the six pro clubs he would play for. Also going to Chicago was centre Pit Martin and minor league goalkeeper Jack Norris.

Gaining lanky centre Phil Esposito was the key for new Boston GM Milt Schmidt. "Espo" was the seventh-highest scorer in the NHL in 1966–67. The Hawks were troubled by his personality. He was flippant and opinionated. Maybe a tad slow and another tad soft. "No big loss," said the Hawks' brass. Accompanying Esposito to Boston were young forwards Fred Stanfield and Ken Hodge. Both would have been left available to the six new expansion teams. So, let 'em go. But if the Bruins are willing to take them—why not?

And we get Marotte? Oh, boy. We've really pulled a fast one on Milty and the Bruins. We suckered him. Maybe next time we should con him into giving us Orr.

Esposito exploded into the number one centre the Bruins had long been seeking and finished second in scoring to Stan Mikita in his first season as a Bruin.

He would spend eight seasons with Boston, winning two Stanley Cups in the process. (It should have been more, but the Bruins loved to party.) He led the league in goals six times, including a record 76 in 1970–71. He was the scoring champion five times. He played brilliantly for Team Canada against the Soviets in '72. He, Hodge, and Wayne Cashman formed the most feared attacking line of the late 1960s and 1970s.

Stanfield enjoyed six productive seasons with the Bruins, mainly as the second-line centre. He was a superb penalty killer and valued power-play specialist who never scored less than 20 goals a season as a Bruin.

Boston became a powerhouse, making the playoffs in 29 consecutive seasons. Such amazing success would never have taken place had not new GM Schmidt seen an opportunity, gambled on the results, and brought in the three former Blackhawks.

Many of the stars of that era, Hall of Famers like Lindsay, Hall, George Armstrong, and Johnny Bower, conceded that today's players are bigger, faster, and stronger. They are enormously better paid. Back then, the average salary might be $10,000. Today, it's close to $3 million. And climbing every minute.

"Wait a minute. They are not faster," the late Hall of Famer Red Kelly told me before he left us. "They are better equipped and better coached. And they have expensive sticks that shoot bullets. But they are no faster than we were."

I almost agree. If we could match the lap times of Mike Gartner or Yvan Cournoyer against the speedsters in today's game, I think the results would be very close.

How many defencemen in today's game would outskate Bobby Orr or Paul Coffey?

Still, I must concede that today's players collectively appear to be a shade faster than the skaters who preceded them. Better skates, lighter equipment, and a superior fitness level lead to astonishing fleetness.

But speed, while important, isn't necessarily a key factor in a player's success. High-speed skating often means snap decisions to pass or to shoot the puck without the certainty it will reach the intended target.

The modern-day NHLer is not tougher, either. None of today's ruffians is tougher or more talented than big Gordie Howe or more explosive than John Ferguson. None more rugged than Milt Schmidt, more dynamic than Rocket Richard, Mario Lemieux, Guy Lafleur, or Bobby Hull.

They are not even more popular, despite the huge amount of TV time they get, the internet exposure, the swarms of media people encircling them. Name me a dozen of today's stars who are more popular than Bobby Orr, Wayne Gretzky, Bobby Hull, Gordie Howe, Jean Beliveau, Guy Lafleur, Dave Keon, Eddie Shack, or Johnny Bower. They were icons in my era.

I do agree the modern players shoot harder. All of them have wondrous wrist shots and slapshots, thanks to composite sticks and modern gloves. Sid the Kid can't be the only one who perfected his shooting by drilling pucks into the family dryer. Passes skim the ice incredibly fast. That's why three-on-three play in overtime sometimes takes your breath away.

Shot speed has always been controversial.

Montreal's big shooter, Shea Weber, once tried to match Bobby Hull's shooting prowess using a retro wooden stick. Weber had his slapshot timed at 108.5 mph at the NHL All-Star Game a few years ago. But when he wore leather gloves and shot with an outdated wooden stick, the fastest he could manage was 91 mph. When he switched back to his current composite stick, his shot jumped to 103 mph.

When Bobby Hull was at his peak in the 1960s, it was reported his slapshot was timed at 118.3 mph. But that figure is suspect. How was

Hull's shot actually measured? Hull fans said he had the hardest slapshot of his era. Hull himself credited brother Dennis with having an even harder shot. One of Hull's Chicago teammates told me that Hull's wife, Joanne, showed up at a practice one day and started yapping at Hull from rinkside. Hull tried to scare her by shooting a puck off the glass close by. When she didn't flinch, he told Dennis, "You fire one at her. You shoot harder than I do." I simply can't believe that Bobby Hull could have approached 120 mph using a wooden stick in the 1960s. Impossible.

One of his shots at Maple Leaf Gardens was memorable. He drilled one over the glass in warm-ups, and it struck Leaf owner Harold Ballard—sitting in his bunker—right between the eyes. Ballard went off for repairs and encountered Hull in a corridor. "Come over here, Bobby. I want to get a photo of us—me with two black eyes." Just then, Blackhawks coach Billy Reay came along and pulled Hull back. "Ballard's the bugger who fired me as Leaf coach," he grumbled. "I don't want you doing him any favours."

I was able to brag about my own shot one day in the '70s. But only once. I broke the glass in Buffalo that day. I was with Ted Lindsay and Tim Ryan with NBC back then, and we were getting ready to play some media guys in a fun game. I went on the ice early and all alone out there took a shot that broke the glass.

I hurried back to the dressing room and told the guys what happened. They laughed. They didn't believe a word I said. "We've all seen you shoot," Lindsay chuckled as he laced his skates. "No sheet of glass ever had to worry."

"But I have a witness," I told them. "The arena manager was right there."

"And what did he say?" asked Ryan.

"Well, to be honest, he said the glass will withstand a thousand shots. And then, for no reason, it breaks on the next one."

"There you go," laughed Lindsay. "You're in the thousand-and-one-shot club."

Today's NHL, with the constant movement of players from team to team, seldom delivers line combinations that perform dazzling feats year after year. Perhaps the best line combination in the '70s wasn't even seen in the NHL. I never saw them perform. I refer to the dazzling threesome of Bobby Hull, Anders Hedberg, and Ulf Nilsson with the Winnipeg Jets, playing in the World Hockey Association (WHA), a rebel league.

It's unfortunate that Hull's big line was seldom seen by NHL fans, and Hull—as I soon found out—resented the lack of exposure. He once blasted me personally for not taking the time to go see him play. This was in a New York bar—Il Vagabondo. Wine flowing like the Danube. "You had lots of chances to see me play with the Jets," he barked.

I told him, "Bobby, I have enough trouble keeping up with the NHL clubs." What did he expect me to do? Fly to Winnipeg and buy a ticket to see him perform in the WHA? Only to find out he was sitting out that game to protest the violence in the game? Or he'd been out carousing until 3 a.m. and playing "guilty"—his word—and only half the player he normally was?

Hull turned to Ken Daneyko that night in New York. Daneyko was sitting across the table. "I want nothing to do with these two," Hull growled, glaring at the McFarlanes. In turning his back on us, he almost knocked my wife out of her chair.

"Look out!" Daneyko yelped.

My wife said, "Bobby, what did I do? Brian made you mad, not me."

I was surprised she didn't pull him over her knee and give him a good paddling. Tell him he was being a naughty boy. Have him go stand in the corner for a minute—a time out.

To his credit, Hull apologized at breakfast the next morning. We mentioned that we had tickets to the theatre that night to a hit Broadway show. He said, "We do, too. And you're going with us." Hull was our friend again. But he was upset. Somebody had stolen his wife's purse with cash and credit cards inside. I gave him half the cash I carried—a hundred bucks. Then a football player with the Giants came rushing over and plopped 10 $100 bills in Hull's hand. "Pay me back someday," he laughed.

People can't do enough for Bobby.

He says, "I met some billionaire last night, and he's sending his chauffeur around to pick us up. You two are coming, and dinner after the show is included."

To our surprise, that evening a vintage Rolls-Royce awaited us, a chauffeur in uniform and a rose in the bud vase in the car. When we stepped out of the Rolls in front of the theatre, people turned and gawked. I expected someone would shout, "Hey, it's Paul Newman and Robert Redford." But nobody did.

A young man did approach me, seeking my autograph. I said to him, "You don't want my autograph. There's Bobby Hull just ahead of us."

"No, I want yours," he said, "I've got Bobby's."

I was surprised. My wife was, too. Only my bank manager asks for my signature.

She said, "Maybe he thought you were Bobby's father. Or grandfather."

I'm certain that Bobby feels that in Winnipeg he played on the greatest line in hockey history. But because his big line never faced NHL competition week after week, there will always be some doubt about that.

I've seen the Original Six teams produce some big lines, too. Some, I'd argue, as dangerous as the Big Three in Winnipeg. Montreal's "Punch Line" (Maurice Richard, Elmer Lach, and Toe Blake), the "Production Line" in Detroit (Ted Lindsay, Gordie Howe, and Sid Abel), Chicago's "Million-Dollar Line" (Bobby Hull, Bill Hay, and Murray Balfour), and Boston's "Kraut Line" (Milt Schmidt, Bobby Bauer, and Woody Dumart), later succeeded by the "Uke Line" (Bronco Horvath, Johnny Bucyk, and Vic Stasiuk) and then Esposito, Hodge, and Cashman.

There was New York's "GAG Line" (Rod Gilbert, Jean Ratelle, and Vic Hadfield delivering a goal a game). Plus, the "Triple Crown Line" of the Los Angeles Kings (Marcel Dionne, Dave Taylor, and Charlie Simmer).

All were often spectacular. And none performing against teams that weren't quite NHL calibre.

Bronco Horvath. Hands up if you remember Horvath. Later, in these pages, you'll find the amazing story of how Horvath almost won the NHL scoring crown (over Hull) one season. And Bucyk triggers another memory. Detroit GM Jack Adams made a horrible blunder when he traded Bucyk to Boston after a couple of seasons as a Red Wing. Close to what the Bruins thought was the end of Bucyk's magnificent career, they held a "Night" for Johnny—about 10 years too soon. He played another 10 seasons, and in one of them—at age 35—he became the oldest 50-goal scorer in NHL history. By then, he was second to Orr in popularity among Boston fans.

Detroit's Jack Adams misjudged Bucyk's talent. Didn't like his checking and dumped him off on the Bruins. Big mistake. A future Hall of Famer sent packing.

In the Big Six era, teams faced one another 14 times a season, and rivalries were often bitter, acrimonious, and great entertainment for the fans. And at bargain ticket prices. Five bucks would get you a good seat. There was no fraternization, no players' association; although Ted Lindsay and Doug Harvey courageously tried to start one, displaying guts few other players had. Ringleader Lindsay was banished from Detroit to Chicago, and later Montreal's Harvey was sent to the Rangers, sending a clear message to all the others: "Don't start anything!"

Back then, NHL players were expected to toe the line, to accept management and coaching decisions without complaint. "Yes, sir, Mr. Blake." And "Sorry, Mr. Imlach. It won't happen again." And "I'll sign, Mr. Adams, and polish your shoes every day, maybe even kiss your butt, if you'll get me a Red Wings jacket." Bitching and bellyaching were taboo. It could lead to a trade to a last-place team or banishment to the minors for an eternity.

Managers and coaches would not tolerate insubordination. Not even from All-Stars.

There was no cozying up with rival players at golf tournaments or hockey schools.

"I hated going to events where players showed up from other teams," John Ferguson told me. "Even after I retired, it took years before I could be civil to guys like Hull and Eddie Shack. They'd always been the enemy. The Canadiens played in Toronto one time, and I had a pre-game meal with my teammate Dick Duff, a former Leaf. Who walks in the restaurant, but Eddie Shack? 'Hiya, Duffy,' he shouts, in that goofy voice of his. I jumped up, threw a 20-dollar bill down and walked out of there. If I hadn't, there might have been blood flying—all over the other diners."

Said Fergie: "And Hull? Hull took me aside one day and suggested we let bygones be bygones. I froze, stuck for an answer. I assumed we'd be lifelong enemies."

Broadcasters had to be careful, too. Some bosses didn't want to hear any grumbling from the hired hands.

Ask for a raise, and the boss at *Hockey Night* would remind you that there were a hundred guys panting to replace you—willing to work for peanuts. Put a knock on the Leafs, and owner Harold Ballard would threaten to ban you from his building—forever.

Yeah, I go way back, a pioneer on the hockey telecasts. And also the first Canadian announcer to appear on an American hockey telecast—CBS—in 1960. I'm quite proud of that. Five years later, I joined *Hockey Night* in Canada. I was there when Ward Cornell was host. Cornell was a big football fan. I'm not sure he even liked hockey. I was there when Cherry broke in wearing a suit that went unnoticed. When Bob Goldham joined us. And Howie Meeker. And Dick Irvin and Dave Hodge and Ron MacLean. And Bob Cole, who outlasted us all and was still going strong after 50 years. And being pissed when told he couldn't get in a few more seasons. How could Cole still be calling games when most of us were going deaf and blind? There must be something in that Newfoundland sea air. Did you know he flew in from St. John's for every telecast? He's spent half his life at 30 thousand feet. And he still indulges in Newfie shin-kicking. Ron MacLean has the bruises to prove it.

CHAPTER 4

WHY WRITE
ABOUT HOCKEY?

My late friend Pat MacAdam, a columnist who toiled for the *Ottawa Sun* and wrote a number of interesting books, once said, "Yeah, I write a book, and my pal says to me, 'I like the look of your new book, Pat. I can't wait for my library to get it in.' I told him, 'Why, you cheap son of a bitch. Go buy a copy, and I'll earn a royalty.'"

His outburst made me laugh. All authors should follow his lead.

Why do I write about hockey? Certainly not because it's lucrative. It was lucrative—well, somewhat lucrative—at one time. But mostly for other writers. When the late Scott Young wrote *The Boys of Saturday Night*, a book about *Hockey Night in Canada*, years ago, I understand he was given an advance of $50,000. Young spent $12,000 of that handsome amount on an assistant, Bob Gordon, a veteran *Hockey Night in Canada* producer, to provide him with background information. Hefty advances were the norm back then. Why wouldn't Young ask me to assist him, you might wonder? Well, I was planning to write my own book about *Hockey Night in Canada*. I did agree to meet with him for lunch one day and told him some tales. But with the understanding I would be holding my best stories back for my own book.

Roy MacGregor, a writer I greatly admire, author of the famous Screech Owls series, was recruited by a publisher to work with Gordie and Colleen Howe on a biography. They agreed on a 60/40 split.

"And the advance was stunning," Roy told me. "It was over $200,000, as I recall. Guys settle for $2,000 advances today. But when the final contract arrived, I noticed a change. The 60/40 had been changed to 65/35, and Colleen had initialled the change. I'd heard about Colleen and her control of Gordie. And how she looked after all the Howe business. I called the publishers and told them to get somebody else to ghost write the book."

Attaboy, Roy! You're another of my heroes.

Remember the time, Roy, when the NHL invited a bunch of us to an event in Quebec City? And they organized a pond hockey game for the writers and broadcasters, most of them young Americans? We played on lake ice that had so many deep ruts, it's a wonder we didn't break our legs. Young guys flying all over, hitting the ruts, and flopping on their faces. We were smart to step aside and watch from a snowbank, sharing a few precious moments together. Old guys who'd seen it all. Old guys bonding.

Roy says, "I played one of those ex-NHLer/media charity games a few years back. It was to raise money for Jocelyn Lovell, the biker who was so badly injured he needed a van for his wheelchair. Ken Dryden and I organized it, and the *Toronto Star* put big promotion dollars into it. Dryden, Gordie Howe, Andy Bathgate, Frank Mahovlich, and others showed up. As did Eddie Shack. The crowd loved him, of course. Molson's came in and dropped off two 24s in our dressing room. Eddie took one of the 24s, put it in his big bag, and left. Somebody shouted after him, 'Eddie, don't be an asshole.' But the door had already slammed behind him."

I had a few problems with Shack, too, which I'll describe ahead. Much of it over a song I wrote about him. But now that he's gone, I find I miss his act. He was never dull.

Today, there are very few publishers seeking hockey books and most want autobiographies only—from the lips of the game's biggest stars or the most controversial personalities. I can't fault them for that. It's a risky business today.

Hockey novels, heavens no. Forget fiction. I have a hockey novel—*The Hockey Guy*—ready for print. Friends say it's really good. One or two said, "This book must be published." But publishers say, "Hockey fiction doesn't sell." I may self-publish it anyway.

Why do I write about hockey? Because it's fun. And I like to share my stories. And because—every once in a while—some reader tells me they care.

Before Christmas one year, Ken Campbell of *The Hockey News* penned a personal article that caught my eye and astonished me. It was about how he received a hockey book when he was a lad—*Brian McFarlane's Hockey Annual*—for Christmas 1973, and how that simple gift changed his life forever. He wrote:

> Prior to getting that book, I was what is known today as a "reluctant reader." But after receiving *Brian McFarlane's Hockey Annual*, I couldn't get enough of the written word. I consumed that tome cover to cover hundreds of times, used the information in it for class projects and speeches and because of it, became a student of hockey history. I swear there were passages from that book that I could recite verbatim. From there, I picked up every other hockey book I could find and read each one voraciously.
>
> And now, when I look back almost 30 years later, I can trace my chosen profession back to that one book. Becoming a reader made me want to write and wanting to write, combined with my passion for hockey, led me to journalism school.
>
> Journalism. I'd call it a job, but it rarely ever feels as though I'm working. I've covered Stanley Cup finals, World Junior Championships and Olympics and travelled the world, in large part because of the seeds that book sowed in 1973. I still own it, in fact. Actually, I've already passed it down to my son Lukas, and he vows to keep it for his son.

Campbell wrote that? I've never received a compliment as meaningful as that one. Even though it took 30 years to reach me.

It's obvious why Ken Campbell's words astonished me. Really. An author—any author—will tell you that words of praise and appreciation, words that talk about a life-changing effect on a young reader—even coming decades after an author's book is all but forgotten—are so unexpected, so rare, that the author's reaction is one of incredulity. He gazes in wonder at Campbell's recollections. How a simple hockey annual, written in haste, propelled a reluctant reader into a voracious reader, how he could recite passages verbatim, how the book was even the basis for Campbell's chosen profession—a career in journalism—hockey journalism. It's a stunning revelation.

An author is blessed if just once in his lifetime he is rewarded with such words from a reader.

I rummaged through boxes of old books in my shed and found a mint copy of the vintage book Campbell cited. Signed it and sent it off. I don't know if he ever received it.

Now this book, possibly a final book. I remember one of the publishers I began with in 1965. While working on my first book, *Fifty Years of Hockey: A History of the NHL*, I met with Jack David, owner and publisher of ECW Press, a small Toronto-based publishing house.

"Jack, I've been thinking I'd like to write King Clancy's autobiography. What do you think?"

"A great idea," he said. "Have you talked to King?"

"No, I'm hesitant. He might laugh at me and say if he wanted his memoirs published, he'd get an established writer to do it—someone like Milt Dunnell, Scott Young, or George Gross—pals of his." Jack said, "Go ask him. If he says yes, I'll be your publisher."

Encouraged, I approached King and told him I'd like to put his life story in book form. His reply surprised me.

"Sure, I'll talk into your tape recorder. Not that anybody will want to read about my life in hockey. And any money that comes from a book, you keep it. I'm sure it won't be much." He was right about that. I'm guessing it brought a payback of a couple of thousand dollars. But it was so much fun to write. And no, nobody like Gross or Young had asked King to write a book. "Why would they?" he asked. "I'm an old guy who played back in the '20s and '30s. Nobody remembers me."

"Oh, yes they do, King," I told him. "You're a legend. A player, coach, manager, referee, and friend to all. I can't believe you're willing to let me do this."

"Brian, Tommy Gorman, manager of the Ottawa club, gave me a chance to play pro hockey in the NHL when I was only 18. Paid me $800 for the season when I didn't think I was worth 10 cents. And it worked out. You'll do fine, even if nobody reads the book."

"Hell, it'll be fun," he added. "Let's get started."

We started shortly after that meeting. Back then, I carried a 16-pound reel-to-reel Wollensak tape recorder around with me. Clancy and I met in the TV room at the Gardens, and the first session delighted me. He had a unique, captivating voice and took me back to his childhood days in Ottawa.

His stories mesmerized me. How his parents bought him a hockey stick for Christmas and hid it under a bed. Clancy found it and took it outside to play street hockey with it—and it broke. He cried when he told his mother—and she cried even harder as she hugged him to her breast. How he broke in with Ottawa at 18 and scored a goal in his first game, a winning goal in overtime in Hamilton. And how the Hamilton goalie screamed "No goal!" because the puck went through a hole in the side of the net. But somehow it counted, and Clancy was on his way.

How proud he was of his $800 salary and how he played every position, including goaltender, in a Stanley Cup playoff game against Edmonton in 1923. In those days, goalies had to serve their own penalties. When Clint Benedict, the Ottawa goalie, was sent to the sin bin, he handed his goal stick to Clancy, telling him, "Take care of this place, kid. I'll be right back." Clancy, who'd already played all three forward positions and both defence spots, took over and was not scored on.

The Stanley Cup he won that spring somehow wound up in his living room for the summer, where it collected cigar butts and bills to be paid. A Clancy teammate borrowed the Cup, then stuffed it away in his bedroom closet and forgot about it. A lengthy search for it ended in success and in time for it to be presented to the new champions months later.

Here's a hard-to-believe Clancy story: Clancy and two other Ottawa Senators, Frank Boucher and Morley Bruce, on a bitterly cold night, were allowed to sit around the pot-bellied stove in the Ottawa dressing room during a game. It meant there were no subs on the Ottawa bench. The subs were playing cards around the stove.

"The coach rigged up a bell, and if he needed one of us, the bell would ring in the room. One ring meant Morley Bruce was to come out, two rings were for Frankie Boucher, and three rings were for me," said Clancy.

"But somehow we got confused, and when the bell rang the wrong player went out. One of us had even taken his skates off. So, the coach was mad and the crowd was mad, and the referee was mad. And the next day, the NHL came up with a new rule. All players must be on the bench during a game, not in the dressing room. Even if they froze their asses off."

Clancy's mantra was: "If you don't have fun, what's the sense in playing." When Clancy died on November 10, 1986, I produced a short documentary about his extraordinary hockey life for *Hockey Night in Canada*, including the wonderful eulogy delivered by Monsignor Robitaille. Don Cherry called the next day to tell me how emotional it all was. "You had me crying," he said.

It's hard to believe that Clancy was not popular in the Leaf dressing room. That some players thought he tattle-taled to Punch Imlach and Harold Ballard everything that went on in there.

It struck me back then that if Clancy could recall tale after tale, stories of mirth and merriment, others must have that same ability. And so, I began lugging that 16-pound Wollensak with me everywhere hockey men gathered. It was the beginning of a lifelong quest for tales of hockey's fascinating past, as told by many of the best on ice— Cyclone Taylor, Milt Schmidt, Ace Bailey, Johnny Bower, Ted Lindsay, Bobby Orr, Wayne Gretzky, and dozens—no, hundreds— more. Yeah,

I became a word collector. Forget hockey cards or autographs. I collected the spoken word and the written word.

Sometimes, collecting words, especially the spoken word, proved to be a challenge.

When I worked for CFRB radio in 1958, I was handed sports director Wes McKnight's weekly show, *Meet the Hockey Stars*. On one show that season, I decided to feature New York Ranger coach Phil Watson. The Rangers, like most teams, stayed at the Royal York Hotel when in Toronto, and I phoned his room one morning. "Mr. Watson, could I tape an interview with you today for my radio show tonight?"

"Sure, kid. But we're going to Maple Leaf Gardens for a skate. Meet me there." The skate was a short one—15 or 20 minutes—and when I arrived a bit late, the players were hustling into cabs, headed back to the hotel. I peered in one cab, saw a man I thought was Phil Watson, and through the open window reminded him of our date.

"Sorry, kid, we finished early. Meet me back at the hotel—in the lobby."

I hustled down to the hotel, lugging my Wollensak, and there waiting for me was a tall individual. He came over and said, "Hello." I thought Watson was a little guy. *Who was this?*

"Let's do this up in my room," he suggested.

I had never met Phil Watson. Just saw his shadowy figure through the window of a cab. And my alarm bells were ringing. The man in the elevator appeared to be larger than Watson. Younger, too. With a craggy face. But he'd been waiting for me in the lobby. *Who else could it be?*

In his room, I fiddled with my tape recorder, stalling for time. Made small talk, hoping he'd give me a clue. *Was he Watson? Was he a player?* I was squirming in embarrassment—starting to panic. Finally, I decided he must be a player. *But which one?* I would have to guess.

I began the interview.

"My guest on *Meet the Hockey Stars* tonight is—Bill Gadsby."

I sneaked a peak. No reaction from my guest.

It *was* Bill Gadsby. His photo in a recent *Hockey News* issue was the only clue. I had no time to wonder how this had happened. I ploughed ahead. Finished the interview and thanked Bill Gadsby for taking time to talk with me. Cursed myself for not asking him about his dramatic rescue at age 12 from a sinking ocean liner, the *Athenia*, torpedoed by a German U-boat on the first day of the war. Or how, at 14, he was almost clobbered by a falling piece of concrete which grazed his body while walking in Calgary. Or how he managed to conquer polio in his early 20s while in his native Calgary. *You dummy, Brian.*

Then I remembered Watson.

As I left Gadsby's room, I asked him, "Say, Bill, do you happen to know Phil Watson's room number?"

"Yeah, he's down the hall—in 225."

Gadsby's door closed behind me, and I walked briskly down the hall. The door to 225 was open.

"Where the hell have you been?" was Phil Watson's testy greeting. "We doing this interview or not?"

I apologized, set up the tape recorder for a second interview.

I even remember some of it. When I asked Watson if he was concerned about the Leafs making a mad dash to the playoffs and possibly knocking the Rangers out, Watson scoffed. "Let me tell you," he said, jumping up from the sofa. "Imlach's never going to knock my Rangers out of the playoffs. You can quote me on that. I don't like Punch, and he doesn't like me. I'm gonna keep his team out of the playoffs, and that's a damn fact." A few days later, Imlach's Leafs rushed past the startled Rangers, coming from oblivion to claim the final playoff spot. It was the spring of 1959, and a decade later, when he was fired by the Leafs, Imlach looked back on all the big games his team had played in winning four Stanley Cups. "That season of 1958–59, and that final game that got us into the playoffs, were the biggest thrills I had in my hockey career."

A postscript. That day with Phil Watson at the Royal York Hotel ended with me asking him about his goaltender, Gump Worsley, who'd been known to enjoy a pint or two after games.

"Let me tell you about Gump," Watson said. "He's going on a hockey tour overseas. Yeah, the Rangers and the Blackhawks—after the season. And he's looking forward to playing in France. He told me, 'Phil, the first puck that hits me in the belly—especially if that kid Bobby Hull takes it—the burgundy's going to shoot out both of my ears.'"

Watson cackled with laughter. I laughed, too, and got a dandy interview for my show.

I never did solve the mystery of having two Rangers—a coach and a player—waiting for me to arrive at the hotel. The only conclusion I could reach was this: when I stuck my head in the cab window, Gadsby may have thought I said "Bill" instead of "Phil." And that's why he was there. I met him many times over the next few decades and never told him how confused I was that day—and how I had to guess who he was. I should have told him.

Years later, Gadsby's wife, Edna, told me a good story—not a happy story—about a date with her famous hockey star husband-to-be: "I was a small-town girl from the Prairies when Bill was in Chicago playing for the Blackhawks. He invited me to come there for a weekend visit, and I agreed. Bill was living in a boarding house, and the owner had two young daughters—pretty girls.

"When I arrived, I had a new hairdo and a new green dress I'd bought back home. I thought I looked really smashing. And I hoped Bill would think so, too.

"We all went out to a club that night—a real Chicago nightclub—and I was amazed at the food and all the drinks and the music. Then I slipped away to the ladies' room, where I sat in the stall. The rest room door opened, and the two girls from Bill's rooming house rushed in, giggling.

"'What do you think of Bill's girlfriend?' one asked the other.

"'Strictly from Hicksville,' the other one said. 'Can't you tell?'

"'Oh, yes,' said the other girl. 'That awful hairdo. Don't they have hair salons in Canada?'

"'What about her dress? You'd think it was St. Patrick's Day.'

"I heard all this and held my head in my hands as the tears poured down my face. And I stayed in that stall for the longest time. Finally, Bill sent someone to find me. I didn't want to tell him how mortified I was. But I recovered, and Bill and I had a good time together. We must have. We got married, didn't we? And we stayed married."

Gadsby was inducted into the Hockey Hall of Fame in 1970. His burning ambition over 20 seasons was to play on a Stanley Cup winner, but it never happened. He was named to *The Hockey News* 100 Greatest Players list years ago—at number 99.

He played in 1,246 NHL games with three of the Original Six clubs—New York, Chicago, and Detroit.

I think it's important to chronicle the shocking stories in hockey. Mike Robitaille, defenceman with the Buffalo Sabres, was so kind to me one day when I was stuck in Buffalo and needed to get to the Buffalo airport—fast.

"Hop in," he told me cheerfully. "I'll get you there in 20 minutes."

And he did.

Years later, I'd be writing, in *Golden Oldies*, about his horrendous experiences in Vancouver, when he was forced to play despite a back injury that could have been life-threatening. How he sued the Canucks and won a huge settlement. How he became a very popular hockey broadcaster with the Sabres. How the team owner he liked is still serving a long jail term.

And I'd be writing about goalie Clint Malarchuk's tale of near-death after a gruesome cut to the throat by an opponent's skate blade in Buffalo one night.

Malarchuk was a minute or two away from death when the Buffalo trainer raced onto the ice, his strong fingers latched onto the goalie's throat to stem the bleeding. His quick action in getting Malarchuk to a Buffalo hospital saved his life. He was hours in surgery and then came back to the game too soon. He suffered from OCD, and he survived another close-to-death experience when he pulled the trigger on a .22 rifle—a suicide attempt?—and the bullet went up through his nose, but stopped just short of his brain. It has not been removed.

Looking back on close to 100 published books, there's one that brought me income I never envisioned. *The Youngest Goalie* was the true story of 17-year-old Albert Forrest, goalie on the remarkable Dawson

City team, that travelled 4,000 miles to challenge a powerful Ottawa club for the Stanley Cup. The team left the Yukon in mid-December 1904 and arrived in Ottawa in 1905.

A syndicate involving Ralph Mellanby, my boss on *Hockey Night in Canada* at the time, and members of the Bronfman family purchased the movie rights to the book for a sum bordering on six figures, and that was a stunning surprise. It was a bigger surprise when they abandoned the project. The movie was never made. They never asked for their money back.

Picture this. A 17-year-old goalie approaches his parents with a request. The rush for gold is almost over. The long winter has set in, and Christmas is only a few days away.

"Mom, Dad," the boy says. "I've been asked to play goal for the local hockey team when they challenge for the Stanley Cup in January. Can I go?"

"Well, I don't know," says the father. "Where will the games be played?"

"In Ottawa."

"Hmmm. That's about 4,000 miles away. How do you plan to get there, son?"

"We're planning to leave on our bicycles for Whitehorse. That's about 350 miles down the trail. If there's snow, and the bikes break down, we'll hitch a ride on dogsleds. Some of the guys will be walking. From Whitehorse we'll take the train to Skagway in Alaska. After that, we'll go by steamship to Vancouver. Or maybe to Seattle. Then we'll get back on the train and go to Ottawa. It may take us a month to get there."

"Hmmm, that's a mighty long way to go just to play hockey, son. Remember, you're only 17 and you'll miss a lot of school."

"And Christmas at home," his mother added. "What's this Stanley Cup thing all about, anyway?"

"It's a trophy, Mom. About the size of a football. Any old team can challenge for it and every team wants to win it. We think our Dawson City team can win it. Please say I can go."

"Oh, I suppose. I don't see why not," said the father. "You'll see a lot of Canada."

"Just behave yourself and don't get hurt," said the mother. "When will you be back, Albert?"

"I have no idea. But sometime in 1905."

"All right, son. Have a nice trip. I'll make sandwiches. I'll write a note to your teacher. Go and win the Stanley Cup."

Does that sound like any parent-teenager conversation you've ever heard? Not likely.

But a discussion just like it must have happened in 1904 just before 17-year-old Albert Forrest left with his teammates for Ottawa and a Stanley Cup series versus the famous Ottawa Silver Seven. The Dawson City players, after a 4,000 mile, 23-day journey by bicycle, foot, tramp steamer, train, and dogsled, arrived in Ottawa without having practised for almost a month. They lost by lopsided scores of 9–2 and 23–2, and in one of the games, Ottawa star Frank McGee scored 14 goals against young Forrest.

The Ottawa crowd had nothing but praise for Forrest. Most agreed if it hadn't been for his plucky play, the Ottawa snipers might have doubled their goal production. McGee's 14 goals in one game remains an all-time Stanley Cup scoring record.

So, in one game played in 1905, one player set an all-time scoring record for Stanley Cup play and another set a record for most goals against. Both records still stand and may never be broken.

After 125 years of playoff games for the Stanley Cup, Albert Forrest remains the youngest, and the most porous, of all playoff goaltenders.

Can you imagine the conversation when he got home?

CHAPTER 5

A KID IN HAILEYBURY

I was born on August 10, 1931, in the Northern Ontario town of Haileybury. Actually, it was at the New Liskeard hospital, another five miles north. Nine pounds, three ounces. A month and a half went by before my parents named me.

My grandfather, John Henry McFarlane, had moved north with his wife, Rebecca, and four sons in 1910. A school principal, he doubled his salary by moving from his former school in the Ottawa Valley. When my father, Leslie, John Henry's oldest of four boys, began his writing career years later, he wrote about those pioneering days. And it was there he wrote some of the bestselling boys' books of all time—the Hardy Boys. But under another name—Franklin W. Dixon.

He writes:

> While automobiles had already appeared on the roads of Southern Ontario, none had appeared in Haileybury—not when the McFarlane family moved there. There was simply no point in being a motorist because there was no place to motor. Nobody could drive a car in winter, especially a Temiskaming winter. If the engine didn't freeze the driver would. At 35 below, both would. In spring and autumn, you

could guarantee that the mud and the ruts would stall any car before it travelled more than a block from home.

In my father's school, I was taught by Miss Flegg, who ruled by fear and stood for no nonsense. Strap in hand, she moved toward me, bent over, and whispered in my ear, "Don't think for a minute because you're the principal's son you can get away with any nonsense."

I almost wet my pants. No, I confess. I did wet my pants.

In winter, blizzards came down from the north and rocked the McFarlane house. It creaked with every gust. My brothers and I slept in woollen underwear beneath a hundred pounds of blankets, huddled snugly and grateful for the home that sheltered us from the icy fury that raged outside. It wasn't a well-built house. Snow often sifted through the cracks and left a white carpet on the kitchen floor. Nobody walked around barefoot. There'd be a thin layer of ice in the water basin each morning.

But winter had its good days for the McFarlane kids. There was skating and sledding. Learning to skate began on bob skates, which were considered childish because they had double runners. Kids discarded them as soon as they managed to waddle around the ice on real skates. Real skates were attached to your boots by screw nails, which were always working loose. There were patches of ice everywhere, and boys of all ages, wearing hand-me-down skates, old magazines for shin pads, mitts for hockey gloves, and heavy sticks—some made from tree limbs—played furious games of shinny after school and on weekends.

The nearby lake, Lake Temiskaming, was tempting but it took time for it to freeze solid. When it did, we could skate for miles. Goal posts for hockey games on the lake might be a hundred yards apart—before the snow fell. The fastest skaters stood out. When a storm dumped a foot of snow on the ice, we brought shovels and cleared a much smaller rink, maybe 50 by 100 feet. The huge snowbanks gobbled up misplaced shots and passes, and the smallest, youngest kid (it was usually me) would be told to "fetch the puck."

He'd take off a mitt and reach bare-handed into the hole made by the missing disc. When he retrieved it, he'd get a gentle slap on the butt with a stick and a "Good going!" from the other players. Saturday afternoons were spent indoors—at the big covered rink adjoining the Plaza Theatre, with the privilege of skidding and sprawling across the crowded surface to the music of a mechanical organ, which boasted two tunes played over and over again. When kids learned to skate upright, skating hand in hand with a girl—often because of a dare—became a romantic adventure. Who knows how many partners in marriage would look back and say, "I remember the first words you said to me, 'Wanna skate?'" Kids spent more time by the pot-bellied stove in the dressing room than on the ice. Eventually, the dressing room fragrances of coal gas and old socks and impish boys farting drove the skaters out again. Obviously, they preferred frostbite to asphyxiation.

Believe it or not, Haileybury had once iced a team in the National Hockey Association, forerunner to the NHL.

Here's how that happened.

In 1909, a new hockey league was formed in Eastern Canada. It was called the Canadian Hockey Association, with franchises in Ottawa, Quebec City, and three in Montreal. The admission fee was $25 per club.

Two teams applying for membership—Montreal Wanderers and Renfrew—were rejected. Hockey men behind these clubs did not take a slap in the face lightly. They quickly organized a new professional league—the National Hockey Association—with two of the clubs in Cobalt and Haileybury. The fiercest battles were the games between these thriving towns: working-class miners living in Cobalt shacks versus millionaire owners residing in posh Haileybury homes on "Millionaire's Row."

Art Ross was recruited to play in the Cobalt Silver Kings lineup in a pair of 1909 games. Ross earned $1,000 for a weekend's play, more than many miners earned in a year. He would go on to manage the Boston Bruins, win Stanley Cups there, and be inducted into the Hockey Hall of Fame.

The referee for the game was a local doctor who made it clear he had no objection to high-sticking or brawling. Then he moved around cautiously. He didn't mind blood, but he didn't want to be splattered with it.

Cobalt won that match and retained the O'Brien Cup, a huge trophy donated by local mine owner M.J. O'Brien, who owned the Renfrew Millionaires.

The following year, the two teams met again, this time in the Haileybury arena. The Cobalt squad would be Stanley Cup contenders if they could just defeat the Haileybury Comets. Noah Timmins was one of the biggest mine owners in Cobalt, but he lived in Haileybury. It's said that he bet $40,000 on the game.

Many working men in both towns bet their entire monthly wages on the outcome, risking the wrath of a quick-tempered wife if they came home with an empty wallet.

By half time (two 30-minute periods in that era) it looked grim for Haileybury. The Comets trailed Cobalt by five goals. Timmins made a personal trip to the hometown dressing room. He pulled a thousand dollars from his pocket and said, "This goes to the player who scores the winning goal."

One hockey historian suggests we owe much of the description of that epic game to young Leslie McFarlane, who was then 10 years old.

My dad looked puzzled when I asked him about that quote.

"I have no recollection of saying those words," He said. "But then, I don't recall anything I may have said at the age of 10."

Five unanswered goals scored by Haileybury sent the game into overtime, and when Haileybury's Horace Gaul scored the winning goal, players scooped up money thrown for them on the ice. Goalie Billy Nicholson found a washtub somewhere, threw cash he'd scooped up into the tub, turned it over, and sat on it. Nicholson weighed almost 300 pounds. Horace Gaul was a hockey hero. He'd served in the Boer War, and later the Great War. In battle overseas, he'd been severely wounded and returned to Canada, lucky to be alive. Years later, he offered to give a McFarlane family member (my cousin Eleanor) his old Haileybury hockey jersey, but she refused. "Who'd want that smelly old thing," she told him. I would have grabbed it with no hesitation.

After the silver boom declined, the Haileybury team was transferred to Montreal and became known as Les Canadiens. Imagine! The greatest team with the most Stanley Cup wins in history got its start in Haileybury—my first hometown.

CHAPTER 6

HAILEYBURY: A HUNDRED YEARS LATER

In mid-October 2017, a dozen McFarlane family members journeyed to lovely Haileybury for a weekend highlighted by Leslie McFarlane's induction into the Order of the North. He was the third son of the North to be honoured for his contributions to the culture of the vast region, mainly because he authored the famous Hardy Boys series. Had he been living, he would have shaken his head in disbelief.

"Any hack writer could have done that," he would have protested.

But no, Dad, they couldn't have.

Sure, he wrote those books quickly. And for a pittance. A hundred bucks a book and with no hope of royalties. With estimated sales over the next few decades of 100 million. But Leslie McFarlane reached out to millions of young readers with his Hardy Boys adventures. Unknowingly, he hooked those countless lads on the joys of reading, me included.

In time, we all would outgrow the Hardy Boys and go on to discover other authors once the seed was planted—Mark Twain, Charles Dickens, and hundreds of others who captured our imaginations. But the Hardy Boys were the spark, the brothers whose exploits turned some of us from casual or sluggish readers to voracious page-turners. How he became F. W. Dixon I'll explain in a later chapter.

He is a deserving member of the Order of the North 40 years after his passing. He should also have received an Order of Canada. But he'll never get one. You have to be living to qualify—I myself enjoyed that honour in 2020.

The splendour of the scenery as our long drive brought us closer to Haileybury featured brilliant fall colours, tall pines, and deep bush. Lovely lakes bordered by jagged rock formations in hues of red-brown, green, and grey. Land that lifts your spirits and chases bad moods away.

There was a big yellow sign, "*WELCOME McFARLANE FAMILY,*" as we neared our destination. "There'll be another sign ready on Sunday," I said at the banquet: "*GOOD RIDDANCE, McFARLANE FAMILY.*"

The following morning, we strolled along the waterfront, where a Leslie McFarlane plaque is prominently displayed and where a street is named after him. On to the curling club for ceremonies honouring winners of the McFarlane creative writing contests. Obviously, there is plenty of writing talent in Haileybury. It was a delight to see the fresh young faces in the hall as they came up to receive their awards.

I introduced family members and said a few words. Tea and cake followed.

Back for the five o'clock dinner in the same venue, and the McFarlane clan filled two tables.

I spoke again and presented Dad's silver tray to the Haileybury Heritage Museum. It had been a farewell gift from his friends when he moved to Whitby, Ontario, in the early '30s to be closer to the Toronto markets. Amy Arnold, my mother, deserves much credit for my dad's success. She steered him away from drink during the gloomy Depression and helped him become the really good person he was. They were devoted to each other. After his death in 1977, I inherited his diaries and was touched by one entry: "I have always been faithful to Amy as she has been to me." Amy, the eldest of seven children, left Haileybury in her late teens to become a housekeeper for a Montreal family—the Fishers. She sent much of the money she earned back home, so that her sisters could get an education. She was a giver, a caretaker, a nurturer. The Arnold family was close knit and highly respected. The five Arnold sisters were all attractive and popular. They often sang together. The Fisher family loved Amy like a daughter.

When my dad was honoured in 2017, there was so much love and affection in the air. Huge hugs and strong handshakes at every turn.

Sunday morning, before leaving, on to the Haileybury Museum, where a knowledgeable man named Paul gave us a tour. Lots of detail about the famous fire that destroyed the town in 1922; a vintage fire engine; the lore of the hockey teams; the little-known Thomas Edison tower that was built early in the last century, one I'd never heard about; beautiful Lake Temiskaming being 700 feet deep; one of the original streetcars; the McFarlane exhibit; mining and farming and the famous ship the *Meteor* that brought hundreds of settlers to the area more than a century ago; Mr. C.C. Farr, who founded the town and named it after the school he attended in England.

We all agreed that the good people who organized and arranged this event were fabulous. All volunteers, they showed us an abundance of the famous Northern Ontario hospitality.

We treasure our daughters, Lauren and Brenda, who drove us there. Time in the car—despite Sunday's fierce wind and rain—flew by as we discussed family matters and relationships. Our son Michael made a surprise last-minute appearance after a six-hour drive from Southern Ontario.

Leslie McFarlane has been recognized with a few honours and awards in his lifetime, but none to match this posthumous award. He loved the North.

My dad's first real job was as a 17-year-old reporter for the newspaper in Cobalt not far from his Haileybury home. He rode to Cobalt on a trolley car. The unique little trolley line was about 10 miles long, from Cobalt to New Liskeard. Within a few months, he was hired in a similar position with the much bigger *Sudbury Star*.

In 1920, Sudbury, Ontario, was a brawling railroad centre and mining town in the middle of a region that produced more nickel than anywhere else on earth. And the smell of sulphur was everywhere.

As a rookie reporter on the *Sudbury Star*, my dad flew about town like a bumblebee, from office to police court to town hall to fire hall to police station and—always—to the hockey rink. Even then, before he was 20, Leslie had no intention of making newspaper journalism a career. He aspired to become an author, like a fellow reporter he encountered from time to time, a chap who toiled for the *Toronto Star*. His name was Ernest Hemingway.

My dad was barely out of his teens when a forest fire raged uncontrolled through Haileybury. The town was gutted, and the house he grew up in consumed by flames. His parents and brothers ran for the shallow beach waters of Lake Temiskaming, waded out, and survived by covering their heads with water-soaked towels and blankets. His story on the *Sudbury Star*'s front page described the disaster in detail, and it wasn't until a relief train arrived from the north with his family members aboard he knew all of the McFarlane clan had survived. Forty-four others perished as the fire swept through 300,000 acres of bush.

His newspaper work left practically no time for after-hours ventures into creative literature. But by staying awake until two or three o'clock in the morning, he did manage to write a few short stories and, to his surprise, sold most of them to the *Star Weekly*. The payment he received for the first story he sold was 10 dollars.

When his editor at the *Sudbury Star*, a demanding, intimidating man named Mason, assigned my dad to the hockey beat one winter, the aspiring author soon learned that Sudbury, like most Northern towns, was about to surrender to a state of complete lunacy for the next four months.

On the night before a big game, fans would huddle outside the arena hours before the ticket office opened. They would congregate in a long line, stamping their booted feet, pulling food and bottles of booze from the pockets of their overcoats. Some would come armed with a bag full of rotten fruit with the expectation that the referee—an out-of-towner—would surely blow a close call and would therefore earn himself a "shower."

Fans would build huge bonfires along the street to warm themselves. The city fire department seldom intervened, even when gusts of wind sent sparks soaring in the air and threatened to burn the arena to the ground.

Les McFarlane knew his hockey. Late at night, hunkered over his old Underwood, he would dash off stories, short and long, about hockey heroes in Canada's Northland.

His hockey yarns would be published by the pulp magazines of the day. Growing up, I read all of them. They take the reader back to an era when scouts roamed the boondocks looking for talent, when 60-minute men were common, when teams had one goalie who played without a mask, when natural ice turned to slush in the spring, when goal judges stood out on the ice behind the net and waved a hankie to signal a score.

Twenty years ago, I found a publisher who agreed to reprint many of his hockey yarns in book form.

In Sudbury, there was rock. Rock everywhere. And the smell of sulphur. Hockey star Eddie Shack, who would later become my nemesis, was from Sudbury, a butcher boy in the '50s—in his youth. And in his speeches later in his life, he'd tell his fans, "Yeah, we planted potatoes in Sudbury. But we'd have to use dynamite to get 'em up."

Long before Shack, the Green brothers, Red and Shorty, were great senior players from Sudbury, and Les would soon get to know them. Both went on to play in the NHL in the '20s with the Hamilton Tigers.

In his diary, he wrote: "Shorty is visiting in Haileybury, back from the hockey season and driving a shiny new car. He stopped by the house and took son Brian for a spin."

So, the first NHL star I ever met was Shorty Green. Alas, I have no recollection of that ride. Shorty made his mark by scoring the first goal at Madison Square Garden and by once scoring five goals in a game.

He was also critically injured during a game in New York in 1927, so badly hurt he was given the last rites by a priest. He recovered but played only 103 games over four seasons. He is the least productive forward in the Hockey Hall of Fame, escorted in with a mere 33 career goals and 20 assists for 53 points as his career statistics. How he won enough votes for induction is a hockey mystery. As for his nickname? At five-foot-ten he wasn't even short.

Ironically, in the hall next to him—alphabetically—is Wayne Gretzky, with 894 goals and 1,963 assists for 2,857 points. But give Shorty credit. He was a warrior. He joined the Canadian army in 1916 and was gassed at the Battle of Passchendaele in 1917. He had guts enough to stand up to German soldiers, who tried to rob him of his life, and guts enough to stand up to hockey owners who merely tried to rob him.

CHAPTER 7

THE PIONEER BROADCASTER

When my dad worked for the *Sudbury Star*, he witnessed some of the best amateur hockey of the era. Amateurism meant that the players weren't supposed to admit they landed good jobs and were paid under the table to play hockey. When Sudbury played Sault Ste. Marie (the Soo), Ontario, diehard fans who couldn't make the 200-mile journey when the game was played out of town demanded instant information. This was provided by the CPR Telegraph people, who offered play-by-play wire service accounts of the games to local clubs and movie theatres.

Because my dad followed the Sudbury Wolves to games in the Soo, he was enlisted to dictate the play-by-play to a nimble-fingered man on the telegraph key. Back in Sudbury, curling matches and Hollywood movies at the local theatre would be interrupted in order that my dad's accounts could be read aloud to a hushed, hockey-mad audience.

Trouble was, he was providing information for the CPR that wouldn't be seen in the paper he worked for until the following day. His boss, Bill Mason, seethed over this perceived conflict.

One day Mason asked my dad how much he earned for his game reports.

"Five bucks a game," he replied.

"Disgraceful," Mason told him. "They're robbing you blind. You've got a gift for that sort of thing. Go and ask for 20 bucks."

Tentatively, my dad approached the CPR's Dan Bowen (grandfather of current Leaf broadcaster Joe Bowen) and asked for a $15 raise.

"We can't pay that," Bowen told him. "And if you're not happy with the current sum, we don't want you working for us. We'll simply have the telegrapher double up and do both jobs from now on."

"So, I lost that job," my dad told me. "And apparently nobody noticed any difference. But I learned an important fact of life that day. Nobody is indispensable."

A few mornings later, Bill Mason arrived at the office in a foul mood. After bawling out a couple of printers, he barged into the newsroom and began a rant. My dad had finally reached the conclusion he was a small-town tyrant.

"The whole paper," he said, "is going to pot. And none of you gives a damn."

My dad mumbled under his breath.

"You, Les, was that you muttering? You have something to say?"

"Not at the moment."

"Well, you better not."

My dad rose from his chair, threw down his copy pencil, reached for his straw hat on the rack, and turned to face his boss.

Then, to his utter astonishment, he heard himself say, "Mason, why don't you go fuck yourself?"

He heard a female reporter gasp. He thought he heard ghostly cheers from former employees who'd promised to deliver the same message to Mason, but never did. By then, he was out of the building and in the street.

As passers-by scattered out of the way, he did an awkward little jig, threw both arms in the air as if he'd scored a Stanley Cup winning goal, and shouted, "Yeeaaah!"

My dad wasn't idle long. He couldn't afford to be. He rented an isolated cabin on Ramsey Lake, reaching it by canoe. No road in, no electricity, no running water. Drinking water came from a small stream. No social life. A skunk he befriended—Geraldine—was a pet. And he began writing in earnest.

He earned a few hundred dollars selling fiction in his first year as a freelancer. It wasn't enough. And when one rejection followed another, lonely and depressed, he thought seriously of walking into the lake. A final walk and a brief swim. No need to pay any more rent.

Somehow, he pushed those thoughts aside and found another job—a reporter on the Springfield, Massachusetts, paper the *Republican*—at 40 bucks a week. Perhaps he'd use that job as a stepping stone to New York. Perhaps he'd become a famous playwright and mingle with the Broadway stars.

Goodbye, dear Geraldine. So long, Sudbury. He thought he'd never return, but he would.

In Springfield, he answered an ad one day: "Writer wanted for juvenile fiction books."

A man in New Jersey named Stratemeyer liked my dad's work and hired him to write a couple of boys' adventure books—popular at the time. The books bore a pen name—pseudonyms like Nat Ridley and Roy Rockwell. "I have lots of books for you to write," Les was told. "You might consider doing this full time."

Even though Stratemeyer offered a flat fee of one hundred dollars per book with no royalties, and with an invisible author getting the credit as the wordsmith, my dad took the bait.

He called a man in Sudbury.

"Is the cottage I lived in still available? It is? Good. I'm quitting my job here and I'm coming back."

A wedding would follow—finally. Les and Amy Arnold would tie the knot.

A friend said, "Getting married, Amy? To a writer? That's all he does? Sits at a typewriter and writes? God help you, my dear."

Les and Amy Arnold met at a dance, where he helped her change from winter boots to dancing shoes. The neighbour's comment about writers was amusing at the time. Later, they realized that her friend had meant every word.

Their courtship was possibly one of the longest in Northern Ontario history. Les had moved back to the cottage on Ramsey Lake with only Geraldine to welcome him back. There he began writing the Hardy Boys for Stratemeyer, and while Amy was uppermost in his thoughts and he kept in touch with dozens of love letters, there is no mention in his diaries of a wedding date. Or even an engagement ring. But he soon packed up and moved to Montreal for obvious reasons.

One of Amy's main concerns was the age difference. She was six years older than Les, and when she turned 30, she must have felt she was destined to live her life as a spinster.

But, no.

On the afternoon of May 3, 1928, the knot was tied in Montreal. Les was 25, and Amy about to turn 32. If my mother were alive to read this, she would cringe. "There's no need to reveal my age," she would admonish me. Mom, nobody cares. You loved each other.

Les was concerned that Amy would soon conclude that marrying a writer was the riskiest and possibly the worst decision she had ever made.

He wrote (as his son might write): "Writers are not good husband material. Not because they are worse characters than men in other occupations. They aren't. Not because they are impractical and untidy. They are. Not because their income is chancy. It is. But they are always underfoot. The presence of a mate who hammers away at a typewriter hour after hour and bawls for silence can become, at the very least, irksome. Every time the woman of the house lays eyes on the pest, she is provoked into considering his imperfections.

"When he reads aloud to her—some happy expression of his genius—she yawns or nods off at her peril. She must applaud and nod approval if she knows what's good for her. Otherwise, the creator's feelings will be hurt and he'll go into a sulk."

After a few months in Montreal, with baby Patricia born a year after the wedding, the McFarlanes were on the move, first to Toronto and then, for whatever reason, back to Haileybury. Son Brian (that's me) came along on August 10, 1931, and another daughter, Norah, followed in 1933. But it seems we had just settled in when my dad decided to settle out. Next destination—Whitby, Ontario. Much closer to the publishers in Toronto.

While reading my father's diaries recently, I stumbled on something really exciting. The date was March 6, 1937.

On that night at Maple Leaf Gardens, my dad became a pioneer colour commentator on *Hockey Night in Canada*.

CHAPTER 8

HAPPY DAYS IN WHITBY

It was in Whitby where I first began to skate and play hockey on the outdoor ponds and backyard rinks. I began by skating alone and sometimes with my sisters on a small patch of ice about the size of my small bedroom. The ice formed in a ditch about a hundred feet from our front door. Then, I discovered other boys were playing shinny on ice in the park about two blocks away and I soon joined them there. What fun it was to discover shinny played on a much bigger surface. And what a surprise to see so many other kids—kids of all ages and sizes—enjoying those scrambly games on ice covered with bumps and ruts. I became hooked on hockey the first day I played there.

I longed to play games in the Whitby Arena someday—an old barn unlike any other rink I ever saw. There were two corridors flanking the hockey ice that were opened for skating sessions. After school once or twice a week, boys and girls would skate there to music.

You'd ask a girl to skate, although I was shy about that, and you'd skate from the main rink through the darkened corridors and you'd find it a bit thrilling. The dim lighting, the music, and holding the mittened hand of a girl. You'd wonder what would happen if you leaned in and kissed the girl. But, of course, you wouldn't dare. But you'd think about it—often. I remember those feelings when I skated with Lorna

Sullivan through those tunnels. Then, to my dismay, the Sunday school teacher announced, "Children, I'm sad to say Lorna and her family will be moving to Toronto." I recall how upset I was—the sense of loss. I never saw her again, but I still remember her name and how much I liked her. I hope you've had a good life, Lorna Sullivan.

But, at that age, I liked hockey as much as any girl—perhaps even Lorna. And listening on the radio to games played at the famous Maple Leaf Gardens in Toronto was also a thrill.

I think my fascination for broadcasting booths, and Foster Hewitt's famous gondola at the Gardens, began in Whitby when I was seven or eight years old. The gondola? I wouldn't have known a gondola from a gorilla at that age. But "the gondola" sure sounded like an exciting place to be.

Here's the exciting event I mentioned earlier. My dad was invited to be a colour commentator on *Hockey Night in Canada* long before I was.

"Mr. Passmore of the MacLaren Advertising Agency called up this morning to invite me to be guest announcer on the Imperial Oil hockey broadcast next Saturday night at fifty dollars for the date."

On Friday, my dad went to the Royal York Hotel, where a suite had been arranged for him by MacLaren. He describes his first adventure into broadcasting the following day:

> Up early this morning to meet Percy LeSueur [a CBC commentator and former hockey goaltending great with Ottawa] and we talked and went over material for the broadcast. Up to the Gardens and then up to the gondola. First period was over quickly which cut down on our time on the air so we had to discard our material and ad lib — a fearful experience for an initiation. Not until I told a story in the second intermission did I manage to loosen up. After the game it was down to a microphone in the dressing room corridor to chat with Karakas, Apps, and Fowler. After it was over my knees melted. Sheer nerves. Back home, Amy and others thought the broadcast was quite good.

Everybody in Whitby seems to have listened with great interest.

What amazes me about my dad's report on his CBC debut is that he makes no mention of the fact the game he covered was historic. It was the game in which the Chicago Blackhawks introduced an all-American lineup. There was Mike Karakas (Aurora, Minnesota) in goal, one of four bona fide U.S.-born big leaguers on the Hawks. The others were Alex Levinsky (Syracuse, New York), Doc Romnes (White Bear Lake, Minnesota), and Louis Trudel (Salem, Massachusetts).

But Hawks owner Major McLaughlin, a coffee baron who knew little of hockey, added five more Yankees to his roster that week—all rookies. McLaughlin boasted his team would become the "New York Yankees of hockey." Some called his experiment "the most farcical thing ever attempted in hockey." McLaughlin was ahead of his time. Nobody today would describe a team of all-American players as "farcical."

I'm not certain why my dad was invited to be in the gondola that night. Perhaps it was because he had a reputation as a skilled writer of hockey fiction. Or because he had been a pioneer broadcaster of sorts, in Sudbury, when senior hockey was big.

The Leafs were lucky to win that night by a 3–2 score. And my dad was there to see it and talk about it. Too bad he was never invited back.

Someone once suggested that, listening to him on the radio that night, I considered the possibility of someday following him along the catwalk that led to that magical place where Foster Hewitt made Saturday night the most exciting night of the week. No, not for a second. If I ever got to Maple Leaf Gardens, I'd want to be there as a *player*, like every other kid I knew. The Leafs were my heroes, and I had the BeeHive Corn Syrup photos to prove it. One year I wore an old blue hockey jersey to my games of shinny on the park ice. I asked my mother to cut out a number from a piece of white felt to stitch on the back. No. 10 was for Apps, my favourite player.

One night, my dad took me by the hand to a smoke-filled room in Whitby. There, my eyes stinging from the cigar smoke, I met the great captain of the Leafs. Over the hubbub I asked him for his autograph. He took my pen and paper, looked down, and smiled, then signed my scrap of paper. My first autograph. When I looked at it, I was thrilled. "Dad, Dad, look! He signed 'Best wishes, Syl Apps.' Can you believe it? He gave me two extra words." Many years later, I often sat next to Apps in the Gardens' press box, on purpose, of course. I may have asked him some goofy questions, but I hope not. I did remind him of that night in Whitby, and how meaningful those extra words were to a young fan. He smiled. I didn't tell him the scrap of paper he signed had disappeared.

In 2016, I was asked to be a member of a select group to pick the 100 greatest Leafs players. Apps was right up there—not at the top, but second to Dave Keon. Ted Kennedy was third.

The hockey broadcasts on radio 70–80 years ago were mesmerizing. When I listened intently to the intermissions, I thought to myself, *How fortunate these men with the authoritative voices are. They get to see all the Leafs games—for free.* I'm sure I was quite surprised when my dad told me they were actually paid to sit around a microphone and talk about hockey. What a fascinating occupation!

Later on, with the birth of TV, the man who ushered them into the studio was announcer Murray Westgate who, at the age of 100, was the oldest living member of those early-day telecasts. But his passing in August 2018 makes me the oldest survivor of hockey games on TV in black and white. I visited with Westgate once a year in the war vets branch of Sunnybrook Hospital in Toronto. He had a photo of us together on the wall of his room. Back then, he was the spokesman for Imperial Oil, the chief sponsor of *Hockey Night in Canada.* And his cheery "Happy Motoring" is lodged in my brain bank to this day. Westgate survived submarine duty during the war. A dangerous, heroic job.

Perhaps the seed was planted then. If I failed to become another Apps, perhaps I could become another Wes McKnight or Baldy Cotton. Or even the most famous of them all—Foster Hewitt. No, I would never have harboured such thoughts at that age. Or would I? For me to play for the Leafs or be a hockey announcer? I had as much chance of that as becoming prime minister of Canada.

I chuckled over another diary item that winter.

"Brian has inherited Pat's [my sister's] old skates. His pride in them is almost pathetic."

They must have been hockey skates. I would sooner have played in snowshoes than wear white figure skates.

It was in Whitby that I was hired for my first two jobs. On our street, a construction crew began building a house. I was about 10 years old when I approached the foreman and asked him if he needed another worker.

"Can you dig a foundation?" he asked me.

"Sure. I guess I can. What's a foundation?"

He handed me a heavy shovel. "You can start right now. I pay 25 cents per hour."

The other men chuckled when I dug in.

I retired early with blistered hands—after collecting 50 cents.

Then I worked in a gas station, filling tanks and wiping windshields. Again, 25 cents an hour. But I got awfully sick one day while sweeping out the station's basement. I was inhaling carbon monoxide and didn't know it. But I knew enough to jump on my bike and cycle home. My mom took one look at my face streaked with shades of yellow and purple, and called the doctor. He diagnosed my problem and said to my mom, "Pedalling that bike and breathing hard may have cleared his lungs and saved his life."

CHAPTER 9

THE WAR YEARS

The McFarlanes moved to Ottawa when Canada entered the Second World War. My dad, then 40, tried to enlist in the army, but was rejected for some reason. Maybe he just wasn't tall enough.

But later, he was recruited to write speeches for the Department of Munitions and Supply. That job prompted the move to Ottawa. As a family, we were sad to leave Whitby. We had good friends there. I missed the old rink as much as anything. (I'd gotten over Lorna Sullivan.)

We moved to Ottawa and lived in half of the house my dad's Aunt Eva owned. Suddenly, because there were seven of us, I had a bedmate, a lanky teenaged distant cousin named Barney who said little and snored a lot. It was a small bed in a tiny room, and Barney soon discovered, to his horror, that I was an occasional bedwetter.

Coincidentally, the bedwetting stopped soon after Barney departed. I place all the blame on him for causing the problem. He made me nervous. And I never got the credit I deserved for freeing up some extra family space.

There was a tiny storage shed in back of that house, and I soon discovered, if I put on my skates in the shed, slipped down the stairs, and skated two blocks down Bronson Avenue, there was a park with a hockey rink. Dozens of kids of all ages and sizes were flying around in all directions, and two or three games were in progress—all on the same sheet of natural ice. Playing with your head down, as I did while learning to stickhandle, could lead to decapitation.

Despite the chaos and the danger, I was enthralled and soon addicted. This was McNabb Park in the mid-1940s. I'd scramble to get there at every opportunity. I had my first concussion there, my first fist fight.

There were meek kids, like me, and tough kids and braggarts and bullies. There were kids who could "dangle" and kids who had no idea how to keep out of the way. Other kids ploughed right through them and over them. The best player on the ice was Larry Regan, who would grow up to be rookie of the year with Boston in the NHL. At age 26. But if you expected a pass from Regan, forget it. He owned the puck. He dared anyone to take it away from him. He laughed at us when we couldn't.

Head down, I got flattened by an older boy one day, and that's all I remember. When I came to, other kids were gathered around, annoyed that I was holding up their game.

"Did he swallow his tongue?"

Somebody—a teenager—shoved a dirty finger in my mouth and moved it around. I almost gagged.

"No, just out cold. He's coming around."

I blinked, struggled to my feet feeling nauseous. I looked around.

There were two players where there should have been one. Two pucks, two nets. Two of everything.

"Guess I'll go home," I muttered.

"Yeah, good idea. Go home, kid."

I was confused. And suddenly awfully tired.

"Which way is home?"

A kid pointed. "That way. That's Bronson Avenue."

Somehow, I got home. My mother again called the doctor, who showed up within the hour. Doctors made house calls then.

"I'm almost certain it's a concussion," the doctor said. "Let's get him into bed."

I didn't know what a concussion was, but it scared me. I didn't have to be told concussions were bad for the brain.

A few days in bed, and I was back up, eager to get back to the games at McNabb Park, determined to keep my head up.

My parents let me go, perhaps with a few words of caution.

It was my first of three or four concussions, the final one coming while playing with the NHL Oldtimers almost half a century later.

I must have learned something about hockey on that scary rink at McNabb Park, because a few years later I was playing on a juvenile team—the Aces—that played off for the city championship on a sheet of outdoor ice covered with an inch or two of water at one end, yet solid at the other. In the deciding game of a three-game series, the Aces had to slog through the water for two periods and couldn't score. Our opponents won the title with a pair of goals scored on the solid ice.

I stumbled upon one of my dad's many diaries recently. He wrote: "To Brian's playoff game and the boys were hugely disappointed when they lost while trying to shoot through pools of water. The ice conditions were wretched. In the best-of-three series, Brian scored five of his team's seven goals."

I did? I have no memory of that.

After the season, all the league's players gathered in a big hall at Ottawa Tech one night, and my name was called out. I proceeded to the stage and was handed a small trophy with my name on it—and with the letters *MVP* underneath.

I was truly astonished. Me—the MVP. That trophy must still be around somewhere. But without the hockey stick the miniature player was holding. It fell out of his hands one day—the goofball—and was lost.

The first school I attended in Ottawa was Glashan Public School. At age 12, I won an essay contest there, and it led to a chance to be heard on the CBC. I wrote about life as a school kid in Ottawa during the war. I don't recall if there was a cash prize, but I do recall the thrill of speaking into a microphone at the CBC studios in the Chateau Laurier Hotel. I was told my recording would soon be heard by kids in Great Britain and Australia.

Decades later, I would be back in a CBC studio in Toronto talking about my dad, and during our chat, the interviewer played back a portion of my childhood essay. Then she asked me about my aims and ambitions when I was young. I told her of wanting to play hockey and wanting to be a hockey broadcaster and perhaps a writer as well.

She then asked a question that baffled me.

"Brian, did any of those early ambitions of yours come true?" I didn't know how to answer without embarrassing her. She had no idea I'd been with *Hockey Night in Canada* for 15 years and had written about 40 books.

After the interview, when someone told her of her gaffe, as they must have, she would have been mortified. As I would have, if I'd been in her place. You must do your homework. My sister Norah and I spent our high school years in Ottawa at Glebe Collegiate, where my kid sister, not to be upstaged, entered and won a short story contest at age 16 in *Seventeen* magazine. Norah received first prize money of $500, beating out hundreds of applicants from all over North America—and her photo appeared over a story in the *Ottawa Journal*.

I have that 1947 clipping in front of me. "I've been writing since I was little," Norah tells the reporter. "I had two poems published in *Maclean's* magazine when I was eight and when I was 12, I sold a story to an American magazine called *Polly Pigtails*. I don't let anyone fuss with my stories when I finish them—not even my dad. I don't type very well so I let him check them for typographical errors. I didn't think I'd win this contest because it's the first one I entered. Golly, isn't it wonderful news."

Norah went on to win awards for some of her novels and continues to write wonderful prose in her late 80s under her married name, Norah A. Perez. Her latest novel is *The Slave Raffle*, and she has just completed *When the Bough Breaks*, a family memoir.

She lost her husband, Lou, recently—a huge loss. And then Jon, her youngest of three sons. But she is coping. She said recently, "All I need is a bed, a book, and a bourbon and I'm content."

Today's teenagers have no idea how war affected our generation. In the summer of '41, while still in grade school, Norah and I stood on a dock at a summer cottage my dad had rented. It was Camp Lorraine in Northern Ontario. I was 10, she was 8, and we had a serious discussion about the ability of the Brits to stave off an invasion by German forces. If Britain fell, we'd be next.

We were frightened little kids who should have been swimming and canoeing and picking blueberries, not fearful of Adolph Hitler soon ruling the British Isles and then shipping his storm troopers over to Canada.

Scary times for kids like us. Our grandkids and great grandkids have no idea how threatened we felt—although the recent pandemic caused much anxiety and fear. Boys and girls just a couple of years older believed that one day they'd be called to active duty.

At Glebe Collegiate in Ottawa, students were already reacting soberly to the reality of an invasion. Nobody laughed when 50 Glebe boys formed a knitting club—the first such club in Canada—and balls of yarn were quickly converted to socks and afghans.

One Glebe teacher told the *Ottawa Citizen* that football players pulled out their knitting needles during assembly, in the cafeteria, and even at football games while sitting on the bench.

Come on, teach, not during a football game.

A number of senior players would soon join the armed forces, no doubt wondering if some quartermaster would hand them a pair of socks they'd knitted while at Glebe.

Across town, at Lisgar Collegiate, the girls actually thought they might be called on to defend their country. A Lisgar Girls' Rifle Club was formed, and a surprising number of girls signed up, becoming regulars at the after-school shooting range. "We'll be able to lick the Hun if he ever comes over here," one sharpshooting lass said defiantly.

I did something novel at Glebe that involved writing. I'm certain nobody but me remembers. I created a sports magazine of four pages—the *Athletic*. Charged three cents a copy; wrote the articles myself. But there were few purchasers, and I got discouraged. After a few weeks I closed it down.

After school, we often got together in the schoolyard and played volleyball, using the high wire fence around the yard as a net. Again, I found a way to get a little attention. After each game, I phoned the

Ottawa Journal and reported the results of the Glebe senior volleyball league. I made up teams and scores, and soon the paper was printing the results. But I got a little nervous, thinking the fraud squad might descend at any moment. Or the principal would catch us goofing around. The volleyball league folded before a champion could be declared.

At Glebe Collegiate, I felt virtually ignored. I can't recall one good friend I made. I earned one A—in art class.

Our high school principal was, I'm pretty sure, perplexed with me. I was the rebel, the kid who suggested to my high school classmates, "See the big clock in the classroom? When it hits three o'clock, everybody cough and sneeze. Watch our grumpy old teacher jump out of his chair."

I was the one, while pretending to study in our school library with the creaky floorboards, who would request book after book from the library shelves. Miss Jenkins, the librarian, would whisper "Yes, Brian, get a book but be quiet." I would set out for the farthest shelf. I would be silent, but the floorboards spoke for themselves.

Creak, creak, creak. What a lovely sound.

I would come back, scan a page or two, and return the book.

Creak, Creak, creak.

I would seek another. *Creak, Creak, creak.* Scan it. Put it back on the shelf. *Creak, Creak, creak.*

Other students would look up and smile. They got my act. Were amused.

Miss Jenkins got it, too. Was not amused. She broke the silence with a loud directive after she slammed a dictionary on her desk, stood, and hollered, "McFarlane, will you please sit down and shut up!" Snoozing students awoke. Heads snapped up. Girls tittered.

"Yes, miss. Sorry. I've got my squeaky shoes on and—"

"It's not your shoes," she barked. "It's your—? Oh, never mind. Sit down and be quiet."

I remember there was one hockey book on the shelves in the school library. It was one of the few ever written to that time. I believe Lester Patrick was the author. I read it from cover to cover.

For a short time, I took after-school art lessons from noted Ottawa painter Henri Masson and I enjoyed them. For my first lesson, he handed me some paint and a brush after placing some fruit on a plate.

"Paint that," he said as he left the studio. He'd been called to dinner.

I painted "that," and it turned out well. He came back, looked surprised, and praised my efforts.

"Very good," he said. "You must continue."

But when I made the junior football team as a halfback and missed practice one day, coach Thornton was annoyed. He ripped into me. "Where were you yesterday, McFarlane? You missed practice."

"Sir, I was taking an art lesson. I go once a week. They cost 50 cents a lesson."

"Art lessons? Forget the art lessons," he barked. "I need you in my backfield."

He did? I wanted to believe him, but he'd paid scant attention to me. I never heard a word of praise from the man, whereas Henri Masson encouraged me to paint. I still have the first couple of paintings I did for him hanging in my office. They are over 75 years old and they are quite good—for a teenaged beginner. Every time I look at them, I think of Mr. Thornton. *Why did I strive to be a football player when I wasn't very good? Why did I let him intimidate me?* I never got much from football. But the world of art has given me countless hours of joy. I waited half a century to get back to it and now I'm pleased with my work. Buyers of my stuff apparently think it's worthy. I'll keep trying to improve, but the sands of time are telling me, "Better hurry. Your vision is failing. We'll be running out on you soon."

I wanted to be somebody in high school. Nobody cared about art, but everybody followed the senior and junior football clubs. I wanted to be a star.

But I was not fast on my feet, and my small hands made it difficult to throw a football with ease. But I could catch one. I spent many hours playing touch football at McNabb Park and I could pluck a long pass out of the air with confidence. Coach Thornton never discovered or noticed this skill. He put me at halfback, but I never was used as a pass receiver. I'd take the ball from the quarterback, look for a hole, and run into two or three huge linemen who enjoyed jumping on my back, smacking me into the mud and grass. I don't remember ever scoring a touchdown or even making a first down.

Opting for football gave me little enjoyment. It led to plenty of pain and frustration, but because of coach Thornton's mocking words I gave up painting and didn't rediscover it for 60 years.

At Glebe Collegiate, I also played for the school hockey team. Now I was where I belonged, but nobody cared. A few parents straggled in to our games. I wore a pair of vintage hockey pants, blue with two white stripes down each side. The white had turned to dark grey over the years, so I took paint and brush to the stripes and—presto—they were dazzling.

That may have been my second step into the world of art. But there was no call for my expertise. I never painted anyone else's pants, although I'd gladly have put a brush to coach Thornton's ass.

I remember Glebe for several reasons. There was VE Day—75 years ago to the day as I write this—when we all leaped from our seats at the news the war was over. We all raced into downtown Ottawa to view the wild celebrations.

At Glebe, there were weekly after-school dances in the gym. I would go, but never danced. I had a crush on a girl named Betty Ann Walker. I never got to dance with her. Decades later, I met a man in Edmonton who was a former Glebeite. I told him about my long-ago crush on Betty Ann and how I hoped she was having a good life. He surprised me by saying, "Brian, I hope so, too. That's the girl I married."

I remember Glebe for long-distance runner Don McEwen, who was a year or two ahead of me. He was a brilliant miler and distance runner and went on to an impressive career in track at the University of Michigan. How I admired him. While there, he won consecutive NCAA men's track and field championships in the two-mile race. In 1950, McEwen won the NCAA championship with a time of nine minutes, 1.9 seconds, setting a new NCAA record. His record lasted for 55 years—until 2008. McEwen also won six Big Ten Conference individual championships in track. In 1951, he set a mark of 4:09.0 in the one-mile run.

I was not a fast runner, but McEwen inspired me to run distances—to develop lung and leg strength and stamina. He had great legs, strong and muscular. Powerful legs. Mine were as skinny as Olive Oyl's—Popeye's girlfriend. So skinny I hated to wear shorts.

I remember Glebe for the boring lessons in history class. So many dates to remember. What was the date of this war, this voyage of discovery? I yawned my way through the classes, unaware in later life I would become a history buff, especially when it came to hockey.

I was at Glebe when Barbara Ann Scott won the World Figure Skating title at Davos, Switzerland, in 1948. The City of Ottawa bought her a car—a yellow '48 convertible. In art class, I made a papier mâché replica of the car, but she never got to see mine or drive the real one. Avery Brundage, the head of the International Olympic Committee, told her he'd declare her a professional if she accepted it. We all hated Brundage. But when Scott won the '48 Olympic title at St. Moritz, Switzerland, she thanked him for helping to save her amateur standing.

Late in our lives, in our 80s, Barbara Ann (she was not a Glebeite) and I became email pals. In one, she told me about the '48 Olympics, and how she was adopted by Canada's Olympic hockey team, and how gold medals were won by both. Writer Frank Orr said to me one day, "Barbara Ann made a whole career out of being pert."

The only teacher who appreciated me was the art teacher, Miss Cushing. She inspired me. "Brian, you have a creative streak that pleases me. I can see you doing well in art. Or maybe the theatre. Or writing."

Recently, I wondered if Glebe ever laid claim to me or my sister or Don McEwen as distinguished graduates. Alas, none of us made the list, although Margaret Atwood did, and Peter Mansbridge. Hell, Glebe didn't even recognize Bill Cowley, who went there, one of the finest centres in NHL history. If I'd been asked to compile a list of famous alums, Cowley would be right at the top.

A quick story about Cowley, and why I considered him a great sportsman. He was awarded an assist on a goal one night and felt he hadn't deserved it. So, he wrote the NHL offices and asked for the point to be deleted from the records. His request was granted, and the point he relinquished cost him a tie for the NHL scoring crown that season. His was the second autograph I sought and got from a hockey star.

On April 5, 1947, at the Bruins' annual breakup party, Cowley unexpectedly announced he was leaving hockey. He was upset when general manager Art Ross left him off the roster for a post-season exhibition swing through Western Canada and the United States. Cowley's wife was from Vancouver, and the tour would be their honeymoon. When he retired, he was the NHL's all-time leading point scorer. And that assist he gave up? He finished with 548 points in 549 regular season games.

CHAPTER 10

A FATHER'S ADVICE

I was 15 when my father took me aside one day. "We have to talk," he said, leading me into his cramped study. This was in the dumpy house we lived in during the war—in Ottawa. At 8 Christie Street. One tiny bathroom. A tub, no shower. My dad's study was prison-sized—about 10 by 10. No door. There were books and files everywhere, a small desk on which perched his steady old Underwood. On this machine, with two chubby fingers striking the keys like a concert pianist, almost magically, he churned out scripts of fiction and fact. There were two novels—*The Murder Tree* and *Streets of Shadow*—he'd published along the way to good reviews, film scripts for the documentaries he wrote and directed for the National Film Board (NFB) in Ottawa, television dramas for producers at the CBC, the occasional article he penned for *Maclean's* and other magazines. On a shelf were bound volumes of hockey yarns full of action and suspense from the pulp magazines of the '30s and '40s. And books of mystery and suspense for boys and girls—the Hardy Boys and the Dana Girls series.

Yes, writing under a *nom de plume*, Franklin W. Dixon, my dad, a shy, jockey-sized man who smoked two packs per day, had authored, in his drinking days, the first 21 volumes in the famous Hardy Boys series. He was a creative but modest man who probably never considered that he could rightfully claim the title of Canada's all-time bestselling author. My sister Norah and I will claim it for him. How many other Canadian writers have sold an estimated 80–100 million books? How many others would write books at all if there were no royalties to be earned and no credit given for those millions of words?

On reflection, he could not have claimed that distinction—not aloud—because he'd signed a pact with his New Jersey publisher—a man he never met named Stratemeyer—not to make any claims about the Hardy Boys. He was never to reveal that he'd written the damn books. He often admonished his three kids, especially me, because I was the chatterbox, never to mention the fact he was, in fact, Franklin W. Dixon. I may have been the only kid in Canada who knew that F. W. Dixon was a fake, an imposter.

My dad wound up disliking the books intensely. "I enjoyed writing the first few books in the series," he once told me. "The publisher would send me a brief outline—a plot—and I tried to make them fun for kids to read, with some challenging words and proper grammar. But then they became boring. It was hack writing. After a few, I vowed I'd never write another one. Then I'd need the hundred bucks and I'd agree to do one more.

"Any one of a hundred hack writers could have written them. I wrote them when money was tight. A hundred bucks put coal in the furnace for the winter. I was astonished when I learned they sold in the millions. Today's editions are a crappy, watered-down version of the originals— and still sell a million a year."

"Don't be telling your pals I wrote those cursed books," he growled at me back then. "What are you staring at?" he asked.

"The books—the Hardy Boys. On your shelf. You should have gotten royalties. A penny a book, and you'd have been wealthy. You could have bought a car, a house for Mom."

"Forget the books. I knew what the deal was. I wasn't cheated. If I hadn't written them, somebody else would have jumped in to do it. Besides, they're history now."

"Dad, no they're not. Kids still read them. Kids still love them. I'm almost 16, and they got me hooked on reading years ago. I'm glad you wrote them. I'm proud of you. And maybe I'll be a writer someday—like you are."

"Okay, so they did some good. Kids jumped from them to better stuff. But we're not here to talk Hardy Boys. Forget about those brats."

Forget about them? Any youngster who read the Hardy Boys remembered them for a lifetime. In 1967, my dad would write about his role in their success in an autobiography—*The Ghost of the Hardy Boys*, which is about to be re-published by a U.S. publisher—Godine.

Obviously, this was a strange prelude to the Big Talk coming between father and son. My instincts told me a serious discussion about the mysteries of sex and condoms and teenaged pregnancy and gonorrhea and syphilis was fast approaching, and so, I fidgeted. The dictionary had already revealed to me that gonorrhea and syphilis were diseases of the genitals.

I fidgeted for another reason. The guys were already on their way to the outdoor rink at McNabb Park, two blocks away. Soon they'd be choosing sides for a game of shinny, and I wanted to be there.

There was only one chair. I sat on a box of books and braced myself for a few cautionary words about unprotected sex, accepting that "no" means "no," and perhaps a few words of sage advice about avoiding men who lust after young boys.

To my surprise, on that day in his study, he had no intention of orchestrating the Big Talk. But he was concerned about something.

"There's a problem?" I asked.

"Yes," he said. "I know you've been skipping school a lot this winter—don't ask me how I know—and I assume you've been writing notes to the teacher in your mother's handwriting."

He was right. *How did he know that? Had he come across scraps of paper where I'd practised writing "Amy McFarlane" over and over?*

"And you've been sneaking into the Ottawa auditorium in the morning with your skates and stick—to play hockey."

Geez—he was right again. My dad was a better detective than Dick Tracy. Or, more appropriately, Fenton Hardy.

I had been sneaking into the old oval-shaped arena, home of the pro Senators of the Quebec League, where I pleaded with any team booking morning ice time there—firemen and policeman, mainly—to let me play with them if they were short of bodies, which they often were. I just learned that Auston Matthews did the same thing. But in Arizona.

After that, all sweaty and happy, I'd trot off to Glebe Collegiate, hand the teacher a note signed by my mother (I could forge her signature almost perfectly), and nod off through my afternoon classes.

Most kids skipped school in the afternoons, when the movie theatres opened.

"This obsession with hockey is not good," my father continued. "You play in the morning and you've got league games at night. And you play shinny at McNabb Park all weekend. It's too much. I seldom see you doing much homework. The only subject you got an A in is art. Art won't get you into university."

"Right again, Dad," I almost said, "But maybe hockey will." But that would be a longshot at best. Nobody in our circle had ever been recruited by a university hockey coach.

It was my mother who wanted desperately for me to go to college. That wasn't likely to happen. No family member had a university degree, not even my dad, who was an established writer and filmmaker. He even taught creative writing courses at Carlton University in Ottawa. So, he was like a professor—almost one—but with a lowly high school education.

He had a final observation that day.

"If you don't give up the game, if you continue to skip school to play all morning, you'll become a high school dropout. You'll never amount to anything. Perhaps you'd better give up hockey. I want you to think about that."

I promised him I would. Think about it. But give up the game? That was unlikely. Unthinkable. Hockey already had a Gordie Howe grip on me. Unshakeable. I knew it would never bring me to the NHL. But where would it take me?

I had no answer. I wish Ted Lindsay or Syl Apps had been around. Or Bill Cowley. I'd ask them why and how hockey had consumed their lives.

I still have my old hockey bag—they were called duffle bags, but nobody ever told me what duffles were—from those early days in Ottawa. With this bag, I'd scramble to get to midget and juvenile games by walking or bicycling. Sometimes I'd get there by bus or streetcar. One day I hopped on a streetcar and found I only had four pennies in my pocket. The fare was five cents. I slipped the pennies into the coin box and hoped the driver wouldn't check. But he did. He called me back.

"You owe a penny, son."

"Sir, I don't have one."

He said nothing. I stood there.

At the next stop, he opened the door. "Get off," he ordered.

And I did. It was a long walk to the outdoor rink, and I was almost late. But I'd learned a lesson. Cheaters get caught.

But my hockey bag was never heavy. That bag, which I still have, was incredibly small. About the size of a large brown paper bag. What could I have put in there? There was no room for pants and barely room for shin pads. I figure I wore my everyday pants to games, no shoulder pads, but I must have had a small pair of gloves. No jock. Visors and helmets were unheard of. My stick would be thrust through my skate blades and carried over one shoulder. I smile every time I look at that brown bag. My name scratched on it near the top. A stout drawstring to hold everything in place. With my gear stuffed inside, it might have weighed all of 10 or 15 pounds.

At the time it seemed perfectly adequate. I don't recall teammates who showed up with bigger bags.

In Florida, where I played with the Snowbirds until I was 84, I brought all my gear in a standard-sized hockey bag. Don Awrey noticed it one day and said, "That's too heavy to lug around. Get yourself a bag with wheels."

I said, "No, it wouldn't feel right. If you can't haul your bag into a rink by hand, you shouldn't be playing." Saying that sounds silly now. Some players today carry bags the size of bathtubs.

When I was a teen in Ottawa, the city was inundated with sleet and rain one winter day. All city streets were closed to traffic when the temperature plunged, and everything froze. I urged my friend Norm Cottee to grab his skates.

"We can skate down the main streets," I told him. "We can skate right up to the Parliament buildings."

It was heady stuff, exciting. We dashed along Bank and Sparks streets, around the War Memorial—not a car or cop in sight. Or any other skaters.

Nobody had ever skated to places we did that day. "Norm, we're making history!" I shouted.

Soon it was time to start back.

But the fun was over.

While we were enjoying our once-in-a-lifetime adventure, the sanders were out. There were rows of sand at many intersections, forcing us to leap over them. Easy at first, but we tired and went sprawling when poor timing and sharp blades hit grit.

But we made it home, nursing bruised knees and nicked blades.

"Was it worth it, Norm?" I asked.

"Every minute."

"Shall we tell our parents what fun we had?"

"Nah. Why bother."

But my morning workouts at the Ottawa Auditorium soon ceased. Mainly because, for the following season, I'd been invited to play with the Junior A Ottawa Montagnards. A good season in juvenile had earned me a tryout with the Monties, and I surprised myself by making the team. I was amazed that someone thought I was good enough to play Junior A.

There was practice time with the Monties (never enough) and a 20-game season played against the other top teenagers in the city. With all games played in the old Auditorium, where the professional Senators played. Occasionally, I'd see Mr. Tommy Gorman, team owner and a big name in hockey—he'd managed the Blackhawks and the Canadiens to Stanley Cups—and now he was roaming the corridors of the Ottawa Auditorium. Today, decades later, I'm friends with his grandson Dave.

I absolutely could not believe I'd reached the Junior A level. No one in our scattered family had ever aspired to be a player. My father had played some as a kid, but not seriously.

"Were you a good stickhandler, Dad?" I asked.

"One day I was. I tied the puck to my stick with three feet of fishing line. They let me play because I owned a couple of pucks."

While he dismissed the Hardy Boys as "hack writing," he did take some pride in his adventure and mystery stories. And even more pride, I believe, in his sports stories—especially those about hockey.

I treasured them because they were written when I was a little kid, trying out my first pair of skates, and when I clung to a faint hope that I'd grow up and be a star on the ice, like the young men my dad wrote about.

Soon after he stopped writing them—among the earliest hockey stories ever published—the pulp magazines vanished from the scene. Reluctantly, my dad's fictional heroes—"Skates" Kelsey, Bing McGonigal, Sniper Jack Parmalee, Diving Danny Wade, and many others, were forced to hang up their skates. No lucrative pensions, no Hall of Fame inductions for these old stars who skated on mythical ice. They simply disappeared.

My dad's diaries reflected his financial plight and his frustration of relying on Hardy Boys assignments to keep the wolves from snapping at our door.

1932: "Not a nickel in the world and nothing in sight. Am simply desperate with anxiety. What's to become of us this winter? It looks black."

1933: "Worked away at the accursed Hardy book. The plot they sent me is so ridiculous that I am constantly held up trying to work a little logic into it."

"Tried to get at the Hardy Boys juvenile again today but the ghastly job appalls me."

"A small advance arrived so I was able to pay part of the grocery bill and buy a load of dry wood."

1934: "I took Brian for a walk downtown today but his shoes fell apart and I had to bring him home."

"The publisher wants me to do another book. I said I would never do another of the cursed things but the offer always comes when we are desperate for money. I said I would do it but asked for more than the $85 offer, a disgraceful price for 45,000 words."

Did he get his raise? No. Did he write the book? Yes.

Hockey has changed dramatically since my dad's involvement in the game. Chicken wire no longer affords a screen behind the goal nets, natural ice is a rarity—if it even exists—in small-town rinks, the 60-minute man and the unmasked goalie have vanished like straight-bladed sticks and the wheeled barrels of water used to resurface the ice before the Zamboni. But the basics remain: the speed, the hard-hitting slam-bang combat, the suspense which makes for good drama.

I trust some of the yarns I like to tell and write—in books and speeches—bring a nod of approval from readers, perhaps even as much pleasure as my father brought to his audience, even to his son, so many years ago.

While never much of a player, my father had always been a devoted fan of hockey. For a time, he served as manager of the Haileybury junior club, and I was always proud of the fact he once served as a guest colour commentator alongside Foster Hewitt. Perhaps I sat in the same chair.

In Ottawa, I met famed Canadian artist A.Y. Jackson one day. It was like meeting a hockey star. I remember sneaking into a tent show at the Ottawa Exhibition with my pal Norm Cottee. And leaving quickly when we discovered the performer was Paul Anka, a kid who lived a few blocks away from us. "He's only 16. He can't be very good," we agreed, the tent skirt flapping behind us.

I had many jobs. I worked delivering ice and piling lumber in a lumberyard. The driver of the ice truck was a good-looking man and was popular with a few of the housewives on our route. Even at 16, I knew he was delivering something warmer than ice when an apartment door closed behind him. While he was being entertained, I was lugging 50 pounds of ice up three floors to an icebox that challenged me to heave the ice into a chamber at the top. My boss had the muscles to do it; I had the muscle cramps.

I spent one summer as a copy boy on the *Ottawa Journal*, where I was pleased when Bill Westwick, the sports editor with a corner office, nodded at me as he passed. I knew about Bill's famous father, Rat Westwick, who had played and won Stanley Cups with Ottawa.

One summer—1947—without telling her, I entered my sister Pat's name in the Miss Ottawa contest, and she won. This triggered a long career for Pat as a top fashion model in the city.

I delivered prescriptions from a nearby drugstore to customers on my bicycle, and one summer, now 17, I sold magazine subscriptions to office girls despite my concern over the zits that dotted my face. Some weeks I made as much as 50 dollars. The job led me to Toronto, where I booked a cheap room on Jarvis Street. My dad saw the address on a letter I sent him and he asked, "Isn't that where most of the brothels are?"

What did I know? And how did he know?

But I did learn a lesson or two on that job. I'd be in the middle of a sales pitch to three or four girls at their desk when an officious male clerk would come rushing over. "Get out of here. You're not allowed to talk to these girls while they're at work. Come on. Move it."

I'd go—but not very far. I'd look for the office of the CEO or someone else with clout. If I gained admittance, I'd tell him how I was trying hard to work my way through college (I wasn't even in college), and how the girls really wanted the magazines, and how the clerk had screwed everything up. Could I please share another few minutes with the young ladies and then I'd be gone?

Often, I'd get permission to finish my pitch. The man would say, "I did what you're doing when I was in college. Finish up, but be quick about it."

And I would—only to have the clerk come rushing back to threaten me again.

And I could tell him I wasn't going anywhere. I had permission from his boss to talk to the ladies. "Go ask him. And leave us alone."

The girls would almost applaud. They'd whisper, "He's such a jerk. I'm glad you told him to fuck off."

I hadn't used those two words. Just thought about it. Today four-year-olds are using them.

I worked as a house painter in Pembroke, Ontario, one summer. That's where I bought my first car—a 1931 Chevy with no brakes. It cost 75 dollars. My friend Art Gallagher drove it to the ballpark, where we had a game that night. After the game, in semi-darkness, we drove it around and around the infield and the outfield while Gallagher taught me how to drive. Satisfied I'd learned the basics, I drove back to my boarding house alone, dripping with perspiration the entire way. With no brakes, I had to learn how to "gear down" to bring the old car to a halt.

I drove it all summer. And without a driver's licence or insurance. Even when we painted the police station offices in town. I parked it next to where the cruisers parked.

I was totally stupid.

My painting partner, Bill, was an older chap. We painted a two-story brick house one day with white paint. We started at the back. We climbed our long ladders, Bill starting at one end, and me at the other. There was one lone window, and it was at my end. I began painting and when I quickly reached the window it opened and an attractive young woman leaned out to say hello. Her name, I soon learned, was Ateji Viss, and she was the maid. We chatted, and she charmed me as I painted around her window, applying one coat on top of another. I was so engrossed I failed to observe my partner's efforts until he moved his ladder alongside mine. He'd painted almost the entire back wall of the house while I was focused on the window—and the pretty young Ateji Viss inside it.

I can't believe I still remember the name of a girl I met once—for an hour or two—almost 70 years later?

Occasionally, my dad would recruit family members for his NFB productions, one of which was nominated for an Academy Award. My sister Pat appears in his film *Here's Hockey!* I watched the film on my computer the other day. My sister Norah had a major acting role in a film called *The Boy Who Stopped Niagara*. My mother was recruited for bit parts in his films. But she was always a reluctant recruit.

CHAPTER 11

SMALL TOWN, BIG DREAMS

After juvenile hockey, it was on to the Ottawa Junior A league with the Montagnards. Indoor hockey, at last, with fast ice and real dressing rooms. First, there was the surprise of making the team and later, to my utter astonishment, after leading the Monties in scoring, earning a second team berth on the All-Star team, behind Bill Dineen of St. Pats, who would go on to play for the Detroit Red Wings with Gordie Howe and Ted Lindsay. Dineen was awesome. He made a last-second rush in a tie game with us one night. I threw myself prone on the ice to block him off, and he leaped over me, stickhandled past everybody else, and scored on us with one second to play. That goal remains clear in my memory after all these years. The Dineen family became famous—and highly respected in hockey circles. I was saddened to hear of Bill's death in 2016. Wish I'd known him better.

I didn't come close to Bill Dineen as a hockey player. No muscles, a skinny frame, small hands and thin wrists. No heavy shot. A lousy fighter. If I possessed any snot, it would be beaten out of me. But I could score goals. And I was rather proud of my passing.

But I was almost sure I'd never be skillful enough to make pro hockey.

I was 16 when my dad took me to see a junior playoff game at the Ottawa Auditorium one night. The powerful St. Pats—the 1948 city champs—would host a team of farm boys from the little town of Inkerman, Ontario. Nobody knew or cared where Inkerman was. The names on the roster meant nothing. They'd be no match for the city champs. But my dad thought otherwise.

"You watch the Inkerman kids," he told me. "Their coach, Lloyd Laporte, has some boys who can skate like the wind. They don't have a league to play in, so they play exhibition games all season against much older fellows—intermediates and seniors. They'll be toughened up. They'll do well against St. Pats."

When I saw the farm boys skate out for the warm-up, I almost felt sorry for them. They were little fellows, most of them. And their hockey pants were too small. Surely, my dad had been misinformed. They'd be no match for St. Pats.

Then the game began, and the Rockets went to work. They whipped the Ottawa boys easily that day with non-stop skating and an energy that was truly impressive. Twins Erwin and Edwin Duncan supplied most of the offence. Leo Boivin, 15 years old, was a standout on the blue line, beginning a career that would take him all the way to the Hockey Hall of Fame. And another 15-year-old, Gordie Brown, from Smiths Falls, Ontario, led some dazzling rushes.

I was captivated by the Rockets. The Duncan twins swirling and twirling, superb little guys who bewildered the St. Pats. Boivin, a little baby-faced kid from Prescott, Ontario, playing the blue line like no other junior I'd ever seen. A riot of noise from the farmers who backed the Rockets and helped fill the building.

I turned to my dad and said, "That's the team I want to play for someday."

"Maybe you will."

Here's the Inkerman story. Lloyd Laporte, a schoolteacher, had moved to Inkerman from Collingwood, Ontario, in the early '40s and he loved hockey. A non-player—he'd lost the sight in one eye when a pair of scissors slipped—he made sure there was a rink next to his tiny schoolhouse. As a young man and an avid fan, he travelled a long distance to buy tickets for the opening game at Maple Leaf Gardens in November 1931.

As a teacher, he enjoyed helping boys get started in the game. So, he had his pupils shovel off a patch of ice in the schoolyard and supervised games of shinny there. Other kids played unsupervised games of shinny under the bridge over the Nation River. Laporte had a good eye for talent.

Later, he coached a team in the Winchester Town league. Winchester was a slightly bigger town five miles down the road and boasted a rickety indoor rink. Larry Robinson grew up in nearby Marvelville, Ontario. But Larry came along later.

At the end of his first season in an organized league, Laporte found himself with a 48-dollar surplus in the kitty. The kitty was composed of five-dollar bills collected from farmers in the area. Laporte figured he might have almost enough to purchase new jerseys for a teenaged team he was organizing.

When he drove to a sporting goods store in Ottawa, it wasn't enough.

But the owner said, "Wait a minute. Last season, a team paid for jerseys they never picked up. There's a big *R* stitched on the front."

"What colour are they?"

"Red and white."

"Will you take 48 bucks for them?"

"I will."

Laporte saw a bargain. "I'll take them," he said. "I'll call my team the Rivermen or the Reds. Maybe even Rockets."

"Yeah, Rockets. That's a good name."

People laughed when Laporte applied for a Junior A franchise— and got one.

"There's not a single Junior A–calibre player in your area," he was told. "And no league. No team is going to play on your rinky-dink rink in Winchester."

"I'll bet they will. And I'll bring in the players," he said confidently.

And, by golly, he did. He recruited farm boys from nearby towns and a few from bigger places, cities like Cornwall, Ontario; Ottawa; and even one from Brooklyn, New York.

I had no idea where Inkerman was. So, I looked it up on the map. I found it finally, a little speck between Ottawa and Cornwall.

The following year, I tried out for the Rockets, but Laporte wasn't interested in a 150-pound high school player from Glebe Collegiate. But he did take three older players from Glebe, which hadn't turned out any hockey players since Bill Cowley back in the '30s. They were centre Lev McDonald, winger Billy Lynn, and goaltender Bert Feltham. Laporte picked well. They were all top-calibre junior players.

But after I turned in a good season and earned an all-star berth with the Monties, Laporte called my folks. Could he come and visit?

A few days later, he stood in our living room at 8 Christie Street.

"I'd like your lad to play for us in Inkerman," he told my parents. "I've seen him play, and he'll fit in well with us. I can pay 25 dollars a week to cover expenses."

"How will he commute?" my dad asked. "I don't drive. Never owned a car."

"He can come back and forth on the bus. But I'll arrange for him to be billeted to a home in Winchester. Inkerman doesn't have a rink. We play our home games in Winchester, five miles away."

"Billeted?"

"Yes, over Gerry Helmer's barbershop. The team will pay his room and board. He'll get free haircuts."

"Is there a school nearby?"

"Of course, Winchester High School. A good school. Within walking distance."

"But I understand you don't have a league to play in."

"We'll play in an intermediate league, and there will be a lot of exhibition games. Even one or two in New York State against teams like the Clinton Comets. We get a bye into the Ottawa playoffs each year."

"Your teams appear to get solid fan support."

"We play home games in an old barn, I admit. Natural ice is sometimes a problem. But our fans fill it for every game, and opposing teams think twice about starting anything. Anyone hits a Rocket with a dirty slash, and six tough farmers will jump the boards and make them pay."

"Sounds like the Northern Ontario hockey I covered when I worked for the newspapers up there." He turned to me. "What do you think?"

"Dad, you know how much I want to play for the Rockets. I'll be rooming with my pal, Lev McDonald. And John McDonald, who lives down the street, may be a teammate, too. He just signed a C form with the Maple Leafs. I can't wait to put on a Rockets jersey."

He looked at my mom, who nodded and smiled.

I was going to be a Rocket.

CHAPTER 12

LIVING OVER A BARBERSHOP

For two seasons, playing for the Inkerman Rockets was hockey heaven. I lived over Gerry Helmer's barbershop, and his mother was paid 10 dollars a week for room and board. Some nights it was so cold that I slept under—I'm exaggerating perhaps—20 blankets. My dad—who'd suffered through the Depression—later told me, "What sold me on the Rockets was the free haircuts."

Me, too. I had lots of hair then.

The Rockets were the talk of the Ottawa Valley over 70 years ago.

Inkerman Rockets? You kidding? Never heard of them.

I believe you. But listen. It's true. No village so small ever produced a team so talented, so popular.

Lloyd Laporte had made me a better offer than one I'd received from former NHL star Bucko McDonald—to join his Sundridge Beavers, a tough but successful intermediate team located somewhere north of Toronto. McDonald "auditioned" me one morning, booking ice time at the Ottawa Auditorium for just the two of us. I did most of the skating. He fired passes to me and had me take shots on the empty net. He worked me hard, and when the hour was over he said, "You can play for me in Sundridge. You're young for senior hockey, but you'll fit in.

I'll pay you 10 bucks a week, and you can go to a school about 16 miles down the road. This is a big step for you."

It was. Too big. At least, that's what my dad thought.

"You'll get killed playing senior hockey," he told me. "You've already lost three front teeth. Bucko's a good coach, and he always has a winning team. But I think you should stick to junior. Much closer to home."

McDonald faded from my life. Years later, ever on the hunt to find another kid like me to coach, he finally found one in Parry Sound, Ontario—Robert Orr.

I see you've stopped reading. You're thinking, *He's kidding, right?*

And McDonald would reappear many years later as my employee, more or less. He was hired to coach a pro lacrosse team I owned—the Montreal Canadiens.

My parents liked Lloyd Laporte and allowed me to sign with him. After he signed me, he went down the street two blocks and signed highly rated defenceman John McDonald, who was envied because of the C form he'd signed with the Toronto Maple Leafs. McDonald and I had played a hundred games of shinny on the ice of McNabb Park—a hundred yards from McDonald's front door. He never made the Leafs, but he became a respected police officer in Ottawa, and we've been emailing each other in recent years. A good man, John McDonald.

Laporte was low key, soft spoken—a schoolteacher. Out-of-towners he brought in to play for his Rockets stayed at his house—three or four at a time. And he had three kids of his own. His wife, Hilda—a big fan—never seemed to mind.

Bob Lunny, a Montreal junior, showed up one day by train and called from the Winchester station.

"Is this Lloyd Laporte?"

"Yes, it is."

"Well, I'm Bob Lunny and I'm here to play for your Rockets. I need a ride to your place."

"What makes you think you're good enough to play for the Rockets?"

"Oh, I saw your team play in Montreal last spring. Don't worry, I'm good enough. Have someone pick me up. I'm carrying a big suitcase."

Laporte had someone pick up Lunny. He brought him home, sat him down at the table. Hilda served him a big meal. Lunny had a friend with him. He sat down, too.

Laporte was puzzled. Lunny's small companion said nothing. But he ate everything on his plate. Then had seconds.

Finally, Laporte said, "Bob, your friend here. Is he a hockey player, too?"

Lunny said, "I don't think so. He was at the station when I came in. He tagged along. I don't know who he is."

Lunny convinced Laporte he was a player. After dinner, he threw his big suitcase in a spare bedroom and stayed for the next three years.

I have no idea what happened to his strange companion. But he left well fed.

That story perhaps reveals why Bob Lunny became the biggest character in Inkerman Rocket history.

A year later, Lunny recruited me as his partner in a money-making scheme.

It was playoff time, and a special train was booked for a big game in Smiths Falls. Lunny and I bought up all the red-and-white ribbon in town, some pins, and a pair of scissors.

We got to the train station early, and when the crowd descended we sold the ribbons for 25 cents. Business was so brisk that Bob, who had the scissors, began cutting his ribbons shorter and shorter. Some fans had ribbons 18 inches long, some had 12-inch ribbons, and late-comers had six-inch ribbons.

When we boarded the train, our pockets were so full of quarters, dimes, and nickels we feared our pants would fall down.

It was my first venture into financial entrepreneurship.

One of our fans fell off the train that night, halfway to our destination. He was walking between cars with a bottle in hand. The train lurched one way, and he lurched the other—into thin air and a snowbank. Somehow he crawled to a farmhouse and took refuge there, cursing because he missed the game.

The Rockets still had no junior league to play in. But an intermediate league accepted the team, and we won the league championship on a goal that bounced in off my head in the final minutes of the final game.

We played exhibition games in places as far away as Clinton and Lake Placid, New York. And one hugely important game in Canton, New York, against the Lake Placid Roamers. How important? Well, I'm getting to that. It changed my life forever.

I would get to play with Gordie Brown, the skating whiz who'd been so impressive against St. Pats at age 15. But you won't know that name. To my amazement, he was done. No more fancy rushes, an enigma, having to beg Laporte to put him on the ice. Embarrassing. Funny how some guys fall by the wayside. I was disappointed not to play with Boivin. Boivin was gone, too, picked up by the Port Arthur Junior A club. He went on to play 1,150 NHL games with five different NHL clubs and was whisked into the Hall of Fame in 1986. I'd never seen anyone skate backwards like Boivin. Or hand out such thumping bodychecks. Not much taller than a fire hydrant, he crushed people. Along the way, he shed his nickname "Nig," acquired when he was a youngster because of his dark complexion. Can you imagine? Ted Lindsay told me he was saddled with a similar ugly nickname, "Buckwheat," when he was a teen—all because he was dark-skinned.

They held a night for Leo in Prescott several years ago, and I drove from Toronto to be the emcee. But I told a joke that offended a clergyman in the audience, and he let me know it. I agonized about it all the way home and decided he was right. I'd ignored my own rule: when in doubt, leave it out. I wished I could have gone back and started over again. But you can never do that. Sorry, Leo. I'm still berating myself all these years later. Boivin, who'd lost his father as a lad, was a little boy lost when the Laportes took him in at age 15. He thrived under the home life and guidance he received and excelled on the ice. He's featured in a documentary on the Rockets produced by Samantha Armstrong, daughter of a Rocket, Percy Armstrong. It's on YouTube.

We played home games on natural ice in that tiny barn of a rink in Winchester. We filled arenas wherever we played because of the Rockets' reputation for clean, fast play. And we could do no wrong on home ice. If some tough old veterans tried to smack us around, our fans would bristle. Some would leap over the boards and pummel our tormentors into submission. No one was ever charged with assault. No, they were cheered.

Conversely, our road games could be intimidating. Teams we played in Ontario towns like Finch, Maxville, Alexandria, and Cornwall didn't appreciate being embarrassed by fast-moving, cocky teenagers. When they caught us, which wasn't easy, they would get in their licks, and we'd take a bit of a thumping. But we always thumped back.

One night in Maxville, we scored the tying goal with seconds to play. Our opponents were so incensed they lashed out at us with sticks and fists. When the referee moved in to keep peace, he was belted to the ice, his nose spewing blood. Overtime was called for, but Laporte told the home team he was conceding. "I won't have my kids trampled to death for the sake of two points," he said. And we scooted out of there. When we reached our bus, we were thankful the hometown fans hadn't slashed the tires.

In Alexandria, we played in the most frigid weather we'd ever encountered. Maybe 30, 40 below. We donned toques and scarves, and our teeth chattered from start to finish. Laporte wisely rotated his lines—two lines on the bench while a third line stayed huddled around the hot stove in the dressing room.

We should have been accustomed to the cold. On our drives to games, we'd often open all four windows of the car, and the first to complain would be the "chicken" in the group. We'd drive for miles, so frigid we couldn't speak.

In one of those towns, our opponents had mayhem in mind when we took a two-goal lead. They hammered us in the corners and in front of the net, slashing, holding, and punching. The referee obviously saw nothing wrong with these fouls that bordered on criminal, and the hometown fans screamed for more.

A fellow named Snider was particularly nasty and aggressive. He moved in with the puck, and I hit him hard, a solid cross-check, and he went down. He lurched to his feet, and his big fist shot out. Bingo! He nailed me in the mouth with a punch that stunned me and rocked me and rattled my teeth. I wanted to shout, "Hey Snider, I already lost three teeth to hockey when I was 16. Pick another target."

"You two, five minutes each for fighting," the referee ruled, his eyes finally open.

Fighting? I didn't even get my gloves off.

Snider and I went to the penalty box—on his team's side of the rink.

We sat shoulder to shoulder. He looked huge. He had whiskers. He looked ugly. He looked mean. He had bad breath.

His pals in the crowd moved in behind him.

"Give the little shit another one, Snider," they shouted. "Lay the pisser out. We'll do it."

He smirked and said to me, "You want another whack in the kisser?"

I didn't know how to reply. I decided to ignore him. Don't poke the bear. I pretended I was deaf. Now—70 years later—I know what deaf feels like.

I could never figure out why some players had to be so violent. Why they didn't just play and enjoy the game. It was so much fun. But no, they had to punch and scrap and curse and rage and not be content until some poor opponent was writhing on the ice, nursing a broken jaw or ankle. Then they could brag triumphantly to their mates, "Well, I fixed his wagon."

My mates would be no help if Snider decided to throttle me. Maybe stuff his glove down my throat. Stick two fingers in my eyes. You never know. My guys were far away across the ice, as far away as Greenland. And the ref was back to his daydreaming.

Five minutes went on forever. Then I was free and emerged unscathed. What a relief!

You know, I never served another five-minute penalty. Never. And I think it's because I feared another Snider might be waiting for me in the box.

"You haven't seen the last of me," Snider sneered and threatened as we were set free.

But it was the last I'd see of him, thank goodness. At least for 40 years.

But I never forgot that punch in the mouth and his eagerness to deliver another one.

Decades later, there was an annual golf tournament in Ottawa for old-time hockey players. I attended a couple of times, and one year I was invited as guest speaker. Aurel Joliat was there, and I kicked myself for not taping a conversation I enjoyed with the great left winger of bygone days. Joliat worked at the train station in town—a ticket seller. I thought of all the people who bought tickets from him, not knowing he was a former hockey great. A Hall of Famer.

"You know who else is here today?" someone asked.

"Who?"

"Remember your old nemesis, Snider? He's sitting right over there on the sofa."

No. Couldn't be Snider. I looked the man over. He was old and portly. He had jowls. His hair was thin and grey. He looked like a harmless old coot, not the villainous tough guy with the thick black hair, the quick fists, and hot temper. That was the Snider I remembered.

I approached him tentatively.

"Are you Snider?" I asked.

He recognized me, smiled, and struggled to get up. He gave me a big hello and pumped my hand.

"I'm so pleased to meet you, Brian," he said, gently. "I watch you on TV all the time and I often tell my pals that I played against you years ago."

We had a good chat, and when I told him why I remembered him so well, he chuckled.

"I don't remember any of that," he said.

But I felt the bond. The bond of hockey guy to hockey guy. Your foe can quickly become your friend. Just like that.

I hope you're still around and doing well, Snider. Sorry I mentioned your jowls. One day I'll learn your first name.

Ottawa Sun columnist Pat MacAdam wrote about the Rockets one day: The two best-known Rockets were the Duncan twins—Ed and Erwin. One was a goal scorer and the other a gifted playmaker. One always knew where the other one was on the ice. How? They attached tiny tinkling bells to their tube skates.

The twins were not averse to on-ice larceny. It was impossible to tell them apart. They were identical twins. MacAdam recalled:

> One night the high scoring Duncan was in the penalty box at the end of a period when the twins switched jerseys in the dressing room. The game officials never caught on.
>
> The Rockets filled rinks everywhere they went. Home games in Winchester were Standing Room Only. If games were scheduled to start at 8:00 p.m. the crowds began lining up at 5:00 p.m. Because it was a natural ice arena, rink management would not allow fans in until just before game time. Body heat would soften the ice.

The Rockets won most of their games in my final season—1950–51—and when spring rolled around, we were in splendid condition, full of confidence for the junior playoff grind ahead. We always met the Ottawa City champs in the playoffs—one year it was St. Pats, the next season Eastview St. Charles.

Before the playoffs began, we were in Cornwall for a game one night, and the most embarrassing moment happened. And I was the goat. I circled our net with the puck and started a rush when I heard a clanking sound. I looked down and noticed the metal cup from my jock had slipped free and fallen to the ice.

I ignored it and carried on, my rush ending with a whistle and a faceoff at the far end of the rink. I figured nobody had noticed my boo-boo. But when I looked back, George Marlin, our top defenceman, was stickhandling up the ice with exaggerated moves, the metal cup on the blade of his stick. He swooped in, picked up the cup, and handed it to me. The crowd roared with laughter.

"You dropped this back there," Marlin said, laughing. As if I didn't know.

I skated to our bench and tossed the cup to the trainer. Reinsertion could wait.

CHAPTER 13

TO STRATFORD AND BACK

I almost missed all the excitement surrounding the best season the Rockets ever enjoyed.

That was in 1950–51. I'd been invited to jump to the Ontario Hockey Association (OHA) with Ontario's Stratford Kroehlers that season, a team that had sent George Armstrong and Danny Lewicki to the NHL. Stratford paid $800 for my release from Inkerman and offered me 50 dollars per week in salary, er, expenses. So, I left for the city that became more famous for Shakespeare than shinny.

But I wasn't happy there. The fun went out of the game.

In Stratford, I was switched from centre to wing. And the new CCM Tacks (skates) they handed me left both ankles bruised and bleeding. It shouldn't have happened. Tacks were every player's top choice in skates. Back then, you got on a bus or a train, you threw your Tacks over your shoulder. Anyone looking up would nod and say, "There's a hockey player. He's got Tacks." My centre and roommate was Bob Bailey, a skilled player with a hot temper. I bobbled a pass from him in practice one day, and he threw his hockey stick at me. "Hey, Bob, you're scaring me," I said. It sailed over my noggin and into the stands, but I got the message: "Smarten up."

Bailey, I felt, would be a big star in the NHL someday, but he struggled there, playing for Toronto, Detroit, and Chicago. He scored only 15 NHL goals. He played for 18 teams in his career and had one monster season with the Dayton Gems. More than 100 points. He was traded three times for Bill Dineen—a bit of hockey trivia.

And Bailey, while a Leaf, was despised by Rocket Richard. They tangled one night and slashed and tried to maim each other. When they were sent to the penalty box, the Rocket refused to go. He was so incensed he wanted one more shot at Bailey.

If I'd been there, I would have said to the Rocket, "Maurice, off the ice he's the nicest man you'll ever meet. Give him a break."

And the Rocket would have said, "*Tabernac!* I'd like to break his neck."

With Stratford, there was one game in Windsor in which I made a modest contribution. Again, I would meet a man who would play a big part in my future, but I had no inkling of that. Ted Lindsay came into our dressing room before the game and said a few words of encouragement. I looked at him in awe. Gordie Howe's linemate. A little man with huge skills. Set for life in Detroit, I may have thought, although that would not pan out. A few years later, he'd be cursed by his boss, Jack Adams, for being an ingrate, a shit disturber, and sent packing to last-place Chicago. All because Lindsay saw a wrong and tried to right it. He wanted to start a players' association. I would work with him on the NBC hockey telecasts, skate with him and against him, golf with him, drink wine with him, and grieve with him when his wife, Joanne, passed away in 2016. She showed great courage in the last stages of her cancer battle and called to say, "Guys, I'm not going to make it" as calmly as if she were cancelling a dental appointment. God rest, Joanne. Teddy, you followed Joanne at 93, three years later. You were one of a kind, the gutsiest guy I ever knew. And staying with us long enough to have an NHL award named after you and to be awarded a doctorate from a Michigan university. Congratulations, pal!

That day in Windsor, I did not play well (a recurring theme in my time with the Kroehlers). But I did get a breakaway and scored a rare goal.

I came back to our bench and said, "Hey, that goalie's not so hot." I knew the goalie's last name was Hall, but that's about all I knew about him. What I didn't know was that he'd soon embark on a fantastic NHL career and, like Lindsay, Howe, Boivin, and Beliveau, become a Hockey Hall of Famer. Glenn Hall was his name, and he would say to me years later, "Come on. I heard when you first wrote about that goal. You said it went 10 feet wide. I'd tell the people the truth if I could, but I don't even remember it. You sure you scored on me? You're not making that crap up?"

I just loved Glenn Hall. Another hockey great discarded by Detroit's quirky Jack Adams.

I never admired Adams, never thought he should have let Lindsay and Hall go; he let Red Kelly get away and was always so dictatorial.

That's why it surprised me one day during my *Hockey Night in Canada* career to get a lovely letter from Adams's wife, thanking me for all the nice things I said about her husband on TV. I did? Maybe so, but I wonder if I'd say them today.

After a couple of months in that top junior league, I found I missed Inkerman. And when the Stratford coach, Pinky Lewis, reneged on a promise I'd play every game (he sat me out for one at Maple Leaf Gardens against the Marlies), I quit the next day. How I longed to play at the Gardens. My dad had travelled some distance to share my joy. Now he shared my frustration when I told him I was being replaced by a kid just out of jail because Lewis wanted to "give him a chance."

The kid never played another game. I'm still pissed the kid got the Gardens game and I didn't.

My dad gave me some good advice that day.

"I know you're upset, but never make a decision in anger," he advised.

I waited 24 hours and made up my mind. No longer angry, I decided to leave the Kroehlers and Stratford, and move back to the Rockets at half the money but twice the fun. It was a tough decision because most people would think I'd been dumped, that I couldn't cut it in Canada's top junior league. If I'd been 17, I might have stayed. But I was 19 and I knew I was not much better or worse than the other juniors I played against. And few of them would make it to the NHL. Six teams with one or two openings a year. And a thousand juniors salivating for those spots. What are the odds?

I never discussed my benching with Pinky Lewis, the first Black person to coach in the OHA. Nobody ever mentioned his skin colour. It didn't make a bit of difference to any of us. I'd angered him in an earlier game in Barrie, Ontario, for something I said to a teammate.

Barrie built up a lead, and after the first period I chatted with my winger in the locker room. His name was Mitchell.

He said, "Geez, Mac, we're behind by five goals. And neither of us has seen much ice time."

I said, "Yeah, Mitch, but if it goes to overtime, we'll be ready."

The trainer rushed out and told Lewis about my smartass remark.

Lewis collared us as we returned to the ice.

"You two are starting, and we've got a penalty. You better damn well kill it off."

Oh, boy. Trouble.

The puck was dropped, the puck came to me, and I passed it to Mitchell and moved up the ice. The puck came back to me, and I shovelled it ahead. Mitchell grabbed it and scored! About 10 seconds had passed. We celebrated our short-handed goal, but Lewis did not. For some reason, he was fuming.

"All right, you two. Get in the room. You're through for the night."

Geez, that was a short shift. It ended well, though. And we're gone.

Perhaps at that moment, I knew my days in Stratford were numbered. You score a goal and you get banished to the dressing room? Come on.

Back in the Ottawa Valley that season, Lloyd Laporte had found a senior league for his Rockets to play in. He welcomed me back from Stratford, had me centre his first line, and we won the league championship in the final game. There was a vote and I was named captain. Then, in the junior playoffs, we moved into the Ottawa Auditorium and knocked off Eastview St. Charles, the Ottawa champs. We travelled by bus to South Porcupine, Ontario, and won a close series with the South

Porcupine Combines, a very talented club sponsored by the Canadiens. On the bus ride north, we were all wearing white cardigan sweaters with *Inkerman* embroidered on the left front. We stopped along the highway for a pee break and we lined up like soldiers, elbow to elbow, admiring the long arcs of pee that fell into a snow-covered roadside ditch. Then, in mid pee, some joker ran along behind us, dumping us one after another, into the piss-covered ditch. What a mix of cursing and laughter as we climbed back on the bus, each of us brushing pee and snow from our new cardigans.

An incident in a South Porcupine restaurant could have played a deciding factor in the series. But, fortunately, didn't. Five or six of us were dining there when some thuggish local guys moved in and, spotting our team jackets, began to jaw at us. I said, "Ignore them, guys. We don't need any trouble." But Grant Horricks, a big rookie on our club, didn't listen and exchanged barbs with the locals. The result was a challenge to settle things out in the alley. We were outnumbered two to one, and they were big, older, physical guys. I envisioned us getting the snot knocked out of us and being too beat up to perform in the opening game the following night. I even considered it might be a setup; these guys were friends of the Combines, with instructions to beat us up. As team captain, I figured it was up to me to deal with the situation. I admit it made me nervous. I nudged Horricks and told him to put a sock in it. I went over to speak to the locals. I told them we had a curfew and were about to be late. And if we showed up beaten and bloodied, we'd lose the opener by a big score. "And because there's so much interest in this series," I added, "If we get in a brawl with you tonight, it will be in the papers in the morning and on radio. There'll be an investigation."

The toughest looking guy in the group said, "Your mouthy guy—the rookie. Maybe he should come out in the alley with me."

"Come on. He's big, but he's only 17. You don't want to beat up a kid. He won't give you any more trouble."

The guy nodded. "Yeah, okay."

We paid our bill and scrambled out of there, lucky to escape with our lives.

Orval Tessier, from Cornwall, was one of the best players on the Combines. Some of the Combines had tears in their eyes when we ended their season in Ottawa. They had their bags packed, thinking they'd be headed to Halifax in a follow-up series.

They went home, and we went to Halifax.

CHAPTER 14

BATTLING BROPHY AND BELIVEAU

Our next series was against the Maritime champs—Halifax St. Mary's. We were accompanied on our junket (by overnight train) by Tom Foley, sports director of radio station CFRA in Ottawa, and his sidekick, Terry Kielty. I would later find a job on their radio station. It was during summer vacations from university, and I stumbled through hour after hour as the all-night disc jockey. And Foley would go on to become a host on *Hockey Night in Canada*. Would have been in the media section of the Hockey Hall of Fame today.

He'd just settled in with the hockey telecasts when he was killed in a traffic accident after a flight to Pearson Airport, leaving four young daughters. His wife had passed a year earlier. He was just 38. It was very sad. A survivor of the crash said a nervous passenger in the right front seat announced he was superstitious. Would someone in the back seat trade places with him? Foley volunteered and was killed five minutes later when a car smashed into the passenger side of the vehicle. Danny Gallivan was in tears when he delivered a eulogy on *Hockey Night in Canada*. I came back from a CBS game that Saturday afternoon and went straight to the Gardens, where I wept when I heard the news. Tom was a great broadcaster and one of my supporters.

As was Terry Kielty, who became general manager of CFRA in 1960, retiring in 1993 after 45 years.

Hockey and football were always prominent in Kielty's life. From 1977 to 1986, he was president of the Rough Riders, a team he knew well, having covered it as a broadcaster. He's a member of the Hall of Fame of the Canadian Football League (CFL).

The Rockets were truly honoured to have these two Ottawa broadcasters call our playoff games. We got off to a fast start against Halifax and were leading by five goals in the opener when Lloyd became concerned about a rout and urged us to slow down a bit. We did, and St. Mary's roared back with three or four goals. "Get going again!" Lloyd screamed. But it was difficult. We'd lost our momentum. We were lucky to win 9–7.

The series see-sawed back and forth, and my dad got upset. He wrote in his diary: "There's something suspicious about this series. There are big gates involved and Inkerman appears to be stretching out the series because of them."

It may have been true, I don't know. Perhaps the series should not have lasted six games, but it did. I remember John Brophy beginning his long, penalty-filled career with the Halifax club. It may have been Brophy who skated past our bench and clipped me on the head with his stick. Foolishly, I tried to leap over the boards and go after him, but a teammate grabbed my jersey, and I fell awkwardly to the ice. I was given a 10-minute misconduct. It probably saved me from being beaten to death by Brophy. Any one of a thousand guys who played against Brophy would say, "You got that right, Mac." Brophy enjoyed a long career as one of the toughest guys in the game. He even coached the Leafs for a season or two. One Czech player, Miroslav Frycer, hated him so much, he refused to play for him and was traded. Brophy and I reminisced about our junior days one afternoon at the Gardens. And in one famous post-game rant at the Gardens, Brophy used the F-bomb 52 times in less than three minutes. A reporter was counting.

Years after his St. Mary's days, Brophy and Don Perry, another brawler, teamed up on defence for the Long Island Ducks in the old

Eastern League, and they were masters of intimidation. Playing at home against the New Haven Blades one night, they clobbered two or three of the visitors on their very first shift. That was enough. The Blades fled the ice, put on their street clothes, and went home despite the promise of a hundred bucks each if they stayed. The game lasted all of 80 seconds.

We were able to knock off St. Mary's in six games and then came our sternest test—a series against the Quebec Citadelles and their famous star, Jean Beliveau, one of the most publicized players in junior hockey history.

Lloyd took me aside and said, "I'm counting on you to check Beliveau."

But I had played poorly in my last game against Halifax. I was not well and I asked to see our team doctor. He examined me and found bumps on my neck. "Ingrown hairs," he assured me. "Don't worry about it."

But my family doctor disagreed with the diagnosis, and I phoned my coach with the bad news.

"Lloyd, the doc won't let me play. I've come down with the stupid measles. I've been confined to bed for the next few days."

So, I missed the first game of the most important series of my life—a best-of-five against Quebec. From my sick bed, I listened to Tom Foley's play-by-play on the radio and remember Quebec had Marcel Paille in goal, Gord Haworth and Camille Henry up front, and big Gord Hudson on defence. And the Great Beliveau. Today, Marcel Paille's hockey card is one of the most sought after by collectors because there are so few of them.

Jean Beliveau and the Citadelles shut us out in the opener. But I was feeling better—that's what I told people—for Game 2 back in Ottawa, and the doc let me get up to play. My legs were shaking when I skated out to face off against Beliveau. I didn't know if it was from the measles or from the anxiety of facing this amazing player and gentleman. I soon realized I couldn't have stopped Big Jean with a bulldozer, and neither could the rest of the Rockets. He was sensational. I took a run at him at one point and slammed into his shoulder. He casually brushed me aside and my legs buckled. Then he took a shot that Diguer, our mask-less goalie, ducked away from. And just in time. Diguer was a star, a game-saver for us. Lloyd thought he'd be an NHLer one day. I thought so, too. But against Beliveau, all of us looked rather ordinary when he was on the ice.

We lost in three straight games and by embarrassing scores. How could that be? We had won so often all season.

Our season was over—my junior days were over—and I predicted that Beliveau's team would beat the Barrie Flyers and win the Memorial Cup Finals. I mentioned I'd played against Barrie twice when I was at Stratford earlier in the season, and we'd beaten them in one game, lost in the second.

But I was wrong about the Flyers being bowled over by Beliveau. Barrie, with names like Labine and Toppazzini and Jim Morrison and Lorne Howes in goal (Don Cherry was not there yet), came out on top in the Memorial Cup battle, and Beliveau felt what I felt—the agony of defeat.

Before our final match with Quebec at the Colisee, the fans pre-sented Beliveau with a number of costly gifts, including a fancy new car—a Nash Ambassador. During the game, we caused a stir when there was a pileup in the corner. Cliff Baldwin, one of our players, slipped the puck under his armpit and skated to the bench on a line change. The puzzled officials searched everywhere for the missing puck, checking inside hockey pants and under sweaters. Finally, they shrugged and called for another puck.

We've been back to Inkerman for a pair of reunions several years apart. Aging Rockets returned from far and near. Well-deserved trib-utes were showered on Lloyd Laporte, then in his 90s. I went over and hugged him hard, but sensed he was not accustomed to hugs from others of his gender. No matter. My dad was similarly inclined. But make no mistake. Lloyd Laporte was the remarkable man who made the Rockets hum. He's in the Ottawa Sport Hall of Fame, of course, but the Hockey Hall of Fame, as it is for so many others like him, is simply out of reach.

Decades have passed, gone like a puck in the crowd. Or a snowbank. Has it really been 70 years since we entertained crowds wherever we played, with our youthful exuberance and our winning ways? The playoff excitement we brewed each spring, with Laporte stirring the pot, satisfied every fan's huge appetite for hockey in an era before TV. We weren't the high-profile Montreal Junior Canadiens, the Toronto Marlboros, or St. Mike's. We were the small-town underdogs without a rink or a league to play in, the team whose trainer retrieved discarded tape from our shin pads and rolled it up, to be used again—don't ask me how—in a follow-up game. Yes, the Inkerman Rockets, forging a small but indelible chapter in hockey's fascinating history book.

There will never be another team like that one. It's not possible today.

The Inkerman Rockets survived for a few more years, but that 1950–51 season was the best. I played all season on a line with Ed Bjorness, one of the first American (Brooklyn-born) skaters to play junior in Canada, and Moe Savard from Cornwall, who went on to a minor league pro career.

I scored 45 goals after returning from Stratford, and my overall stats may have caught the eye of a 23-year-old Norwegian by way of Brooklyn—Ollie Kollevoll—the first-year coach at St. Lawrence University in Canton, New York.

When Inkerman played an exhibition game at Appleton Arena in Canton late in the season, against a solid Lake Placid team, it became the *huge* game I mentioned. I recall many of us were sick with the flu, and there were as many fights as goals. Kollevoll approached me afterward.

"Would you like to come here next year? We'd like to have you."

I'd seen the campus and was impressed. There was a university radio station, and that excited me. And the arena was spanking new. The boards were varnished, not painted, and that was a revelation. The fan support was great, and oh, yes, there were girls on campus. I didn't tell Kollevoll I was half-committed to Hamilton College, an elite school for men in the middle of the state. I'd been persuaded to consider that option by my Inkerman pal Lev McDonald—an All-American there as a freshman.

I thought of my poor high school record. No respectable Canadian university would want me. *Why was Hamilton even willing to give me a shot? And now St. Lawrence.*

I put out my hand.

"If you can get me in, I'm your guy," I told the young coach. The decision would change my life dramatically.

A few weeks later, I was on a bus in Ottawa and sitting across from me was my high school vice-principal. He was staring at me.

Uh-oh.

"Well, McFarlane," he said in a booming voice, "What are you going to do next season?"

"Sir, I'm going to a U.S. college on a hockey scholarship."

He burst out laughing, and heads began to turn.

"You? Going to college? That'll never work. You plan to skip all your classes?"

CHAPTER 15

YOU? GOING TO COLLEGE?

In October 2017, Joan and I spent a truly memorable weekend at our alma mater—St. Lawrence University. I was there to be honoured as a hockey pioneer. Imagine that.

We met on campus there on the first day we arrived in 1951, unaware at the time that the four best years of our lives were about to follow. She was a New Jersey girl and had chosen St. Lawrence because she liked skiing. She was shocked when she saw the ski hill. Jack and Jill could have walked up it easily. Zdeno Chara could have stood on his toes and looked right over it.

She'd never seen a hockey game, never been to Canada. Now when we watch a game together, she sees things that I miss. I was there on a hockey scholarship, loved hockey, and hoped to do well as a "pioneer" of the game on the ice of beautiful Appleton Arena. I was so proud to play inside those varnished boards wearing St. Lawrence colours.

I worked hard that fall, jogging every day before the season, often alongside a big defenceman from Brooklyn, New York—Ron Fee. Obviously, Fee was a Rangers fan. He wore a Rangers jersey when we jogged—and talked about his days playing defence in the New York Met League. I was hoping he'd be as good as he indicated he was— when we finally hit the ice.

On the first day of tryouts, he strutted out wearing full New York Rangers regalia. And so eager to make a good impression, he was first man on the ice. Fresh ice had been made, and the two doors in back of the net were still partially open. Icemakers were dumping slush and snow into a large hole in the cement floor. Fee barrelled toward the net in a sprint, but lost an edge. He slammed into the doors, went sailing through, lost his footing, and went face first down the hole. I was close behind and saw two legs in Rangers colours sticking up. What a debut for Ronnie Fee! He might have drowned in his first few seconds on the ice. Or choked on a snowball. The icemakers pulled him out by the legs, got him upright, and brushed snow and slush from his body. He returned to the ice despite the howls of laughter he'd triggered and skated around at a much more sedate pace, totally embarrassed.

Did he make the team? No. Unfortunately, he was among the first to be cut.

Before my first game against Northeastern, I was concerned. I'd read about the visitors' All-American goalie and how brilliant he was. I'd be upset if he shut us out to begin our season.

But my worries were needless. During the game, I had two good chances to score, and both times I gave their goalie a little deke and he slid awkwardly to the side, leaving a big gap between pad and post. I had two quick goals, and my college career was underway.

I went on to score 101 career goals with 10 hat tricks and three five-goal games, which remain university records to this day. But it didn't mean much back then—really, it didn't—because we were pioneers and we weren't matching or breaking previous records—there were none.

Those records should have been broken—a couple of dozen St. Lawrence grads have gone on to pro hockey careers, some in the NHL, like Jamie Baker, Gary Croteau, and Rich Peverley, a Stanley Cup winner with the Bruins. Obviously, they had much more talent than I did.

We played a schedule of 20 games back then—half of what they play today—and we finished at 15–5. That earned us a spot in the Final Four with games played at the Broadmoor Ice Palace in Colorado. You can bet the traditional hockey powers in the East, teams like Boston

College and Boston University, were ticked off that a small college in upper New York State was chosen ahead of them. Yale was the other representative from the East.

We bussed to Syracuse and joined the Elis on the flight to Colorado—a first flight for most of us. I had torn cartilage in my knee in our final regular season game in 1952 and postponed an operation until the tournament was over. But I shouldn't have played. Every time I fell down, I had to turn over and get up on my "good" side, losing precious seconds. We lost 2–1 to Colorado and lost again to Yale in the consolation game. A powerful Michigan team won the trophy.

We didn't lose often. The university had recruited a top forward from the Montreal Junior Canadiens—Neale Langill. Langill had played on a Memorial Cup team and had spent a year playing in England before enrolling at St. Lawrence. He had a huge season and was a big factor in our 15–5 record. But we were further handicapped in the Final Four tournament when Langill required an appendectomy.

Back then, the NCAA had strict rules against any student athletes who'd played professionally. But Michigan had a defenceman named Mike Buchanan, an Ottawa boy who'd played one game with the Chicago Blackhawks (1951–52 season, no goals, no assists). For some reason, he remained eligible to play while our star, Neale Langill, prior to the next season, was banned from college hockey because he'd played in England for a few weeks. Seems to me hockey in England was a lot less professional than the NHL. Maybe pro is pro, no matter what or where. But Buchanan played, Langill did not.

After my freshman year, back in Ottawa, there was a knock on our front door one night. Joe McLean, a kid from across the street, stood there.

"Brian, can you get me into that university where you're playing hockey?" he asked.

I was surprised. Joe was a poor kid brought up by a single mother. Not the best-behaved boy in the community, but not a real rascal, either. And I'd played hockey with him at the local park. He was fast, clever with the puck, but I'd never seen him play organized hockey. There's a big difference between scrambly shinny at the park and disciplined league play. I told Joe I'd think about it and get back to him.

I told my mother, "Joe McLean wants me to recommend him for St. Lawrence, Mom."

She turned and said sternly. "You bring him in, and they'll throw you out."

Young men should always listen to their mothers. Listen, but not always obey.

I recommended one or two other boys in the area and all three—McLean, Ron O'Brien, and Lee Fournier—were accepted and awarded scholarships. For three years they formed one of the best lines ever in collegiate hockey. After graduation, McLean went on to become a millionaire in the oil business in Calgary, and O'Brien taught and coached and became a world-famous magician. Two years later, I urged Ottawa junior Pat Presley to attend St. Lawrence, and he did. He became an All-American defenceman and a Chicago Blackhawks prospect.

Mom, I did the right thing.

McLean tops my list as the funniest teammate I ever had. His quips and quotes became legendary. In one game, Fournier was knocked flat by an opponent and was groaning in pain when McLean skated over. He leaned in and said, "Lee, if you die, can I have your skates?"

Another time, a year after I graduated and new coach George Menard had replaced Kollevoll, McLean and his mentor had a disagreement.

"If you think you can coach this team better than I can," huffed Menard, "Tell the athletic director. Tell him you want my job."

When Menard arrived at the rink for a practice session the next day, all the players but McLean were in the dressing room. McLean, wearing a long overcoat borrowed from a six-foot-five defenceman, a fedora hat, thick eyeglasses, and smoking a foot-long cigar, sat in the coach's chair in the office adjacent to the room. His feet were on the desk.

"What the hell are you doing in here?" snapped Menard.

"George, I got the job," said McLean calmly. "The athletic director appointed me head coach. But don't worry. I'm keeping you on as my assistant."

The boys in the room howled when they heard this exchange. And Menard began to roar with laughter, too.

That was Joe McLean.

I was so proud of him for making me look good. And for making his mother so proud. And for bringing so much good humour to the university. He left us much too soon. But he left us all laughing.

In my junior year, with the kids I brought down from Ottawa forming a solid second line, we finished 18–3–1—the best record in the East. *Sports Illustrated* sent a crew to Canton, and we earned an article in the magazine's first swimsuit issue. Surely, we would earn another invitation to the Final Four tournament in Colorado Springs. But no, the selectors in the East considered us to be "up in the boondocks" somewhere and chose RPI and Boston College, instead. RPI, coached by Ned Harkness, won the event with a 5–4 overtime triumph over Minnesota in the title game. Gord Peterkin, my high school right winger, scored the winning goal. Peterkin, I discovered years later, also holds the NCAA record for most points in a game—14 against Springfield. Springfield? Has anyone ever heard of Springfield hockey?

In Colorado, Boston College was horrendous, losing both their games and being outscored 3–21—the worst ever performance in tournament history. St. Lawrence would have been the better choice. Much better.

I suffered a serious injury in a game that season. Derio Nicoli, a player with Michigan State, drilled me into the boards from behind with a cross-check, and I was hauled off the ice on a stretcher. It was a bad concussion, and after a hospital stay, a local couple—Ferris and Doris Caldwell—took me into their home for several days while I recovered. Over the years, I have often wondered how much damage was done inside my skull from that and other concussions.

When I left the Caldwells for my dorm, Ferris Caldwell slipped a blank cheque in my hand. "Fill in the amount you'll need to get you to graduation," he told me.

"Aw, Ferris, don't do this," I said, handing back the cheque. "My dad's helping me out. I'll be fine."

All these years later, I remember that moment, that generous offer.

In spring 1955, my senior year, we went back for another try at a national championship.

Again, the injury bug slapped me down. Another knee cartilage problem. Another surgery postponed. Tape from thigh to ankle to keep things in place. And another double loss, to Michigan and then Harvard. Plus, a shot that struck me in the face late in the game, causing a small break in my jaw.

After shaking hands with the Harvard men, I exchanged jerseys with Terry O'Malley, a star forward with Harvard from St. Catharines, Ontario. O'Malley would go on to a solid career in Toronto advertising and his firm—Vickers and Benson Advertising—became a staunch supporter of the NHL Oldtimers.

A highlight on the flight out was conversing with Harvard coach Cooney Weiland. The seat next to him was empty, so I plopped into it, introduced myself. I was well aware of his impressive accomplishments as a pro and a coach.

In 1923–24, he took the Owen Sound Greys to the 1924 Memorial Cup. He scored 68 goals in 25 games that season and his team averaged 9 goals per game. In 1928-29, as a rookie, he helped the Boston Bruins win their first Stanley Cup. Ten years later he played on a second Cup-winner and captured a third as Boston's coach in 1941.

At Harvard he would coach seven All-Americans, including two-time pick David Johnston '63. The kid from Sudbury, son of the owner of a hardware store, the kid who'd played under-17 hockey with Tony and Phil Esposito in the Soo, and went on to a brilliant post-Harvard career that saw him appointed as Canada's governor general in 2010. Of course, I didn't know all that at the time. I graduated four years before Johnston arrived at Harvard.

Perhaps I should have applied for the governor general's job. I didn't know they were scouting former U.S. college players. Cooney Weiland was good company, and I wished I could have recorded his recollections of NHL life. Wished I'd asked him why he was named "Cooney." It was the first time I began thinking like a hockey historian.

In the time it takes to slap a puck into a net, my college career was over. So, you failed to win a national championship. So what? You've done well. Ninety percent of university teams never even get to the Final Four. A few million players never make a college or university team.

You were a lucky guy, McFarlane.

You enjoyed working on the university radio station, doing play-by-play of football and baseball games, getting experience as a disc jockey and news reader. Taking speech courses. There was the time you got up to make a speech to a class of about 20 students. You started well, but when you looked to the back of the room, fellow student Jack Elmer was holding up a sign that distracted you. *YOUR FLY IS OPEN!* The little bugger.

Being college hockey pioneers meant there was no training table for hockey players like there was for the football team. The sticks we used were meant to last. Heavy shafts and straight blades. Made in Cornwall, just across the border. Our coach—there was only one coach—Ollie Kollevoll—was primarily a baseball coach. He was a friendly, good-looking young man with Norwegian roots whose hockey career consisted of a couple of seasons with the Clinton Comets. And he'd been a pro baseball player, a catcher for Ogdensburg in the Class C Border League. I'd seen him play in Ottawa. (The star player in the Border League, by the way, was Doug Harvey, outfielder with the Ottawa Nats and the best defenceman in the NHL.)

I liked Kollevoll as a coach, but I came to question some of his decision making. He gave me a new winger one season. A kid from Montreal. Excellent skater, but he did nothing else but skate. I was proud of my passing, and in nine games despite some fine setups that left him in the clear, he scored no goals. I asked Kollevoll to consider replacing him with my roommate, Bud Saunders, a big kid from Brooklyn. Saunders was a so-so skater, but he had good hands around the net.

"No, no," said Kollevoll. "Canadian kids are always better than Americans. The Montrealer will be fine. He's a great skater."

"So is Barbara Ann Scott," I should have said.

He was never fine. With each shift, he became more jittery, more apt to fumble a pass, screw up a scoring chance. A misfit.

Kollevoll finally realized it and replaced him—about a half season too late.

In the Stouffville Arena recently, I talked with the father of a defence-man on the Aurora Tigers junior club. He said his son was going to Western Michigan on a scholarship, where Andy Murray was the coach, where he had special tutors standing by and a personal chef to make him any meals he desired. His scholarship was worth $30,000 to $40,000 a year.

At St. Lawrence I recall getting a $600 scholarship and a job as head of the wait staff in the men's cafeteria, which paid my room and board. I was thrilled with that arrangement. I even had a dog, borrowed from a family in town. Spot (what a name for a Dalmatian) lived in the dorm with me for two semesters each year and went home for Christmas and summer vacations. He even attended most of my classes and liked to annoy my fellow students and the professor by suddenly breaking wind while pre-tending to sleep. His farts were legendary, breathtaking. Probably because we fed him cafeteria food. I was so proud of him and his mischievous sense of humour. You could hear him chuckle when he farted. Honest.

Alas, he was struck by a hit-and-run driver barrelling through cam-pus one day, and the entire community grieved his sudden passing. I'm certain Spot is the only dog in history to earn a two-column obituary in the local paper. The vehicle that caused his death was traced to Syracuse, and the surprised driver was apprehended and fined 15 dol-lars for the hit and run. I think he got off lightly. Should have been a life sentence.

I buried Spot down by the river where Joan and I often walked. And when we go back for reunions, we try to find his gravesite.

In our first season, we were playing a weak club and held a 5–0 lead. While making a line change, Kollevoll barked at our line, "No more goals, guys. Their coach is a good friend of mine. Let's not embarrass him."

So, I get a breakaway. *What to do? Throw the puck in the net or throw it into the crowd.* I'd seen 5–0 leads disappear in a hurry in junior hockey.

And the rival coach wasn't my friend. I threw the puck in the net to make it 6–0.

Our line sat for the rest of the game, and I was ticked.

So was my coach. Because I'd scored.

In 2017, on the weekend I mentioned at the top of this chapter, I find myself the recipient of one of the greatest honours an old-time player can receive—acknowledged as one of the Legends of Appleton. And to share the honour of being an initial inductee with my long-time friend and former teammate Bill Torrey, an icon in the NHL, architect of four Stanley Cups with the Islanders, is a huge bonus. It made the whirlwind weekend awesome and extraordinary.

Torrey revealed an interesting recruiting fact that I had never known. In 1951, Bill Dineen, an all-star in the Ottawa Junior league, was on the verge of accepting a scholarship to St. Lawrence. But at the last minute, Detroit GM Jack Adams called him and turned him pro. He went on to play with Gordie Howe and Ted Lindsay and enjoyed a stellar career in the pros as player and coach. But if he'd followed through with his near decision to play at St. Lawrence, we might have been invincible.

To hear the respectful plaudits from presenters Ray Shero and Randy Sexton, both former SLU stars, and the tributes from beloved President Fox, and the applause from the fans when Torrey and I were introduced on the ice before a game at Appleton, were stunning, head-swelling, hard-to-believe revelations. How could anyone deserve such recognition—deserve such a tribute?

To receive well-framed jerseys with our names and numbers on the back—a first for us both—and jackets embossed with the St. Lawrence crest—another first—were gifts to be cherished like no others.

Obviously, the weekend took much planning by an energetic team of enthusiastic and considerate workers, and the result was a masterful agenda with the two *B*s—holding tight to our emotions—constantly in the spotlight. We were thrilled, amazed, humbled, and overflowing with gratitude, not to mention awash in fond memories of campus life in the '50s and hockey experiences of seven decades ago.

Bill Torrey and I agreed the weekend in Canton was absolutely perfect—one never to be forgotten. It was like no other.

Then, out of the blue, a few weeks later, shocking news that Torrey had passed away. He was headed out the door of his Florida home, but he never made it to the door. He dropped dead in the vestibule where his driver, waiting outside and fearing he'd miss his flight, came in and found him. A huge loss to hockey, for he was universally popular and respected. Bill and Torrey family members have donated millions to St. Lawrence over the years.

After his college days, he went from Pittsburgh to Oakland to the Islanders, establishing a reputation as a good young hockey man, a quick learner, a fellow with a keen eye for talent.

He did a phenomenal job with the Islanders, a bare-bones team, making astute decisions like hiring coaching whiz Al Arbour, at the draft and in trades and, in almost no time, making hockey history with four Stanley Cups.

I admired him from afar in those days, catching up with him occasionally at various events. He made me feel special. He told me great hockey stories. Here's one.

"When I attended my first governor's meeting, Stafford Smythe and Harold Ballard were facing jail time for fraudulent acts. One of them—I think it was Stafford—said to the governors, 'We'll soon be able to make licence plates for you guys when we're in the pen.'"

Here's another Torrey tale.

"In Florida, I woke up one morning and found Bob Pulford standing in my driveway. He said, 'Bill, good news. I just purchased the house next door. I'm your new neighbour.' I said, 'That's great, Pully.' Then I went down to Home Depot and bought a *FOR SALE* sign and planted it in my front lawn."

I think it's amazing that we were honoured together on two separate occasions. In 1995, it was the Hockey Hall of Fame. In Torrey's case, induction was a no-brainer. In mine, it was another of those hard-to-believe-it's-happening-to-me moments. We were like brothers. I never had a brother. Bill Torrey would have been a great one.

Bill told me how, as a young lad growing up near the Forum, Camille des Roches (a man with 19 siblings) and a popular Habs employee, trusted Bill to deliver photos of Montreal players to various houses in the vicinity—on his bicycle. Bill said it was his first job. In return, he was allowed to slip through a side door and watch the Canadiens at practice. Those sessions got him hooked on hockey.

Recently, I ran into one of my old-timer teammates—Howie Menard—at a player's luncheon, and we talked about Bill Torrey.

"I was traded to the Seals," said Howie, "and was in the dressing room on my first day there when Bill Torrey strolled in. I'd known Bill from my minor league days and he came right over to say hello. I said, 'Bill, what the hell are you doing here?'

"He leaned over and said quietly, 'I'm the team president, Howie.'"

A final thought about Bill: when he joined the New York Islanders as their first general manager, he couldn't find his office because there was no office. "There wasn't a desk, a phone, or even a pencil," he once told me. Bill rolled up his sleeves and went on to win all those Stanley Cups. He might have done the same with his first club, the California Seals, if the erratic owner there, Charlie Finley, hadn't been so impatient and interfering. And such a non-believer in my friend's hockey wisdom.

Looking back, university fulfilled me, matured me. I had little use for the fraternity system (I didn't drink or party) and while pressured to join one of the half dozen fraternities on campus, I passed on joining any of them my freshman year.

The following year, I bowed to the pressure and joined the ATO house. But I never lived in the house or felt comfortable being a "brother." Especially so in the spring of my senior year, when I discovered the fraternity quietly discriminated against Jews and Blacks—even though there were few Jews and no Blacks at that time on campus. They even dismissed my friend Bill Sloan as a potential member because "he has a soft handshake." I was pissed. Sloan, a Cornwall boy, was a brilliant student, an All-American goalie, and a baseball star. He was offered a contract by at least one major league ball club. Those soft hands served him well in goal and on the diamond.

My favourite professor was Dr. Herbert Bloch, who taught sociology and criminology.

"Dr. Bloch, I have a request. May I submit an audio tape of a habitual criminal locked up in the Canton jail in place of the term paper that's due soon? He's a recidivist about to be sent back to Texas, where he faces a life sentence."

"Yes, McFarlane, you may."

My submission was a success. The criminal was witty and intelligent and candid about his inability to fit into normal society, his downfall an addiction to car thefts. "I'd never steal a car from an individual," he told me. "Only from dealers who can better afford the loss."

The class listened attentively to my half-hour "documentary." Dr. Bloch awarded me an A.

Then there was the play in my senior year, *Of Mice and Men*. I auditioned and won the role of George. It never occurred to me I'd become an actor, like Kirk Douglas, who'd graduated from St. Lawrence as Issur Danielovitch Demsky 20 years earlier. Douglas was the last great movie star of his generation. He died at 103, outliving the likes of John Wayne, Gary Cooper, Henry Fonda, Cary Grant, Charlton Heston, and his buddy Burt Lancaster. Younger audiences probably know him better as Michael Douglas's father than as a star in his own right. But for a long time, he was among the brightest in the Hollywood firmament.

And a huge contributor to the university, where, like me, they gave him—a ragman's son from New York—a chance.

As they did actor Viggo Mortensen more recently. But I wanted to try performing. Joan played the female lead, and I played the lead—George. We rehearsed our lines together hour after hour in the spring of our senior year. I was certain I would forget my lines and the play would bomb.

The play drew full houses for three nights.

There was one unexpected interruption on the final night, when most of the parents attended—it was Parents' Weekend. George and Lennie are onstage conversing. Loud footsteps can be heard in the hall.

The main door to the theatre is thrust open. A loud voice shouts for all to hear, "Everybody, go and get laid!" The door slams shut, someone runs away, laughing hysterically.

George and Lennie eye each other, not knowing whether to laugh or cry. We pick up our lines and carry on. Nothing can rattle us.

It's final semester, time to focus on other things in life. But first, there's a final bill to pay. It's for 50 dollars, my tuition fee for the semester. Gotta be a mistake. I must owe more than 50 bucks. I get a call from the admin building. "Brian, can you come in, please. Someone made an error in your final bill."

"I'll be right over. I figured there was a mistake."

At the admin building, I'm told the error was on their part.

"We overcharged you by 40 dollars. Here's a refund cheque. Sorry about that."

I must be the only student in history who paid a mere 10 bucks for his final semester.

The comfort of university life was over, and graduation upon us. My mother, in the final stages of her cancer battle, lived to see my sister Norah and I graduate together. Lived to see my sister Pat marry Bill McCauley, a man who went on to a successful career in the world of music. But Mom was too ill to attend the wedding of my sister Norah to Lou Perez, who went on to get a law degree at Cornell.

My mom was so proud to see her son and daughter—two Canadian kids—voted class president and vice-president—both making the Dean's List.

Too bad Spot wasn't there to see me graduate. And too bad nobody thought to award him an honorary degree. Apparently there was a rule. Four legs disqualified you.

I wanted to bring my diploma back to Ottawa and thrust it in the face of the vice-principal who said I'd never make it through college. But he died when I was a sophomore.

University life is quickly over. Career choices must be made, jobs sought and undertaken. Courtship is leading to marriage. It's a Time of Big Decisions. So, take a deep breath and plunge right in.

But just before I did, there was a final problem to deal with. The fact that I did not drink alcohol bothered me. On a date with Joan, someone spiked my soft drink with a stiff shot of booze at a local bar while I was in the men's room. When I returned and took a swallow, I exploded in anger.

"You bastards had no right to do that," I told my pals. "We're out of here." I pulled Joan with me to the door and vented outside. Joan sympathized with me, but also thought I'd overreacted.

The next day I bought a six pack of Coors and went to my room. I popped a can and—my arm froze. My hand held the beer, but my elbow refused to bend—until I forced it to. I drank the can of beer. Then another—to make sure I'd solved my problem.

CHAPTER 16

ON TO SCHENECTADY

Four years on campus went by in a blur. I never wanted them to end. But, of course, end they did. With me in the hospital.

A few days after graduation, I faced another knee surgery and recuperation time. Joan flew off to Wyoming to take a flight attendant's course with United Airlines. I feared she'd meet some handsome millionaire and I'd lose her forever.

Somehow, still on the limp, I stumbled onto an acting job with an Ottawa company—Crawley Films, earning a hundred bucks a week playing the role of a young screenwriter in a film called *Picture Province*, sponsored by the New Brunswick government travel bureau. As mentioned, I had some acting experience in university, but I had no plans to make it a career. I wanted to be a sportscaster—preferably a hockey commentator.

While working in New Brunswick, I received a telegram one day from the manager of WRGB, the TV station in Schenectady where I had worked for a couple of summers as a cameraman. Management at the station knew I wanted to pursue a career in sportscasting and they were willing to take a chance on me. Americans are good that way.

The telegram read, "Plan to begin a nightly sportscast here. Are you available? Starting salary is 75 dollars per week."

I sent a telegram back.

"I'm your guy. When do I start?"

Another telegram caught up with me.

"You can start Oct. 10 [1955] and we'll pay a hundred a week."

There was no explanation for the 25 extra dollars.

When the *Picture Province* film was complete—I never saw the finished product—I went back to Ottawa, where I was devastated when my mother passed away in September 1955—she was only 59. She'd been a great mother, encouraging me not to smoke or drink, to be a good person. I'm not proud of some of the things I've done—some she knew about—but she was a forgiving person. One of her tenets was: "If you don't have your health, you don't have anything."

And as kids growing up during the war years, when things looked grim for the free world, we were comforted by her optimistic words: "Right will conquer might."

I stayed with my dad for a few days, both of us quietly grieving, then drove to Schenectady in the 1939 Mercury that Joan and I had purchased jointly—for 75 bucks—in our senior year. A lovely vehicle I hand-painted one afternoon with a brush—in double blue—unaware that at sundown, a thousand bugs would be attracted to the paint.

With a sparse wardrobe and a few US dollars in my wallet, it was time to clear my head, find my way to WRGB—and get to work.

My nightly sportscast was 10 minutes long and was sponsored by a major department store chain—Montgomery Ward.

The Brooklyn Dodgers had just won the 1955 World Series over the Yankees the week I began, and my first guest was Dodger pitching hero Johnny Podres, who lived in a town not far away.

Initially, the biggest problem I had was leaving my desk to deliver a live commercial midway through each 10-minute telecast. I'd pitch everything from snow tires to refrigerators after delivering scores and results, and showing film clips from games played the day—or even two days—before, depending on mail service from New York.

But those commercials were a challenge.

I watched how some of the other announcers—the veterans—did them and how I envied them. So smooth and comfortable on camera.

One man in particular excelled at cigarette commercials. On live camera, he'd extol the virtues of a brand, then inhale a lungful of smoke, pause, and exhale contentedly, as if the cursed smoke was nectar. I said to myself, *I could never do that. Never. I'd choke and gasp and go all teary-eyed. Maybe even throw up and mortify the sponsor, who would fire me on the spot.*

I relied heavily—as did the others—on a new invention—the tele-prompter—to get through my commercials.

One night, I strode into the commercial set adjacent to my sports desk and was about to tell my viewers why they should run to Montgomery Ward and purchase a kitchen table and chair set when I looked at the teleprompter.

UTICA CLUB BEER IS THE FINEST BEER IN NEW YORK STATE read the teleprompter.

Damn it. The wrong commercial.

I had to ad lib.

"Folks, look at this fine table." I didn't know if it was pine or oak or made from palm trees.

"Isn't it nice? And these chairs. They're so—so—sturdy. And yes, comfortable, too."

What else could I say? I was done. On the verge of brain freeze.

"Folks, this nice table and chair set is available at Montgomery Ward."

I didn't give the price. I didn't know the price.

It may have been television's shortest ever ad.

I walked back to the sports desk, shaken and embarrassed. I said, "Turning to football—"

One of my all-time favourite interviews took place while I was at WRGB. It was with baseball great Stan Musial, filmed at Cooperstown, New York, on Hall of Fame day there in 1956.

He agreed to a brief interview with me and it went well, until my cameraman said to me, "Sorry, we didn't get it. The film didn't thread properly."

I scrambled after Musial and explained my plight. Would he come back and do another?

"Sure, kid," he said. "Even I make an error every once in a while."

We did a second interview, and my cameraman stamped his foot. "Damn!" he said. "I still didn't get it."

By then, Musial was in the outfield, warming up.

I trotted out there. I needed that interview for my sportscast that night.

Once again, I explained the situation, told him our technical problem had been corrected. Would he please come back for a third time?

He walked off the field with me, one hand on my shoulder.

"Let's both try to get it right this time," he said with a smile.

I almost kissed him.

We faced the camera once more, and this time everything clicked.

I'm certain he forgot the interview two minutes later. I'll remember it for a lifetime. And when young broadcasters sometimes thank me for giving them time for a coffee and conversation, I tell them, "Let me tell you about meeting Stan Musial."

I met Ty Cobb that day, an early-day baseball superstar, and interviewed him as well. The film of our interview has been preserved. But alas, the Musial interview has not.

While in Schenectady (not much hockey interest there, folks), I was asked to referee a few games at RPI in Troy, New York, where Ned Harkness was head coach. But officiating was not for me. I thought I knew the game, but soon discovered I wasn't certain of all the rules. And in one game, when I scooted over to pick up the puck, I ran headfirst into the other official, almost knocking myself out. I decided to bow out before I made a complete fool of myself.

Besides, it was time to think of more serious, long-range decisions—like getting married.

Joan and I had been together since the first day of college. It was time to tie the knot. She was willing to give up her job with United Airlines, and we set the date, July 7, 1956, in her hometown of Hillsdale, New Jersey. Everything went well, although I forgot to kiss the bride, and a couple of the Inkerman Rockets showed up at the last minute, uninvited, and crashed the dinner, and Joan's brothers put my car over a pit and wired a dozen tin cans to the axle. I had to take off my rental suit, climb into the pit, and remove them, sweating and swearing as I laboured.

We honeymooned in a campsite near Lake Placid. Slept in sleeping bags in a small tent. Fished for trout in the Ausable River. Drove up through Muskoka and visited my dad for a day or two in Montreal. We'd budgeted a hundred bucks for the trip and came home with almost half that.

There were two junkets to New York while at WRGB. Joan and I enjoyed our first big-league baseball game at the Polo Grounds (free press passes from the Giants): Robin Roberts of the Phillies against Johnny Antonelli of the Giants—two of the game's premier pitchers.

And then another trip to Madison Square Garden for a Rangers home game. A balding defenceman for New York caught my eye—Ivan Irwin. I never thought I'd meet him, much less get to play Oldtimers with him and become a close friend for the past 30 years. Irwin's gone now—a wonderful man. He always kept small paper-wrapped candies in his pocket, which he handed out to almost everyone he met. Who does that today? I was glad I went over to him at an Oldtimers' luncheon a few weeks before he passed and told him how much I admired him and, yes, loved him like a brother. He gave me a hug that left me gasping. In Schenectady, within a year, we had our first-born, Michael, who made his TV debut a few hours after his birth (a few seconds on film) on my sportscast the night of his arrival.

One hockey story from that era makes me smile in the telling. We started an amateur team in Schenectady on a rinky-dink rink built in a city park—Central Park. A lumber company donated the boards. I was named player-coach. It was a short season—January to March—all games played on natural ice, which could be a mix of slush or muddy water at times. We practised when a rush of cold air moved in from Canada, and I made my player selections from about 20 candidates. One young fellow approached me and told me he'd played for the Toronto Marlboros. *What great luck,* I thought. *A Marlboro in Schenectady. He'll surely be a starter.*

"Your name?"

"Simmons. Herb Simmons."

"Got your skates?"

"No, they're at home."

"Come out Sunday afternoon. We're playing Utica. You'll be one of my starters on defence."

Before the Sunday game, I gave the rink manager a rule book with a rink diagram and measurements inside.

"Could you paint some lines on the ice—blue lines and a red line?"

"Sure."

When we showed up on Sunday for a game versus the Utica Stars, I discovered he'd painted the lines, all right. The centre ice line was a bright red—but the blue lines—he'd paced off 60 feet from the centre line and splashed a blue line across the ice about 10 feet out from the goal. Then he did the same thing at the opposite end.

We had the biggest centre ice zone in the history of hockey. About 120 feet. And the smallest-ever defensive zones.

We used our skates to try and erase the blue lines, but our efforts failed.

So, we played a game with no concern for blue lines and somehow got through it. The referee said later, "That was easy. I didn't call an off-side all day."

I've forgotten the score and even who won (I think we did), but our warm-up was unforgettable—all because of Herb Simmons, the Marlboro, and the one guy I was counting on. Simmons geared up and skated out. He looked a little wobbly on his blades, but then he made a beeline for our goalie and, unable to stop, crashed into him. The goalie, yet to face a shot, fell back in his net and lay there, moaning.

Simmons staggered to his feet and stumbled away in another direction. Gathering speed, he barrelled into the side boards headfirst and rebounded off the lumber, striking his head on the ice. He was out cold and bleeding. A couple of his buddies at rinkside came to hover over him. They carried him off to a nearby car. One of them shouted at me, "We're taking him to the hospital!"

I shouted back. "Was he really a Marlboro?"

The guy said, "What's a Marlboro?"

One of our players quipped, "Hopefully, they'll take him to the mental ward."

It was the last time I saw Herb Simmons.

But not the last time I would hear from him.

For the next 30 years, I received letters and clippings and religious tracts in the mail—all from Simmons. And dozens of photos of him in full hockey gear, standing on a deck, posing in front of a toilet. Wearing green, yellow, blue jerseys. He talked of planning visits to past stars like Syl Apps and players out west. He promised to come and see me one day, but he never showed up. He told me he'd written a book about the Schenectady Generals—*The Boys of Winter*. He sent me a draft. It was about six pages long—game summaries. One day the letters stopped, and I realized I'd looked forward to them. What happened to you, Herb? I still have your photos.

In Schenectady, I learned that every once in a while, a fellow has to stand up and be counted. I learned that lesson at a meaningless softball game. The game was between the station's softball team and a team from city hall.

When I organized the team and asked my boss, Ted Baughn, the late night newscaster, if he wanted to play, he laughed. "No way," he said. "Not interested."

So, we're playing the city hall before a couple of hundred fans, when a baby-blue Cadillac pulls up along the third base line. Out steps Ted Baughn in his three-piece suit. He saunters across the infield while play stops and he waves to the crowd.

People wave back. "Hi, Ted. Good to see you."

He stands by our bench watching play resume, and a guy in the crowd yells out, "Grab a bat, Ted."

My boss takes off his jacket, rolls up his sleeves, and picks up a bat. "I'll hit next," he tells me.

I'm forced to react and I'm not sure how.

"Ted, why don't you wait an inning or two," I suggest. "You showed no interest in playing when I first asked you. The other guys have shown up for every game and every practice."

He glares at me and then turns to the crowd.

"Hey, the young sportscaster doesn't want me to play. Guess he thinks I'm not good enough. So, I'm outta here."

He retreats across the infield, hops in his Caddie, and drives off.

I tell my wife when I get home, "Be ready to move. I think I just lost my job over a stupid softball game."

But, surprise. A week later, the station fired Baughn for some reason.

And a few weeks after that, when the station programmers decided to cancel all sportscasting at WRGB, I was forced to make a major decision.

What to do next?

I went to New York to investigate opportunities there and found one. A college friend, Bill Creasy, told me a new network, ESPN, was in the planning stages and would be seeking good young announcers. He would be there as a director.

"But the timing isn't right," he informed me. "Why not go to Toronto and get somewhat established? Then come back here before we go to air."

It made sense. I drove to Toronto, stopping in Rochester and Buffalo to enquire about TV opportunities. There appeared to be some opportunity for an eager young sportscaster in Toronto so I returned to Schenectady and discussed the situation with Joan.

We decided to move even though it was December, when business decisions are often put off until the New Year.

We put our belongings in a U-Haul and with six-month-old son Michael securely bundled in back, we moved to Canada. Surely, I was ready for a role, any kind of a role, with *Hockey Night in Canada*.

CHAPTER 17

BAD LUCK, GOOD LUCK

In Toronto, I couldn't land a broadcasting job anywhere. We lived in a cheap motel for a few days, Joan warming Michael's baby's bottle under a hot water tap. Then we found a modest unfurnished apartment in Scarborough at one hundred bucks a month. We ate off cardboard boxes and sat on the floor—no chairs. Our narrow bed was held together—at one wobbly leg—with black hockey tape. Luckily, there was a crib for Michael. Our savings began running out.

At Christmas, I waited until the lots closed and came back with a leftover tree. I bought Joan a broom and a pair of red panties.

I hustled around Toronto, landed a few bit parts on the CBC, acting in commercials, including one for Imperial Oil, which appeared on Saturday night on *Hockey Night in Canada*, one which had me off on a weekend with my actress wife, two kids, and a dog to Niagara Falls, with a stop at a filling station to "fill it up with Esso." Then, on Sunday night, on the *The Ed Sullivan Show*, I appear again in a commercial and once again I'm off to Niagara Falls. This time, I'm driving a new Chevy and I've got a blond lady next to me—my bride. I thought the Alliance of Canadian Cinema, Television and Radio Artists (ACTRA), the union I'd joined, would chastise me for being with my TV bride one night, a wife and kids the next. Nobody said a word.

In another commercial, I was a catcher on a ball team. Wearing a mask, of course. In the studio, a man stood 10 feet in front of me and threw baseballs at my head for a couple of hours. *Bing! Bang! Bong!* Baseballs bouncing off my mask. The mask was protecting my face as much as the sponsor's toothpaste protects my teeth. Any ball player watching would have fallen down laughing. Or shouted, "Catch the damn ball, you idiot!"

But another cheque went into the bank.

A soap company hired me. They filmed me showering before a date, using the company's soap. My actress date may have been showering, too—I don't know. They filmed us at dinner, almost cheek to cheek, probably inhaling the scent of the soap.

The commercial never made it to air. The CBC regulators ruled it "too sexy."

In 1959, the Whitby Dunlops were gearing up for the World Hockey Championships in Oslo, Norway. I'd played junior in Stratford with Gordie Myles and Doug Williams and against Oshawa's Bobby Attersley—all three on the Dunnies—and thought of asking manager Wren Blair for a tryout. But we were down to our last few dollars. I decided I must put family first and find a real job. I was depressed, but I came up with a backup plan. I would sell pots and pans door to door.

My wife said, "You will not. You are a broadcaster. A good one. I won't allow you to sell pots and pans." She helped me get my first "real" job in Toronto. She saw two new names on the lobby mailbox—George and Nina Retzlaff.

"Didn't you mention his name recently?"

"Yes. George is the sports director at the CBC. I met with him."

"Well, he and his wife are living in the apartment downstairs."

"That's incredible."

"When I do the laundry in the basement I'll make sure Nina Retzlaff is there. I'll tell her what a great announcer you are. It may help." It did. Nina told George he'd better find something for me to do. He let me do a sportscast one night. Fifty bucks.

I called all the radio stations in town and told them they might want to check me out on the CBC. An audition of sorts. The following day, CFRB called. "Come in and see us. We're looking for a late-night sportscaster."

Wes McKnight offered me the job at a hundred a week. I told him how well I was doing in the freelance world (hah!) and suggested he sweeten the pot.

"All right. Gordon Sinclair doesn't come in on Saturdays. You can do his newscast and two hours of disc jockey work. We'll make it $130 a week."

But I was cool. I told him I was doing well freelancing and would have to check my schedule. Could I get back to him?

I left the station and almost turned a few cartwheels on Bloor Street. I was ecstatic. The number one radio station in the country wanted me. I had five bucks in my pocket.

I waited a few hours and called back to accept the position.

I was very happy working at CFRB for the next few months. There I worked with hugely popular announcers like Jack Dennett, Gordon Sinclair, and Wally Crouter. I had lots of freedom to express my views on my 10-minute sportscast. I was assigned to cover the opening of the Burlington Bay Skyway linking Fort Erie with Toronto. High winds almost blew me off the damn thing. McKnight had me join him for "live" coverage of golf tournaments back then, like the Canadian Open and Ontario Open. I even initiated an hour of country music on my Saturday afternoon DJ shift. Almost 60 years later, I remain the only DJ to play country music hits on such a prestigious station. And my show was fully sponsored.

Some people found fault with my role as a country music DJ. Gordon Sinclair, CFRB's most famous newscaster, was one. Sinclair, who was a panellist on *Front Page Challenge* for years and also wrote a column for the *Toronto Star*, wrote after my first stint playing country music, "Brian McFarlane, a young broadcaster, was playing country hits on CFRB on Saturday. But every record was sung by an American. Why didn't he play even one song by a Canadian country music star?"

I accosted Sinclair outside Wes McKnight's office on Monday and told him I thought his comment was unfair and ridiculous. We raised our voices in argument until McKnight's door opened, and he stepped out. He heard me say to Sinclair, "If you're so smart, name me one top Canadian country singer."

Sinc's mouth opened, but no name came out. Finally, he said, "How about Mayor Mackay of Calgary? He rode a horse through the lobby of the Royal York on Grey Cup day."

McKnight and I both laughed. We knew that the Calgary mayor was no singer.

"I got you, Sinc. You can't even name one."

McKnight took my side and told Sinc he thought he was a bully for knocking me before I'd even been on the job a week.

The following week, Sinclair gave me a glowing compliment in the *Star* for my work on CFRB sports. From then on we were friends. He headed off to the CBC one night and stopped to chat. "Can you believe they pay me $400 a show to be on *Front Page Challenge?*" he said.

I believed him, thinking there was no way anyone would ever pay me that kind of money.

A few months later, I was a guest on *Front Page Challenge.*

I enjoyed working with Wes McKnight on Toronto Argonauts games, home and away. There was major interest in CFL football back then, and McKnight was a big-name broadcaster of Argonaut games. Big Zeke O'Connor, a former Argo, was third man in our booth. And a man named Joe Wright was also there for most of the games.

McKnight was a serious guy who frowned on any frivolity during his broadcasts. But one night in Montreal—Argos at Alouettes—he stumbled over a few words, and we all but fell off our chairs laughing.

Cookie Gilchrist, a big Argos fullback, plunged for a touchdown and stayed on the field to kick the extra point. "The extra point is good!" shouted McKnight. "Keekie Goolcrease keeks the confert."

O'Connor, Wright, and I kept a straight face—for a second or two. But we were all jammed into this small booth, and I could feel O'Connor's big body begin to twitch and shake, and I heard him trying to hold back a snort. McKnight gave us a grim look, and that did it. O'Connor, Wright, and I all burst out laughing. We threw off our mics and turned away, but I'm sure the radio audience heard all this guffaw-ing in the background. McKnight was not amused. He gave us another withering look before carrying on.

I thought he might drop me from future broadcasts, but he didn't. In fact, he promised me I would be doing the play-by-play the next season. But he reneged on the promise and decided to stay on. "One more year," he said. It was one reason I decided to take a position when it was offered some time later as sports director of a new TV station in Montreal—CFCF-TV.

The CFRB job changed my attitude about working in commercials. I got a call one day from an agency and was asked to report for a film shoot for Eaton's catalogue. When I arrived at the studio, somebody threw a set of long johns at me.

"Change into these," I was ordered. Five other guys were there, stripping down, pulling on the long johns. Ready to pose. I made a quick decision.

"Sorry," I said as I tossed the underwear back. "I just got out of the modelling business."

CHAPTER 18

BRING YOUR SKATES

My friends are often surprised when I tell them I was first hired to broadcast NHL games—not on the CBC and *Hockey Night in Canada*—but on CBS. In 1959, CBS was about to televise 11 NHL games (beginning in January 1960) and had hired a play-by-play announcer, but had no colour commentator. I had been given an opportunity to audition for *Hockey Night in Canada* beginning in 1959–60, but I failed the test. I'd done well in my audition—interviewed King Clancy—but a few days later, Ray Arsenault, a MacLaren executive, delivered the bad news.

"Brian, sorry to tell you this, but MacLaren Advertising is looking for an older, more mature announcer. We think you're too young. We've hired Ward Cornell."

And I said, "Don't sweat it, Ray. I've just been to New York and back. CBS has hired me as a commentator for their NHL *Game of the Week*."

He looked astonished. But he was able to mutter, "Congratulations."

That was the season Montreal goalie Jacques Plante introduced the goalie face mask. His coach, Toe Blake, didn't want him to wear it. But when he was hit in the face in a game in New York, Plante refused to go back on the ice without his mask. Coach Blake shuddered to think he'd have to replace him with Rangers standby goalie Joe Schaefer. You could shoot turtles past Schaefer.

Plante wasn't the first to wear a mask. Clint Benedict of the Montreal Maroons wore a crude leather face protector briefly during the 1929–30 season, and a woman goalie from Queen's University, Elizabeth Graham, wore a wire fencing mask during games even earlier—in 1927. My research even turned up a turn-of-the-century goalie who wore an iron mask in a few games.

If I had to miss any of my radio sportscasts because of the new opportunity with CBS, I found a willing replacement in Bob Hesketh, a Toronto sportswriter. I paid him 10 dollars per show.

When Hesketh later complained to my boss—McKnight—that it was a rather small fee, McKnight called me in.

"How come you're paying Hesketh a mere 10 bucks a show?" he asked.

I said right back, "Wes, that's what you paid me when I subbed for you. You set the standard."

Hesketh and I laughed about that exchange. I should have paid him more, but then his initial radio work soon led to much bigger things at CFRB, where his show, *The Way I See It*, became a popular program, syndicated across Canada.

I soon found out how the CBS position fell my way. Fred Cusick, the voice of the Boston Bruins, was an obvious choice to be the CBS play-by-play announcer, and he was asked who he'd like as a colour man. "Remember," the producers told him, "Your partner will be doing interviews on the ice, so he has to be able to skate."

Cusick said, "I know a young sportscaster at CFRB in Toronto—Brian McFarlane. He's a former college player at St. Lawrence University. He made All-American there and he might fill the bill."

"Does he have any TV experience?"

"He does. He did the late sports on a TV station [WRGB] in Schenectady for a couple of years. *Hockey Night in Canada* has been talking to him but they think he may be too young."

"Well, we think hockey on TV is a young man's field. Let's get him down here. Somebody give him a call."

Joe Gallagher, a CBS producer, called. Would I be interested? Would I fly to New York to discuss the position? Absolutely. Air Canada got me to New York—down and back in a matter of hours—where I met all the big wheels at CBS sports—even Bill MacPhail, the top gun. Joe Gallagher met me privately and offered me $200 per game to fly to weekend games in the four American cities in the six-team league— New York, Boston, Chicago, and Detroit.

I could still keep my job in Toronto as a sportscaster on CFRB, the top radio station in the country. That was important because several private TV licences were about to be granted by the Board of Broadcast Governors, and CFRB was in the running for the coveted Toronto licence. I'd been promised the sports director's job with the new station—if our bid was approved.

Before I flew back to Toronto, someone advised me to meet with the people at MCA, a major talent agency. When I gave them the details of the contract I'd just signed with CBS, I remember one of them snorting, "Jesus, what turnip truck did you fall off. If you'd come to us first, they'd have paid a lot more than that."

I signed with MCA, resisting the temptation to say, "Don't rock the boat, mister. Getting the opportunity with CBS is huge. Who cares what they pay?"

While I was celebrating my good fortune, Joe Gallagher called to tell me the first game on the schedule would be played in New York early in 1960. And I'd be working with a kid just out of Columbia—Chet Forte— who'd supply me with stats and be the "gofer" on the show, running around to make sure my guests arrived for intermission interviews. Then, a major snag. After joining the American Federation of Television and Radio Artists (AFTRA), the performers' union in the US, and getting a social security number, I heard discouraging news from CBS. "There's been a protest from AFTRA," Gallagher phoned to say. "They insist we hire an American announcer to be the colour commentator."

"And?"

"We told them we required an announcer who could skate. None of the American guys can do that. Any one of them would fall on his ass. We're sticking with you."

But the dispute with the union caused me to miss the first game.

Muzz Patrick, Rangers manager, agreed to fill in. My banishment from the opener caused surprising repercussions across Canada and howls of protest in Toronto. The *Toronto Telegram*'s front page, amid photos of famous U.S. singers, dancers, and actors, proclaimed: "They Can Work Here, But McFarlane Can't Work There! Why?"

Crusty Gordon Sinclair blasted the American union, noting that I was a fully paid-up member of ACTRA, the Canadian counterpart of AFTRA. A photographer from the *Toronto Telegram* stopped by our small apartment on Hubbard Boulevard, which borders Lake Ontario. My wife Joan and baby son Michael were snapped holding the *Telegram*'s front page.

As suddenly as the controversy flared up, it subsided. CBS made peace with the union, and I was told my next assignment would be in Chicago. And my first guest would be the NHL's premier player—Red Wing great Gordie Howe.

Much of the CBS season was a blur. Finishing my late sportscast Friday night, rushing home to get a few hours' sleep, then off to Chicago on the morning's first flight. To the Bismarck Hotel for a production meeting, to a dinner with CBS people and Rudy Pilous, the Chicago coach; Tommy Ivan; and other Blackhawks' officials I'd never met. The game the following afternoon was against Gordie Howe, Red Kelly, Terry Sawchuk, and the rest of the Red Wings. I worried about wardrobe—I had none—and at dinner I had concerns about manners and etiquette. I'd never dined on four-course meals. I didn't know a Merlot from a Pinot Grigio. I recall feeling so awkward at the table that night, and at many similar dinners in other cities that followed. I'd listen to what the chap beside me ordered from the huge menu and say, "That sounds good. I'll have the same." Worse, I'd been away from NHL hockey for almost six seasons—four while in college, when I had little time to keep up with the game, then for two years in Schenectady, where there was virtually no hockey.

In fall 1954, I'd wangled a tryout with the Blackhawks and I thought I might see a few NHL regulars on the ice at the camp in Pembroke, Ontario. But my tryout was mainly with minor leaguers who had about as much chance of sticking with the Hawks as I did. And the Hawks were a last-place team. And it was clear they didn't think much of college players. There were none in the NHL. And none on the ice that day—except me. What's more, I was fully aware that I could be suspended from college hockey for even skating with a bunch of pros.

I came away from that camp knowing I'd never skate in the NHL.

And so, in 1960, after a couple of years in Schenectady and gambling that a move to Toronto would put me in a position to find an opportunity with *Hockey Night in Canada*, I began my hockey network broadcasting career as a neophyte and a pioneer—back in the States—high in the booth over the Chicago Stadium ice with the giant Barton organ blasting away somewhere behind me.

Fred Cusick helped break me in. Cusick was a good man and an excellent broadcaster. We clicked. He had commanded sub chaser 1322 during the war, often in dangerous waters, and told me it was "the best duty in the navy." Others called it "a lonely, stinking, dirty job." Cusick talked about night duty, when porpoises swam alongside a ship leaving a phosphorescent wake. Often the porpoises came right at the ship, causing many a rookie sailor to jump in terror, because it looked so much like the wake of an oncoming torpedo.

Cusick earned so much respect in his long career that he was the recipient of the Lester Patrick Award, given by the NHL to persons who make major contributions to the game in the United States. He also was the first American broadcaster to be inducted into the Hockey Hall of Fame in Toronto.

With three minutes to play in each period, I'd make a frantic dash to a back stairwell and rush down a hundred steps to rinkside. One wrong turn, and I could have wound up outside the building. Chet Forte had my skates ready, and I'd throw them on, just in time to barge through the gate, microphone in hand, and interview the great Gordie Howe.

But Howe didn't show.

I'd prepared well, had rehearsed the four or five questions to ask the Great Gordie. A Red Wing skated across the ice as I began to panic.

The guy had red hair. It wasn't Gordie. It must be Red Kelly. There was only one redhead on the Red Wings.

"Gordie was injured late in the period," Kelly told me. "He asked me to come on in his place."

So, okay. The camera's red light flashed, and I talked to Kelly. About what I have no recollection. But I got through the few minutes. I'm sure I asked him to demonstrate some skill or fundamental. Otherwise, why be on skates? It would have been to show how he takes an opposing forward out of the play. I would have come in on him with the puck, and he would have steered me gently into the boards. Not much more than that.

I recall a post-game incident in Chicago. Forte and I, both strangers to the Windy City, wandered into a country music bar after a game there. Sitting around a table were several of the Montreal Canadiens, drinking beer and listening to the musicians onstage. They recognized us and waved us over, shifting chairs to make room. I sat down and glanced at the player next to me. *My God—Rocket Richard. One of my boyhood heroes.* What good fortune. To sit next to an icon, watching his fingers tapping the table in time to the music. I relaxed, sipped on a beer, and felt so privileged, so grateful that these great pros would allow a couple of tenderfeet into their fold. If some seer or visionary had whispered to me that night, "Brian, someday far in the future you will play at Maple Leaf Gardens and the Montreal Forum against some of these same players at this table—including the Rocket. Do you believe me?"

"Absolutely not," I would have replied. "Don't be ridiculous. There's no way that will ever happen."

But it did.

Former NHL referee Red Storey and I had many conversations over the years about the Rocket. "There'll never be another Rocket," he said, "even if they're playing hockey a thousand years from now. I refereed a few thousand games and have seen a lot of dedicated men. I never saw one like the Rocket, never saw one born to score goals like he was born to do."

CHAPTER 19

INTERVIEWS ON CBS

Some interviews from that brief season on CBS are well remembered. I chatted with Gordie Howe, who was in his 14th NHL season, and I asked him how much longer he planned to play. He said, "I'd like to get in 20 years, but that's a long haul for any pro." Incredibly, the man played 26 seasons in the NHL and six more seasons in the World Hockey Association before retiring at age 52. Howe is often said to be the most complete player to ever play the game. Forty-eight years after our interview, I found myself onstage with him in Toronto, introducing him as the inaugural recipient of the NHL Lifetime Achievement Award in 2008.

And I can't forget his impish nature. One night, preparing for a pre-game interview rinkside at the Gardens, Howe skated past us in the warm-up and flicked a handful of snow off his stick over the glass and all over our nice blue jackets.

What respect the man earned. John Tonelli told me how he played alongside Howe in the WHA. After one shift, Howe reached over and blew snot all over Tonelli's sleeve.

"I didn't say a word," Tonelli said. "I mean—it was Gordie Howe."

"Another time," Tonelli added. "a guy wrestled Gordie's son Mark to the ice, and Gordie skated over and said, 'Let him up.' The guy didn't listen, so Gordie reached down, put two big fingers in the guy's nostrils, and pulled him off Mark. The guy was howling in pain."

I interviewed both Richards on those CBS games—the Rocket and his kid brother, Henri. I had been told that Henri was shy and introverted. When I asked coach Toe Blake if he spoke English, he smiled (a rarity for Blake) and said, "Hell, I don't know if he even speaks French."

That day in Chicago, drinking beer with him, I probably told the Rocket exactly where I was on March 17, 1955, the night of the famous Richard Riot at the Montreal Forum. I was in my dorm at St. Lawrence University, my senior year, listening to Danny Gallivan call a game in the final series for the Stanley Cup—Detroit at Montreal. And what I heard left me stunned, almost like hearing about JFK's assassination and forever knowing exactly where you stood when the grim news hit you. Richard fans were so furious with NHL president Clarence Campbell after he suspended their hero for attacking a Boston player in a previous game, they rioted. Campbell was assaulted at the Forum, the game with Detroit lasted only one period, tear gas was thrown and fans outside the building went on a rampage, destroying property and looting stores along rue Sainte-Catherine.

I didn't converse much with the Rocket that day in the country music bar. I didn't want to invade his space and then become a pain in the butt with a string of questions. But on camera, I'm sure I asked him why his famous temper got him in so much trouble in his career. But I'm not sure I got much of a response. And his brother Henri was so shy and uncertain about speaking in English, he was happy to give me "yes" and "no" answers.

Years later, I would get to play against Henri, too—at the Forum. He would even lend me a pair of his skates—two sizes smaller than mine—to make sure that it happened.

As for Red Kelly, he was the first player I interviewed on network TV. And a month after the interview, he was traded to the Rangers—and refused to report. President Clarence Campbell threatened him with banishment from the game. The Leafs wooed him, made a quick deal with Detroit (for Marc Reaume), and that career change turned out well. For Kelly, at least. And a berth in the Hall of Fame. That was a career change that turned out well. For Kelly at least. Reaume played just 47 games for Detroit.

Years later, I would play on the same ice with Red in old-timers hockey at the Herb Carnegie Arena in North York, Ontario, until his cardiologist asked him to stop.

On his 90th birthday, in summer 2017, a year before he died, he paid me a compliment I'll never forget.

"On the ice you surprised me," he said. "I had no idea you could play that well."

Over the years the McFarlanes and Kellys would become fast friends. Everyone loved Red and Andra, the former figure skating champion. Both were champions on and off the ice. Red was the only non-Canadien to win eight Stanley Cups—four with Detroit, four more with the Leafs.

One interview I did that season stands out. It was with Jerry Toppazzini of the Bruins at the Boston Garden. Topper does have a way with words. I asked my first question and never got to the second. He rambled on about the Bruins for at least three minutes and was still talking when the TV producer frantically began calling for a commercial break. Before throwing the cue, I said, "Jerry, you are without doubt the easiest player to interview I've ever encountered."

Toppazzini was always good for a quote. Years later, on the golf course, I said to him, "You got a quick story for me, Jerry?"

"Sure. I'm the only NHLer who scored all four goals in a game in a 2–2 tie: two on the Montreal goalie and two on ours."

Another interview on CBS was with Tommy "Bomber" Williams of the Bruins. Williams was a Duluth, Minnesota, native who starred for the 1960 U.S. Olympic team, stunning winners of a gold medal at the Olympics in Squaw Valley. Williams got a lot of attention that season as the only American-born player in the NHL. He earned his nickname "Bomber" after he jokingly told airport officials in Toronto that he had a bomb in his hockey bag. That major "no-no" cost him a one-game suspension.

During my one season on CBS, I interviewed, at centre ice in Boston, the Bruins top scorer—Bronco Horvath, pivot of the famous "Uke Line" of Horvath, Bucyk, and Toppazzini. Horvath told me he was determined to beat out Bobby Hull for the scoring title and at one point, he looked heavenward and called on God to help him in his quest. His plea was noted by others, and the interview became a focal point for columnists like Scott Young, who took umbrage with Horvath for praying for special attention from the Almighty instead of a more concerted effort from his two sturdy wingers.

But it appeared that God was a Horvath fan because as the season closed, the Bruin sniper led Hull in the race for the Art Ross Trophy.

On March 20, 1960, the Bruins and Blackhawks met at the Boston Garden in the final game of the year. Horvath was on the verge of snaring the NHL scoring championship. With 60 minutes to play in the regular season, he still led Hull by a single point.

Horvath, who had never been in such lofty company before and never would be again, knew it might be his only chance to capture one of the NHL's top prizes. At age 30, he desperately wanted to beat the 21-year-old Hull and win that trophy.

But midway through the first period, Boston defenceman Bob Armstrong (our team captain in Stratford) fired a shot from the blue line that hit Horvath squarely in the jaw. He fell to the ice, unconscious, and then was rushed by ambulance to the hospital. On the way, Horvath came to and begin screaming, "Go back! Go back! I want to play!"

At the hospital, he refused to take off his uniform. X-rays were taken, and it took time for the medics to examine the film. Good news. Horvath's jaw was severely bruised, but not broken.

Horvath bolted for the door. He rushed back to the Garden, threw on his skates, and played the final few minutes of the game. Alas, his slim lead in the scoring race had evaporated. Bobby Hull had recorded two points in a 5–5 tie to win his first scoring crown.

Horvath was in tears. He would never challenge again. The following year he slumped to 30 points—50 fewer than his banner season.

A hockey oddity earlier in that season also contributed to Horvath's missing out on the scoring crown. Playing against the Blackhawks on November 8, Horvath was tripped from behind on a breakaway. Referee Dalt McArthur awarded a penalty shot to the Bruins, but in a bizarre interpretation of the rules, he allowed the Blackhawks to nominate a Bruin to take the shot. Chicago coach Rudy Pilous chose a utility forward named Larry Leach to take the free shot, and he missed by a mile.

McArthur should have allowed Horvath to take the shot. That missed opportunity may have cost Horvath a tie with Hull in the scoring race. McArthur's glaring gaffe cost him his job; his contract was not renewed.

The man who helped immensely in arranging these interviews was Chet Forte. Forte and I were newcomers to NHL hockey and in the same age bracket. We became fast friends. Both of us were new to imbibing as well. I had my first beer at age 24, after college hockey was over and before graduation. Beer and cigarettes had little interest to either one of us. Chet Forte went on to a fabulous career in television.

When we first met, I recognized his name. I rarely followed basketball back then, but I was aware that Chet Forte had been a huge star at Columbia, an All-American, one of the greatest players in the school's history. And when I found out more about his achievements, I could barely believe it.

The thing is, the guy was about as tall as Dr. Anthony Fauci (who was a high school basketball star). Maybe a bit taller than Fauci, at five-foot-seven. About 160 pounds. Forte held 11 school basketball records. In 1956–57, his senior year at Columbia, "Chet the Jet" led the nation in scoring with a 28.9 average, beating Wilt Chamberlain, then a seven-foot Kansas sophomore. That seemed impossible.

When he graduated, he barnstormed with the Harlem Globetrotters.

In Boston for a Bruins game, famed Celtics coach Red Auerbach asked me to bring Forte around. The revered coach held up his thumb and forefinger, inches apart. The coach told Forte, "Three or four more inches, son, and you'd have been a major star in pro basketball."

Forte stayed five years with CBS before switching to ABC, where his broadcasting career took off. He made his mark as the director of *Monday Night Football*, which made its debut in 1970 with names in the booth like Frank Gifford, Don Meredith, and Howard Cosell. It quickly became the most popular sports show on TV. Ratings were sky-high.

Forte won 11 Emmy Awards in his 25-year career at ABC, where he was producer-director of the 1968 and 1984 Summer Olympics. But he was unable to find a job in television when he left the network in 1987.

Why? Because of an addiction that ruined his life. Forte was a betting man. He had gambled away nearly $4 million and lost his multi-million-dollar home in New Jersey.

He was attracted to gambling in the early 1960s, shortly after our stint on CBS. Later, he admitted to defrauding a New Jersey business-man of $100,000 to get more gambling money. By then he was in deep trouble with the IRS.

In 1992, Forte was sentenced to five years' probation, community service, and fines. The judge said he avoided jail time because he had co-operated and begun treatment for his addiction. "I lost a fortune, I lost all respect," Forte said when his career was in shreds. "I hurt my family and I hurt my friends."

He moved from New York to San Diego, California, where he worked as a talk-show host for an all-sports radio station. He started at $58,000 a year. At ABC, he'd been earning close to a million a year.

In 1994, I was relieved to hear he hadn't gambled in more than six years and was attending Gamblers Anonymous meetings regularly. But for much of his adult life, he couldn't keep his hands from rolling dice or turning cards, the same hands he'd used to make himself a magician with a basketball.

He died early, age 60.

CHAPTER 20

MONTREAL, HERE I COME

The CBS season ended on a sour note. At CFRB, Wes McKnight pulled me aside before my final game.

"You won't be going to Detroit to do the final game for CBS," he told me. "We talked to CBS and told them we need you here this weekend—for the Board of Broadcast meetings."

"How could you do that without discussing it with me first?" I asked. I was really angry.

"Never mind," was the reply. "You'll be speaking to the governors as our sports director and telling them of our plans for sports coverage if we get the TV licence for Toronto."

"But you're our sports director, Wes, not me."

"And you will be soon. It's all been decided."

So, my first season on network TV ended with me missing the first and last telecasts and with me still unsure whether I was CFRB's sports director or not. And with CBS possibly wondering about me. Can we count on this guy to show up?

McKnight's decision helped me decide to move on after we lost our bid for a licence. Montreal station CFCF-TV—the successful bidder in Montreal—called to offer me the sports director's job there, and I accepted it.

The CFRB guys held a going-away party for me and presented me with a voucher for four snow tires. Nice.

"You'll need them in Montreal," one of them said.

In Montreal, I ran into a near chaotic situation. The new TV station, owned by Marconi, wasn't nearly ready to go to air. And I was forced to take a dramatic cut in pay before I even got to the station.

At the airport, two executives met me. "Brian, we have disturbing news," one said. "We've been told by Marconi that we can't pay you the $15,000 we promised you."

I took a deep breath. "How come?"

"Well, it's more money than the head of the tube department makes at Marconi."

"So? I'm not in the tube department."

"Of course not. But we'll have to pay you a couple of thousand less than what was offered and we'll try to get you the rest under the carpet."

What a strange beginning. And it got worse.

I immediately questioned my decision to join CFCF-TV. Like others, they reneged on their promises.

But there was no going back. And it would be months before there was a carpet to peek under.

I shrugged and went to work. And I quickly found out my two years of TV experience in Schenectady was hugely helpful. Most of my fellow employees had a bare minimum of experience in front of or behind the cameras.

I rented a house in Lachine and brought my growing family to the city. Daughter Lauren had been born before I left Toronto. Brenda would soon be on her way.

Later, we purchased a beautiful home in Gables Court, Beaconsfield.

The station grudgingly allowed me to hire an assistant and my choice was Dick Irvin, and that started him off on his Hall of Fame broadcast career. When I told my boss Irvin was my choice, he said, "Good. He's local. Offer him 75 bucks a week."

I said, "I can't do that. He's worth much more. He'll have to give up a much higher salary to join us."

The boss shrugged and said, "Send him to me then."

Irvin met with the boss and was persuaded to take the job—at 75 bucks per week.

"I thought the glamorous world of TV sports would be more rewarding than that," said Dick said. "Good thing I'm single and living at home."

I think I surprised Dick by doing some wacky things on the sportscasts. One day I drove a fast trotter in a harness race. Then I went up in a glider with a cameraman flying alongside. Dick and I dressed up in football uniforms at the Alouettes' training camp and posed as two "All-Americans." Turns out we couldn't throw or run with a football, stumbling around until we took off our helmets to reveal "the two goofballs" from CFCF-TV.

We enjoyed working together on the play-by-play of a kids' hockey series—Montreal Minor Hockey—with the always-entertaining Red Storey as our third man in the booth. I vividly recall a pint-sized kid named Bobby Lalonde starring in the series. He was tiny. But he went on to win two Memorial Cups with the Montreal Junior Canadiens and played a dozen years in the NHL—the smallest forward in the game at five-foot-five. Lalonde never saw a parade—until he was in one. And four decades later, I found myself playing right wing with him in our Sunday morning Oldtimers games.

A great role model and inspiration for kids—much like Tampa Bay great Marty St. Louis—kids who wonder if their small stature will deny them a chance in pro hockey. St. Louis was fitted with one of the smallest Hall of Fame jackets when he was inducted in 2017.

No team wanted St. Louis when he finished a sensational college career at Vermont. He went undrafted. Calgary gave him a chance but little ice time and discarded him.

Tampa Bay snapped him up and, after a modest start, he began piling up points. He would collect more than one thousand points in just over one thousand games, win a Stanley Cup, two Hart Trophies, and a Lady Byng. How good is that for a kid whose head came up to Zdeno

Chara's elbow? And Bobby Lalonde, even smaller than St. Louis, was almost his equal. Yes, almost. And in a six-team league.

Of course, the Canadiens were front and centre most of the time back then. But it wasn't easy getting any of them to guest on our shows. When I met with the Habs PR man Frank Selke Jr. to ask the team's policy, he said, "Brian, we'll give you players to interview—but in order of their jersey numbers."

"What, Frank? That's ridiculous. If Beliveau scores a game winner, or Geoffrion has a hat trick, and it's Phil Goyette's turn to be on TV, we have to talk with Goyette? Because his number is next?"

"Sure. He can talk about Geoffrion and Beliveau."

In time, common sense won out, and the policy was changed.

Selke Jr. would later take a position as GM of the expansion California Seals before joining *Hockey Night in Canada* as an executive. The Seals were desperate for fans. I'll wager he pleaded with the TV stations in the area to interview his Seals—never mind their jersey numbers—in an effort to promote the game.

In the studio at CFCF-TV, we often used elongated microphones called giraffe mics. But our boss, Sam Pitt, kept referring to them as "kangaroo" mics, which drew a few chuckles.

When I met with Pitt one day and told him of my frustrations—how cameramen couldn't seem to shoot film in focus, and other bothersome and frustrating job issues—he surprised me by asking, "How are the tires on your car?"

"What? Tires?"

"Yeah, tires. I felt like you do just last week and then I checked my tires. I needed four. Bought some Firestones and I feel like a new man. You should go to the parking lot and check your tires."

I actually wandered out to the lot shaking my head. My tires were fine.

It was at CFCF that I began to let stress and frustrations overwhelm me. I had a confrontation with Bert Cannings, the news director, and accused him of monopolizing the cameramen who were available for both news and sports assignments.

I told off Cannings, and he actually took my accusations rather casually. In fact, he lauded me for standing up for myself.

But I could sense a breakdown coming. It may have followed an order from my boss to be on hand at a downtown banquet honouring former Alouette quarterback Sam Etcheverry.

"It may run late, so have Dick Irvin do your sports show that night," I was told.

For some reason, the station was paying me for each on-air performance.

"If the Etcheverry dinner runs late, and I miss my sportscast," I asked, "I'll still get paid, right?"

"No, if you don't perform, you don't get a fee."

"But that's absurd. You insist I be there. But it will cost me to be there."

"That's the way it is. Live with it."

I began to think I couldn't live with the asinine decisions coming from management. I'd had a heated debate with Pitt over who had final say on the film shoots we were doing. I was at Irving Grundman's bowling alley and I saw our cameraman setting up in the lane—directly in front of the bowlers.

"Get your camera off to the side or behind the bowlers," I ordered. "Are they going to bowl through your legs?"

He was miffed and told Pitt I'd embarrassed him.

Pitt astonished me by saying, "Brian, the cameraman always has the final say in where he sets up."

"No, he does not," I fired back. "I'm the director. I tell him what I want and how to do it. I take full responsibility."

Pitt insisted he was right, and I was wrong.

The cameraman we discussed was the same guy I sent to the Forum one night—to film Boom Boom Geoffrion's attempt at a 50-goal season. He had 49.

"Follow Geoffrion's every move on the ice," I told him. "It'll use up a lot of film, but it'll be worth it if he scores."

He came back from the game and did not look happy.

"What happened?"

"I did what you said and shot film of Boom Boom on every shift. He came close to scoring in the third period, and a fan leaped up in front of me and knocked my hand into the camera lens. I was nursing my hand, looking for a cut, when Geoffrion scored his 50th."

"Don't tell me you missed it."

"Yeah, I missed it. But I've got shots of people celebrating it."

And that's what we used on my sportscast that night. The celebration, but not the goal.

I prepared my late-night sportscast one night, and luckily, Irvin was at the station.

I felt sick and tired. I thrust the copy into his hands and said, "You're going to do the late sports. I'm not well. I'm resigning. I'm getting out of here."

I went home and never went back.

Sure, I handled it badly. I should have requested a leave of absence. Maybe seen a psychologist. Or a hypnotist. Or a vet. Maybe a witch doctor?

I'd battled anxiety and depression once before, when I was working for CBS. At that time, a doctor was treating me for a thyroid issue, which I didn't have, and the pills he prescribed knocked me on my butt.

My state of mind in Montreal was equally as disturbing, and I just wanted out. Even if my paycheque stopped on the day I walked away. And I thought: *Looks like that's it, you wimp. You'll never be able to face a camera again. Better think of selling pots and pans again. Modelling long johns? No, you're too old for that and you look like crap.*

But soon, recalling my mother's words, "Time is a great healer," and finding much to be thankful for when our baby Brenda arrived, I stopped walking the beach in front of our Beaconsfield home. I decided to pick myself up and start all over again. Good song title, that.

I placed a call to John Bassett, owner of the *Toronto Telegram* and CFTO-TV in Toronto.

"Mr. Bassett, Brian McFarlane calling. You may not remember me, but I was at CFRB in Toronto. Now I'm here in Montreal and I just walked away from my job as sports director of the TV station here. I was hoping you might help me."

"I remember you, Brian. I hear you. You were a candidate to be sports director here at CFTO-TV when we hired Johnny Esaw. Leave it with me."

And he was gone. Our conversation lasted 30 seconds.

The following day, Johnny Esaw, Bassett's sports director at CFTO called. He was in Montreal at a hotel. Could we meet?

Esaw got right to the point. "I can get you back to Toronto and CFTO-TV. You'll have to do anything and everything I ask and the most I can offer you is $8,000 a year. Interested?"

"Yes, I am, Johnny. Will you pay moving expenses?"

"No."

"Can you sweeten the pot a bit? Your offer is about half what I've been making here."

"No. Make up your mind."

"I'll take it."

CHAPTER 21

TORONTO AGAIN

Things went badly at CFTO, where I felt Johnny Esaw had hired me only because John Bassett had directed him to. When I joined, I expected I'd be doing sports. Instead, I was told I'd be holed up in a tiny announce booth for much of each day. Every half hour I'd open the microphone and deliver four words, "This is CFTO-TV, Toronto."

At night I'd prepare a sportscast to follow the news and weather, much like I'd done in Montreal and Schenectady. I was deeply conscious I was lucky to have a job of any kind, but in time I dared to complain about my booth role to an executive, Ray Arsenault, stating, "Why can't we tape the station breaks? I could be doing something else much more worthwhile."

His answer: "No, the tape might break. Or some techie might push the wrong button. Just stay where you are."

It sounded like something I might have heard before—at CFCF-TV. Ridiculous.

I'd escaped the announce booth and was doing the late sportscasts, when I found myself running out of breath and desperately trying to inhale without the viewer noticing. A self-concocted remedy was to make use of photos and film to cover my embarrassment and discomfort. I could breathe easier when unseen by my audience. I felt every viewer was staring at me, saying, "There's something wrong with that announcer." As a result, my sportscasts had more photos and film on screen than most. I was definitely trying to hide. I was ashamed and embarrassed. And I had only myself to blame.

I was terribly upset about this condition and wondered if I'd ever successfully combat my demons. I even tried hypnotherapy with a qualified doctor.

The worst night ever was the time I had a well-known skier as my guest and I allotted plenty of time for our interview. He'd brought a short film of a ski race to complement the interview. But he was a nervous wreck on camera—more so than I was. I thought he was about to faint and when I introduced the film and it popped up, he whispered, "I've got to go" and he slipped away and slumped into a chair off set. The film ended, and I had three or four minutes to fill. How I filled them will forever remain a mystery. Perhaps I just simply stammered and stuttered until my time was up, wishing I could juggle or do a few magic tricks to show my audience I wasn't a complete jackass.

But I persevered, struggling through, and, when not on air, it was a relief to help produce filmed vignettes for the show.

Long before I began to play with the NHL Oldtimers hockey club, I decided to feature them on one of my telecasts. They were playing a fundraising game against the media at George Bell Arena, and I brought along Jack Vandermay, a top cameraman, to cover the event.

In goal for the media was Toronto mayor Don Summerville, 48, a former practice goaltender for the Leafs. On defence was Al Boliska, a well-known disc jockey on CHUM-AM. Summerville looked fit—despite a heart attack he'd suffered two years earlier—and was obviously having a good time, when suddenly he bolted from his goal net and headed for the gate to his team's bench. But Boliska, thinking the mayor was quitting, intercepted him and playfully wrestled him to the ice.

Not good. The mayor was on the verge of another heart attack. He clambered unsteadily to his feet, staggered off the ice, and went straight to the dressing room, where he frantically searched his pockets for his nitroglycerine pills.

Vandermay covered the entire sequence with his camera, including the call for an ambulance, and the collapse of the mayor as people rushed from all directions to assist in the emergency.

Mayor Summerville, who was immensely popular, did not make it. After an agonizingly long wait for an ambulance, he died shortly after he was rushed to a nearby hospital. It was one of the biggest news stories of the year. Vandermay and I raced back to the studios in Agincourt, and CFTO had exclusive film coverage of the tragedy on the 11 o'clock news.

The *Toronto Star* had a blazing but tacky headline the following day: "MAYOR SUMMERVILLE SKATES OFF ICE TO DIE."

Boliska, who was a zany, popular morning man at CHUM radio, also died young. A heart attack on the eve of his 40th birthday took him.

A victim of my hiring at CFTO was Tim Ryan, whom I'd worked with a couple of years earlier at CFRB. Ryan was smart and ambitious and was constantly told, "You look too young to be doing this work."

Ryan and I worked Toronto Maple Leafs baseball telecasts and junior hockey games from Maple Leaf Gardens, when Bobby Orr was a brush-cut kid playing for the Oshawa Generals.

We were paid a pittance, hardly enough to pay our expenses in travelling to these venues.

When I complained to Esaw that the $3.60 "travel fee" was scraping the bottom, he countered with, "When we get a sponsor for these telecasts, we'll reward you appropriately." We never got a sponsor. But at the ballpark, we could wolf down as many hot dogs as we wanted.

And it was true we were getting much-needed experience.

I don't recall if we got extra pay for covering hockey—I don't think so—but it was hockey. And when the Oshawa Generals came to play—they played some home games on Gardens ice while a new rink was under construction in Oshawa—there on defence was the small kid from Parry Sound—Bobby Orr—wearing No. 2. So, Orr's first TV appearances were on CFTO.

In his recent book—*Orr: My Story*—he tells of how proud he was of the new suit he wore—part of the contract he and his dad negotiated with the Boston Bruins. And how his teammates kidded him about how ill-fitting the suit was, forcing him to pay for some adjustments.

And how they chuckled in training camp, when Orr took his turn getting on the scales.

"One hundred and twenty-five pounds!" someone shouted. "That'll scare the crap out of a lot of forwards."

And how, when he broke a stick and asked trainer Stan Waylett for a replacement, Waylett asked, "What lie, Bobby?" Orr was stumped. He didn't know about lies—the degree of curve between the shaft and the blade. The lads around him chuckled when he answered, "Left."

One of my assignments for Esaw was to pick up and deliver guests for his show *The Sports Hot Seat*. It was a popular show featuring Esaw as host and a panel of sportswriters interviewing a major sports celebrity. I was the chauffeur. It was my job to drive to the airport, meet the celeb, and get him to the studios northeast of the city in Agincourt.

What Esaw didn't know was that I brought my handy tape recorder with me. I would interview the celeb en route and sometimes in the men's room at the TV station, wait a few days, then go to CBC Radio downtown and sell the interview for 35 bucks. Did I feel a conflict of interest? Was I breaking some unwritten rule? Of course. But I confess I did it, anyway. I was making ends meet. And it was a badly needed source of income. Better than modelling long johns on the side for the Eaton's catalogue. Better than selling pots and pans. Although there's nothing wrong with that. Mike Ilitch, long-time owner of the Red Wings, started out that way. He switched to selling pizzas and became a multi-millionaire.

I was spinning my wheels at CFTO and battling depression and panic attacks. I often thought of a man I met during my Inkerman days, wishing I'd taken his advice. "Brian, you should join my insurance company. You could be earning $10,000 a year in no time."

Then Morley Kells called. Morley Kells? A lacrosse man who worked for MacLaren Advertising.

Over lunch, Kells asked if I had any good ideas that might be incorporated into the *Hockey Night in Canada* telecasts. I was flattered and tempted to say, "Yeah, Morley. Hire me as Bill Hewitt's colour man."

But instead, I said I thought the first intermission could be improved with the introduction of a Hockey College for Kids. Kells and I discussed airing hockey tips from players like Keon and Horton and Bower, Beliveau, Harvey, and Plante. Youngsters could join the Hockey College and win contests by having their mom or dad always fill up at the Esso sign. Imperial Oil would be the major sponsor, of course.

Kells bought the concept and so did MacLaren. My depression was eased in a subsequent meeting when the bigwigs at MacLaren offered me 20 grand a year (did I hear right?) to become dean of the Esso National Hockey College. I quickly accepted and turned in my resignation to Esaw at CFTO-TV. Esaw was upset and proposed a raise of a thousand dollars, thinking that might change my mind, but, of course, it didn't.

I was also miffed at Esaw because of an incident at the annual Telegram Indoor Track and Field Games held at Maple Leaf Gardens. Tim Ryan, Lloyd Percival, and I were calling the events. Esaw would have been there, but he was out of town. Bill Crothers, an elite Toronto distance runner, won the major race of the night to an eruption of applause and promptly collapsed in a heap over the finish line. I hurried over to him and stood by with microphone handy, waiting for Crothers to climb to his feet, when the microphone was pulled from my hand. Esaw had returned from his trip and hurried to the event. He arrived late and raced onto the floor to replace me as interviewer.

"I know this kid," he told me. "I'll do the interview." He bent over and chatted with a winded runner who could barely talk.

I walked off the floor and out of the building, thinking Esaw worked his way into the show for two reasons. He'd bask in Crothers's victory and he'd also earn a performer's fee.

"Let him finish the damn show," I told my wife as we headed out.

But we didn't go home. We attended a post-game party for all involved, and when Esaw walked in I refused to speak with him, afraid a meeting might come to blows.

But on Monday morning, we had it out. He said, "As sports director, I felt compelled to take the mic away from you. I know Crothers well."

"So do I, John. No, you were thinking of the spotlight and you were thinking of the fee you'd earn. If I were conducting an orchestra, and a guy ran onstage and yanked my baton away, you'd know how I felt."

In retrospect, it seems like a minor disagreement. But it was big at the time. And I'm certain Esaw was head and shoulders above me when it came to the business side of TV sports.

The offer from MacLaren came shortly after. Looking back, I feel badly how things went at CFTO. Basically, Esaw was the right man for the CFTO position and we put our differences aside in time. I was mentally stressed when I was there. I was worried sick that I'd never again feel comfortable in front of a camera. I felt I was a failure, weak for not being able to control my emotions, a dreadful broadcaster. I thought it was time to move away from the studio and change the direction of my life.

CHAPTER 22

MacLAREN

When *Mad Men* captivated TV audiences in North America, it took me back to my days with MacLaren Advertising in Toronto in the early '60s. MacLaren was so similar to the TV show. I never thought I'd wind up working there. One executive, Hugh Horler, had a suit of armour standing in his office. I had a meeting with him one day and was tempted to ask, "Do you slip into that on rainy days? Won't it rust? Can our goalie borrow the helmet?" But somehow I controlled my smartass tendencies. The guy had clout.

MacLaren created *Hockey Night in Canada* in 1931 when it was given exclusive radio broadcasting rights for games held in Maple Leaf Gardens. Through the 1950s and '60s, it was the largest ad agency in Canada and its staff produced 85 percent of TV network programming when the CBC started television broadcasting in 1952.

The men who hired me—Bud Turner and David Rae—said, "You'll be working on the fifth floor—in the broadcast department—and we want you and Kells to keep an eye on the people up there and report back to us from time to time." They made it clear they were concerned about those in charge of *Hockey Night in Canada*.

"Pardon me? You want me to be a spy? I'm not comfortable with that."

The request was never mentioned again.

Kells and I got busy organizing the Esso National Hockey College, which would be introduced on *Hockey Night in Canada* the following season. But it never happened! Executives at Imperial Oil decided to postpone the idea indefinitely.

If I thought I was spinning my wheels at CFTO-TV, I soon found myself busy trying to keep those same wheels from whirling pointlessly at the ad agency.

It began well. No microphones or cameras to face. A new attitude, a healthy mental state. Kells and I began by talking to hockey men with experience in the amateur game. Naturally, CAHA officials—Gordon Juckes and others—were excited about our plans.

But meetings with Imperial Oil did not go as well. A man named Burkholder, initially excited about the hockey concept, seemed to be cooling on the idea. For an executive, Burkholder had an office desk that intrigued me. It was spotless. No loose papers, no stapler or note-pad. No suit of armour guarding it. Not even a coffee cup. Did he hastily shovel everything from his desk into a paper bag—maybe an old duffle bag—and hide it somewhere before our meetings? I would never find out. But I was tempted to ask.

"Our Tiger in the Tank campaign is very popular," he told us. "We may carry on with it for another year or two. Perhaps we'll have to postpone the introduction of a hockey college indefinitely."

Meanwhile, I learned that MacLaren did very little in-house production. Everything was farmed out, then returned ready to be delivered to the client with a 15 percent markup.

With the Hockey College in limbo, Ted Hough wanted to meet with me.

"Looks like the hockey college is dead in the water," he said. "We're not sure what to do with you. I'd like you to come and be my assistant. Someday you may succeed me as head of *Hockey Night in Canada*."

I said, "Well, that's interesting. Let me try it for a couple of weeks."

I did, but I soon decided it wasn't going to work. Hough and I were on different wavelengths. My decision was made one night in New

York, when I found myself running from bar to bar with him. It was bizarre. He shouted over his shoulder when we hit the final bar at about 3 a.m. "Not a word about this around the office."

Back in Toronto, I said to him, "Ted, I'm still a broadcaster at heart. Why not put me in the gondola with Bill Hewitt—as his colour man? And I'll form my own company and produce intermission features for you."

He thought about it and agreed it might be a good idea.

"But if you don't want to work with me, who'll I get as my assistant?"

"Call Ralph Mellanby in Montreal," I suggested. "He'd love that kind of position."

Hough made the call, and Mellanby signed a sweet deal with MacLaren as executive producer of *Hockey Night in Canada*. I often wondered if I'd been a dumbbell for turning down such an opportunity. Probably.

But, no. My relations with Hough were frosty for the entire time I worked for the agency. Perhaps word seeped through to him that Kells and I had been asked by his superiors to "keep an eye on the broadcast department" and report back to them.

There was no reporting back. But Hough may have thought there was. He was no fan of Kells, either.

Was I ever going to find a boss I respected, someone I could enjoy working for and with? Yes, but it would come later, when I joined NBC and met Scotty Connal. He was the best boss I ever had—by far.

And somehow I knew that if I could find my way to the gondola at the Gardens, any fears that lingered of facing a camera again would be surmountable. Perhaps the excitement of being part of *Hockey Night in Canada*, the absolute joy of being in the gondola at Maple Leaf Gardens, the most famous building in Canada, covering the most popular hockey team in the nation—maybe in the world (now, now, Habs fans)—helped me get back to normal, back to the professional announcer I once was. I felt confident, optimistic, and anxious for the new NHL season to get underway. If I had one nagging concern, it was that I'd never played in the NHL. Would millions of viewers—and the NHLers themselves—dismiss me as "just a college player. He can't know very much about the pro game"?

I was determined to be fully prepared—to read all the sports pages and the weekly *Hockey News*, to listen to all the sportscasts, to attend morning "skates," and to mingle with players and coaches asking questions—all kinds of questions. To tape the answers, so that I could say on air, "I was chatting with Johnny Bower yesterday, and he said—"

My thirst for knowledge even brought me to the Leafs' training camp in Peterborough, Ontario, where I could watch and listen and learn. The Leafs players were still a little giddy after winning their third straight Stanley Cup in the spring of '64, ousting Detroit four games to three in the final series. Bobby Baun, who'd scored a game-winning goal in overtime in Game 6 to prolong the series, while playing on a "broken ankle," was still drawing a lot of attention. So was his pal Carl Brewer, even then a bit of a rebel, who announced he was retiring from hockey to go to university. But he changed his mind and signed a contract with the Leafs—possibly with long-distance help from his friend Al Eagleson. At training camp in Peterborough in 1964, Leaf goalie Johnny Bower had saved enough money to have his car painted. Punch Imlach said, "Johnny, I know a guy in town who'll paint your car, and it'll be cheap. Give me the keys." "Cheap" was a word Bower adored. A day later, the paint job was finished, the car delivered. It was painted in every conceivable colour: red, green, purple, orange. Bower had to drive it—with George Armstrong a passenger. At every bus stop in Peterborough, Army would talk to people on the curb. "This is Johnny Bower's car. You like it? He picked the colours himself." Bower sneaked back to Toronto with the car. His wife, Nancy, took one look and ordered him back to Peterborough. "You tell that coach of yours I'm furious. Tell him to get the car repainted, or I'll come down there and paint his car. And I bet he won't like it."

I got to know many of the men I'd be talking about on TV and I established a pattern of preparedness I followed for as long as I was a hockey broadcaster. There was no predecessor to tell me what to do and how to do it. And no need for one. You just used common sense.

I was ready for a chair in the gondola, where I'd join two broadcasting legends—Foster and Bill Hewitt.

CHAPTER 23

THE HEWITTS: CALLING THE SHOTS

Well, here it comes, the chapter I worry about most. I hope what I write about the Hewitts—Foster and Bill—is both revealing and fair. I worry that Hewitt fans—and certainly members of the Hewitt family—may cluck their tongues. And that's fair, too.

During my 17 years in the famous gondola at Maple Leaf Gardens, working alongside Bill Hewitt and his father, Foster, I formed some strong opinions on these two broadcasting legends. Both are enshrined in the Hockey Hall of Fame, as is Foster's father, W.A. Hewitt, who served as the head of the OHA for an astonishing 63 years. Think of it. A man heads up amateur hockey in a province for 63 years. Incredible. And one family producing three hockey Hall of Famers—not one of them a player, coach, manager, or referee. Even more incredible.

But I must be honest here. Working as Bill Hewitt's colour commentator required patience, tolerance, and an ability to deal with quirky situations and surprises. There were two major surprises in my very first game with him.

When the 1964–65 NHL season got underway, Bill Hewitt welcomed me to the famous gondola. I was surprised to find it cramped and unimpressive. Occasionally, you sensed that it might crash down on the ice at any second. There was no bathroom. If a game went two or three periods of overtime, you'd better look around for a jar. A simple empty coffee cup wouldn't do. Especially if you sipped from a cup during a game and were forgetful. No phone to call home or anywhere else. Staggering along a narrow catwalk to get to the gondola could be daunting. George Raft, the tough-guy movie actor, was Foster's guest one night in the old radio days and almost fell in a heap as he contemplated the trek. Conn Smythe would never venture up there. By the time I became a regular, safety measures had been taken. It was more fun getting there than frightening.

We shared a small booth in that hallowed place and in similar booths around the NHL for the next 17 years—until I uttered a few words in Minnesota one night that enraged Harold Ballard, and he had me evicted. It could have been worse. He could have come up and thrown me bodily onto the ice below.

As a colour man, I was supposed to fill in when Bill stopped talking. I would give statistics and talk about goals that were scored, discuss personalities and reveal interesting facts about the players and the game. However, if I'd listened to a bizarre edict delivered by my boss, Ted Hough, I might have had very little to say. Before my first game, he entered the gondola and said, "Brian, I think you should speak three times a period. That'll be a nice balance between you and Bill." He held up three fingers. I couldn't believe Hough would place a quota on my comments. What was the man thinking? "Three times, Ted?" I said. "Ted, what if six goals are scored?"

He said, "Talk about three of them," he snapped. Then he turned and left. I decided to ignore his edict and broke it in the first few minutes in my first game. Hough was never happy with me. And I think I know why. He knew that I never thought of him as a hockey guy.

Hough—Ballard called him "Huff and Puff"—complained to Mellanby once that while watching games at home the camera angles seemed distorted. What could Mellanby do about it?

Mellanby paid a visit to Hough's home, took one look at his tiny TV set.

"For God's sake, Ted, buy yourself a new TV—a big one. No wonder the picture seems distorted."

Later, I would receive further instructions: "Don't talk about the fights, don't get Ballard mad, and don't talk to Bill because he doesn't listen to you, anyway."

Can you believe that last edict? Don't talk to your broadcast partner?

Another oddity happened in that first game. At one point, the puck squirted right across the Leafs' goal line—from post to post—and it stayed out. Bill turned to me and said, "Brian, as you know, any part of that puck on the line, and it's a goal." That was stunning news. Surely Bill knew that the puck must cross all the way over the line to count. I certainly wasn't going to correct him while we were "live." But during the next commercial break, I said, "Bill, you made a little mistake there. The puck must be over the line to count."

"No, it doesn't."

I grabbed my handy rule book and thumbed through the pages. I showed Bill the rule.

"See, Bill, it says the puck must be completely over the line, or it's no goal."

He studied the page for a few seconds and then said, "Well, they've changed that rule."

And then he went right on with the play-by-play. That story is somewhat amusing because the "over the line" rule has been in the books since day one.

Unlike me, Bill Hewitt never gave his employers any problems. He was excellent at what he did—play-by-play. He was not much of a contributor to other aspects of the telecast and was quite uncomfortable on camera, even more so than Foster. They were extremely close as father and son, and one came away with the impression that Foster was a huge controlling influence on Bill's career and on his life in general.

Bill had a fear of flying, so he took flying lessons at Buttonville Airport. I suggested we film Bill on the day he went up solo, and we did.

I hopped aboard, and there we were, at three thousand feet, bobbing up and down, and a second plane with our cameraman in it a few wingtips away. Bill seemed a bit nervous, and that made me a bit nervous. Hell, I didn't know if he even drove a car. Or a bicycle. Or a scooter.

We landed—*bump, bump, bump*. I kissed the ground and then I thought of a humorous ending for the piece. I found some vintage film with a plane either crashing into a barn or flying right through a barn—I've forgotten which. On my voice-over, I said, "Here's some film of Bill's second solo flight." It got a chuckle from everybody but Foster.

"Somebody mocking my son like that. Disgraceful. Whose idea was that?"

Silence. Nobody squealed on me.

You may think in all those seasons Bill and I would have become fast friends—buddies. Not so.

Bill didn't make friends easily, not among the broadcast team. To his credit, he didn't have any enemies, either. He was the Walter Mitty of the crew, the least likely to be consulted or to contribute anything but play-by-play to the telecasts. It was a major contribution, one to be commended. Unlike me, he was never a troublemaker. He was the least likely to be controversial and possibly the least understood by the rest of us.

And this will surely surprise you: Bill had a bodyguard. A large, affable ex-cop named Arthur was always nearby wherever Bill appeared. Why, I often wondered, did Bill need a bodyguard?

Arthur may have posed as Bill's "good friend," but it was pretty obvious to us that he was around for a reason—to look after Bill.

Yes, Bill was a pleasant person, a nice man but—dare I say it—a vanilla man.

One season in the '60s, I helped put together a hockey team of *Hockey Night in Canada* personnel. Even Ward Cornell suited up, and he could barely skate. But a good sport. When our touring club was bussed to a game in Wallaceburg, Ontario, one Sunday, Arthur came along with Bill. En route, we stopped at a restaurant for lunch, but Bill and Arthur opted to stay on the bus. Didn't even get off to stretch their legs, breathe some fresh air. They'd packed a brown bag with ham hocks and ate by themselves. That was odd, don't you think?

Bill played a fair game of hockey. Apparently, he'd been an athlete of sorts at Upper Canada College. Earlier, Foster had been a top boxer—a flyweight—at the same institution. Yet neither looked like an athlete. I couldn't envision Foster ever having a bloody nose. Or throwing a solid punch in anger. I couldn't imagine Bill in a hockey dressing room, kibitzing with his teammates. On the ice, any check he threw at an opposing player would have been a gentle one. I doubt he ever saw the inside of a penalty box. But playing alongside him, I found him to be a fair skater and stickhandler.

Another surprise. In all those years, on Leafs road trips, Bill seldom travelled on the same flight as the rest of us. He seldom stayed at the same hotel. I had two meals with him in 17 seasons of travel. I never had a post-game drink with him in the bar when the game was over. Not once.

Bill and Foster were aboard our flight to Chicago one day, prompting Morley Kells to quip, "I feel totally safe aboard. God wouldn't dare let Foster Hewitt die in a plane crash."

Bill was very much a loner—as Danny Gallivan was. Journalist Frank Orr told me Bill often left his hotel room door open a few inches. He sat on his bed hoping someone would come along, poke his head in and talk to him. So, why didn't he ever join the rest of us at the bar for some friendly banter? Orr's comment didn't make sense.

On game day on the road trips, Bill would arrive at our hotel room for a pre-game meeting, seldom contributing a word, except to ask each of us the same question, "Hi, what time did you get in?"

At one of those meetings in Calgary one day, Dave Hodge threw him a curve.

Bill said to Hodge, "Hi, Dave, what time did you get in?"

Hodge said jokingly, "Bill, you always ask me that question. Do you really give a shit when anybody gets in?"

Bill was taken aback. When the meeting was over, we walked down the hall to the elevator together. Bill was upset. He wondered why Hodge had spoken so sharply to him.

I said, "Dave has an odd sense of humour. He was just kidding you. He didn't mean to hurt your feelings. Don't sweat it."

"Oh, okay."

We made small talk while waiting for the elevator.

One of our crew came along and joined us. Bill turned to him and said, "Hi, what time did you get in?"

I almost burst out laughing. Instead, I said, "Bill, you've got to stop asking that."

Bill's strength was play-calling in the booth. Then he'd hurry out of the building and vanish into the night. Gone like a gulp. Game over and forgotten. No small talk, no good nights, no post-game visits to the dressing room to chat with the players, or ask some questions. None of that. Gone!

Come to think of it, this may have been the ideal way to erase another Leafs defeat from memory. There were lots of losses back then.

On one occasion, four of us—not unlike the panels who fill time on *Hockey Night* intermissions today—Jack Dennett, Dave Hodge, Foster Hewitt, and myself, were asked to name the highlight of the half season. I only recall Foster's answer. "I think the highlight was my radio station going to fifty thousand watts," he stated. And he was dead serious.

Luckily, we were taping it and could start over. Hodge jumped in and reminded Foster we were looking for a hockey highlight. Hodge could be cutting. He might have said, "Who the hell cares about your radio station's wattage, Foster? We're on *Hockey Night in Canada*. Give us a hockey highlight." But he didn't. Foster had earned a lot of respect. From everyone but Ballard and the Smythes.

Foster paused for a moment, then recalled a hockey highlight.

During a game, there was minimal conversation between Bill and myself. He was confident and accurate with his descriptions of the play—with few exceptions. But conversing during a break in the action seemed to unnerve him. That was my perception. I believe he feared I would ask him something that would leave him stuck for an answer.

He said some startling things on air.

An example: One season the NHL brought in a new rule governing the tape on the knob of goaltenders' sticks. I had to nudge Bill's elbow to gain his attention. "Bill, there's a new rule in the book for this season. NHL goalies must have a half inch of white tape on the knob of their goal sticks. It's called the Billy Smith rule."

His reply: "Right, Brian. And there's also a rule about having more tape on the knob of the goal stick."

Hmm. Didn't I just state that? Visions of guys falling off barstools across Canada filled my mind. Guys laughing and pointing at the puny TV screens of the era. "Listen to those two a-holes. They don't know what the hell they're talking about."

Another time I nudged Bill and said, "Bill, the All-Star votes are in, and Bobby Orr was a unanimous choice for a First Team berth."

"Right, Brian," came his answer. "Almost everybody voted for him."

Almost everybody? So much for the meaning of "unanimous."

One night, producer Ralph Mellanby told Bill to stand by. On the next whistle he'd be showing Audrey Phillips in the crowd. Phillips was a popular production assistant on the show, and on this night she decided to sit in the stands, close to the Leafs' bench, and cheer on her favourite player—Dan Maloney.

The whistle blew, and Phillips's beaming face filled the screen.

Mellanby said in Bill's earpiece, "Bill, there's Audrey in the crowd."

Bill stared at the screen and was lost for words.

Mellanby repeated himself.

"Bill, there's Audrey in the crowd."

Bill swallowed and stammered, "There's, uh, Audrey, uh, in the crowd," as play resumed.

On the following whistle, Mellanby had me explain who Phillips was and mention her fondness for Maloney.

Mellanby had a surprise for me one night. He came all the way up to the gondola and thrust a paper in front of me. The whistle stopped play, and he mouthed the words "Read this!"

I started to read aloud.

Oh my God. It was a release written by Stan Obodiac, Ballard's PR flack, a release we'd all laughed at prior to the game. Ballard had been set free from prison the previous day and was back in charge. Obodiac was Ballard's biggest fan and the lowest-paid PR director in the NHL. He hailed his boss's return in a press release, extolling all of Ballard's so-called virtues and how the captain was back at the helm, etc.

I simply could not read the release verbatim and I tried to edit as I went, deleting much of the praise, but stumbling my way through the lines. I almost choked on the words and I felt like choking Mellanby. I stopped midway through, before viewers started throwing shoes at their TV set. I was ashamed of myself for not telling Mellanby, "You read it if you feel this bullshit must be heard."

Later, I was told the whole thing was a practical joke gone wrong. Nobody wanted to tell me the full story, but I was told that Dave Hodge, when the release was distributed before game time, told Mellanby that Ballard had left orders that it must be read on the telecast. Mellanby believed Hodge and rushed up to the gondola to insist I be the messenger. Not funny, guys. Not at all.

I was told by one producer never to talk when the puck was about to be dropped on a faceoff, or Bill would get really upset. The norm today is for a lot of back-and-forth chatter between the colour commentator and the play-by-play announcer—at any time. Not back then—not in Toronto. There was never a good reason for Bill—or any play-caller—to monopolize the microphone during the action on the ice. But he did for years. Like his father did before him. In fact, Foster preferred to work alone. Only recently did I learn that when colour commentators were assigned to work radio with Foster, as I was, they were told to stick to a "three comments per period" rule. That did not happen in my case.

My work with Bill would have been so much better—and more informative—if we'd covered the on-ice action in a common sense, natural way.

In a June 2006 *Globe and Mail* article, years after Bill's passing, William Houston wrote about him.

Here's [something] that just makes you shake your head. The NHL Broadcasters' Association has never selected Bill Hewitt winner of the [Foster Hewitt] award.

All Hewitt did was call hockey on radio and television for 30 years. For about 20 years, he was the voice of hockey, along with Danny Gallivan, on Canadian television. He called countless Stanley Cup finals, including the Toronto Maple Leafs' four championships in the 1960s.

Hewitt, who died in 1996 at age 68, had weaknesses. He didn't relate well to his colour commentator. Others of that era didn't, either. Off the air, he was reclusive.

But he was an outstanding play-by-play man. He had the Hewitt crackling voice. He was accurate, anticipated the plays and was fair.

Houston's comments were accurate. And timely. A few months later, Bill Hewitt was ushered into the media section of the Hockey Hall of Fame, finally a winner of the award named after his father. At a Hall of Fame luncheon, I was pleased to say the words that ushered him in, thinking, *Don't be a hypocrite*. Houston's column may have prodded the Broadcasters' Association to name Bill as an inductee in 2007.

The Hewitts were good—but mysterious—people. And Foster especially deserves all the accolades he's been handed over the years. He was the man who set the standard for all the play-by-play announcers who followed. Old-timers across Canada still place him on a pedestal 10 feet high—and so they should.

Foster hit the jackpot early—when people didn't realize there was a jackpot. When he was signed to be the voice of the Leafs, he said, "Sure, but I'd like to be the producer as well. And when the new Maple Leaf Gardens opens, I'd like the right of approval over anyone who wishes to broadcast or film events at the arena."

Owner Conn Smythe agreed to the requests. So, it was Foster, through Foster Hewitt Productions, who negotiated fees with sponsors and promoters. He'd take a cut of the pie—a hefty cut—and turn the rest over to Smythe.

Foster, along with Boston's Fred Cusick and Montreal's Rene Lecavalier, were the first media inductees into the Hockey Hall of Fame. They went in as members of the Hall, not as media members. I may have been the last broadcaster to be inducted as a member in 1995. It says *Honoured Member* on the crest on my jacket. Each year in November, when I wear my jacket to the Hall's induction ceremonies, I hope nobody notices. I fear someone from the Hall may run up, rip off the crest, and replace it with *Media Member*.

If Bill Hewitt felt ignored by the Hall selectors, how does Don Cherry feel? He's had a huge impact on the broadcasting of hockey games and he's still waiting for the Hall to call. Perhaps it never will.

CHAPTER 24

THE LEAFS OF THE '60s

Obviously, the modern-day NHL player is, in almost every way, superior to the men who preceded him. But in one area, they fail miserably—in signing autographs. Yesterday's stars had better penmanship and took the time to show it off.

You read and admire the signatures of Johnny Bower and Jean Beliveau and Bobby Hull. Today's players go *flick, flick, flick* with a pen, and you can't read the damn name.

The names Bower, Beliveau, and Hull take me back to my Toronto days in the '60s, one of my favourite eras in the game. How can anyone who witnessed NHL hockey in that decade not feel they watched some of the most dramatic and spectacular hockey ever played? That's the way I feel about hockey as I saw it—and lived it—when I first joined *Hockey Night in Canada*, in the long-ago '60s.

It was particularly true in the early years of the decade, when Leafs fans witnessed three Stanley Cup triumphs in a row. Then there was that delicious surprise in 1967—a Centennial Year win over the mighty Canadiens, with Montrealers salivating over a chance to display the Stanley Cup at Expo, with the whole world looking on and showing utmost admiration and respect.

Habs fans were incensed when the hated Leafs, a team of ageless wonders, the oldest team in playoff history, sent Les Glorieux reeling, dashing their Centennial dream.

Every week at Maple Leaf Gardens, NHL hockey in the '60s brought new thrills, generated by players representing only six clubs. Teams with lengthy traditions, players whose names and numbers were familiar to millions, visited regularly. These were not faceless strangers with unusual names, performing as Ducks or Sharks or Panthers. These were bare-faced, helmetless men we'd recognize on the street, whose linemates we could name, whose stats we could recite, whose skills we could try to emulate on backyard rinks. Their faces graced our hockey cards, as familiar to us as the mugs of our classmates, our cousins, our fellow Cub Scouts. Everyone knew the NHLers of the '60s.

Seven times a year, the Leafs would host five old rivals at the Gardens, the yellow-brick House that Smythe Built in 1931. One challenge would come from the hard-shooting Blackhawks with Bobby Hull, Stan Mikita, and Glenn Hall, the goalie who played in 502 consecutive games—a streak that ended on November 7, 1962. The Hawks also had hot-tempered, squeaky-voiced Reg Fleming, a crewcut battler who once accumulated 37 penalty minutes in a single game.

Hall would save his most magnificent performances for the bright lights of the Gardens. One night, he stopped a Leaf player's shot with his chin at the north end. He staggered and fell, blood dripping from the wound onto the iconic logo that decorated his jersey. Slowly, he skated off to the medical room. Fifteen minutes and 20 stitches later he was back, patched up and ready to play again.

I followed Hall's career with keen interest because I'd played against him in junior hockey.

In Hall's era, nobody seemed to care that frugal owners declined to hire backup goalies. There were always volunteers if a regular puck-stopper took a puck in his bare face and had to be replaced. A team trainer, a junior, a college netminder, or even a minister would rush down to the dressing room and fill in for the regular guy. If the sub allowed five goals and cost his team the win—and two points—nobody complained.

It wasn't like an opera. If the diva came down with laryngitis midway through act one, and someone from the audience was recruited to finish the performance, there'd be howls of outrage and demands for ticket refunds. Not in the NHL.

Professional backup goalies finally became mandatory in 1965. And about time.

Early one season, the Canadiens announced the signing of a backup—burly Jacques Beauchamp, 32-year-old sports editor of *Montréal-Matin*. Beauchamp had been a senior hockey goalie and was more experienced than the backup goalies who—when needed—were plucked from the stands or the trainer's room in the five other NHL cities. "Those men are far from adequate," stated Habs GM Frank Selke Sr. "Beauchamp travels to all the games for his paper. We can count on him." Beauchamp served for years without ever getting into action.

His name almost made it to a scoresheet one night in November 1959, one month before my first game on CBS. In a game against the Rangers, goalie Jacques Plante took an Andy Bathgate shot to the face. Plante was bloodied, but not bowed. He went to the dressing room and came back wearing a homemade Plexiglas face mask, with coach Toe Blake looking on with disdain. Old-schooler Blake was tempted to toss Plante's face protector into the nearest garbage can. And might have, if Plante hadn't played so brilliantly after donning the device. Plante was a versatile guy. He also knit toques and undershirts, and travelled from his net to explore his surroundings, a modern-day Jacques Cartier on skates.

If coach Blake were on the verge of calling the press box for Beauchamp that night, he didn't follow through. Plante finished the game wearing his mask, and soon, face masks for goalies became a familiar addition to NHL hockey.

Andy Bathgate told me during our days together with the NHL Oldtimers that he was angry with Plante that November night. "He whacked me with his goal stick, and I got back at him by shooting the puck high at his head. I'm not proud of the fact he got hit in the face. But in a way, I helped introduce the mask to hockey."

Like Blake, most NHL coaches and managers were suspicious of goal masks. In New York, Muzz Patrick, Rangers GM, said, "We have a lot of women watching games, and they want to see the players' faces. And the hair—blonds, redheads, even bald spots. If the goalies wear masks and helmets, soon the defencemen will demand them, then the forwards. It'll take a lot away from the game."

All NHL goalies could recount tales of concussions and kayos, blows that forced them to leave games for bodily repairs. Most times they managed to come back to finish the contest. On that November night in 1959, Jacques Plante changed goaltending forever.

Perhaps the next Leafs home game would feature the Red Wings and a potent lineup that included Gordie "Mr. Hockey" Howe, Alex "Fats" Delvecchio, slick playmaker Norm Ullman, and the master of the shutout, goalie Terry Sawchuk. Sawchuk's stern mug bore more stitches than an old quilt.

One night, Howie Young, a noted Red Wing reprobate, appeared with his head shaved mohawk-style. More frightening than his looks was his penchant for dispensing two-handers to any Leafs player who crossed his warpath.

The New York Rangers would be the next visiting club—led by handsome Rod Gilbert, slick Jean Ratelle, Harry Howell, Leapin' Lou Fontinato, and that popular and irrepressible pug-nosed puckstopper, Lorne "Gump" Worsley. "What team gives you the most trouble, Gumper?" someone would ask. "My own," was his famous reply.

Gilbert, as popular with the ladies as football superstar Joe Namath, was always good for an amusing quote.

Watching Gilbert getting dressed after a game—the clean shave, the slicked-back hair, the expensive suit, shirt, and tie—a teammate asked, "Where you headed tonight, Rod?"

"Oh, nowhere special. Just out galvanizing."

"That's Quebec speak for 'gallivanting,'" the teammate explained.

A Boston invasion usually meant a high-scoring performance by the "Uke Line" of Horvath, Bucyk, and Stasiuk. But the Bruins, like the Rangers, despite an interesting mix of players, seldom struck fear into the hearts of the Leafs. Only in the late '60s, when a kid named Orr signed on, would the Bruins move to the front of the NHL pack. By then, Orr knew all about the lie of a hockey stick.

Best of all would be the seven matches at Maple Leaf Gardens each season against the Montreal Canadiens. On those nights, there'd be enough electricity in the building to light up Yonge Street all the way north to Barrie.

Those clashes produced incomparable, crowd-pleasing hockey— guaranteed! Bower against Plante; Keon and Kelly versus Beliveau, Geoffrion, Moore, and the Richards; and the genius of veteran coach Toe Blake (wearing the black fedora) pitted against the savvy and brashness of newcomer Punch Imlach (wearing the white fedora). One night, in a blatant display of nepotism, Imlach started his own son Brent at centre ice, No. 9 on his jersey, facing Beliveau! Brent was not NHL calibre. What chutzpah! Number No. 5½ would have been more appropriate. Another time Imlach started five defencemen against the Habs. The man pulled more surprises out of his fedora than Mandrake the Magician. And he was superstitious. I offered to buy him a beer in the Hot Stove Lounge shortly after he arrived in Toronto. I tossed a two-dollar bill on the bar. Imlach grabbed the bill and ripped it in pieces, stating, "Two-dollar bills bring bad luck." He was right. It was my bad luck to lose two bucks.

Fans who've witnessed modern-day hockey's many dramatic changes fondly recall those glory years of Original Six hockey in Toronto—not just the team total of four Stanley Cup triumphs in the decade, but also the abundant skills of individual favourites. There are memories of ancient Allan Stanley—old "Snowshoes"—forcing slippery Henri Richard to the outside, then slamming the gritty little Hab into the side boards; Tim Horton, the strongest Leaf, outmuscling anyone who challenged him in the slot, a big brother protecting agile but fragile Johnny Bower, the stingy antique netminder who patrolled his crease with tight-lipped determination and never gave his age. But we knew he was ancient because he'd served in the war at age 16 or 17.

There was Bob Baun, a fearless defender, blocking shots and bouncing intruders wearing red, white, and blue jerseys off his massive chest, and Carl Brewer, a sly opportunist, snaring the loose puck and racing nimbly away with it, deking and darting with nifty little moves, then throwing a perfectly timed pass across ice to speedsters Keon or Duff. Brewer was the first NHLer to befriend me, to tell me I was doing a good job on CFRB. The friendship lasted decades. He came to visit one day—on August 24, 2001—to return a manuscript I'd wanted him to read. It was a Friday, and Joan and I planned to drive to our country place, ahead of the traffic. But the conversation with Brewer turned to mortality and a dozen other fascinating subjects. We stayed. Early the following morning, Sue Foster, Brewer's companion, phoned.

"Carl died in his sleep in the middle of the night," she told us in a hushed voice. "He suffered from sleep apnea and tossed his device aside. When I went up to wake him this morning, he was gone."

I told Brewer one day I thought he was worthy of a Hall of Fame induction, but might not get it because he was such a rebel.

"I call it the 'Hall of Shame,'" he snorted. "I'd turn it down because Eagleson's in it." (Eagleson resigned after his conviction. Had he not, a dozen Hall of Famers would have turned in their jackets.)

Sometimes, in these '60s confrontations, there'd be a dozen future Hall of Famers on the ice—at the same time. But nobody was thinking Hall of Fame back then.

When the Habs added John Ferguson to their winning mix, it was akin to throwing a time bomb on the ice. Tempers were bound to explode. Whenever Eddie "The Entertainer" Shack or Bob Pulford or any other player wearing a leaf on his jersey dared block Fergie's path to the goalmouth, he'd come at them like an enraged bull. Some spectators swore they saw steam emerging from Fergie's generous nose. If he failed to score, he'd charge through the players guarding Bower's crease, stick high, elbows flailing. His message was clear: "Get the hell out of my way, or I'll skate right over you!"

Mike "Shakey" Walton, who joined the Leafs in '65, recalls Fergie running over him three times in one game. Finally, Walton drummed up enough courage to do something about it. "The next time he came at me, I whacked him with my stick. Cut him for about six stitches. Geez, was he mad. He grabbed me by the throat and then everybody piled in. He had me down on the ice and he was choking me and shouting, 'Shakey, I'm gonna kill you!' Geez, was I scared!"

Oh, there were some dandy punch-ups in the days when clubs met 14 times a season, and there were no rules covering "third men in." "They're clearing the benches!" Bill or Foster or Danny would shout into their microphones, and a vast *Hockey Night in Canada* audience would sit a little closer to their black-and-white TV sets as a dozen players from each team leaped over the boards, tossing gloves and sticks aside, and plunging headlong into battle.

Hockey fans recall the '60s as being very special. It was a decade when everything stopped on Saturday night. The Toronto cast of *Hockey Night in Canada* included Jack Dennett, Eddie Fitkin, Bob Goldham, Ward Cornell, and—midway through the decade—me. Murray Westgate, everyone's friend, with his gravelly voice, his broad grin, and his Esso service-station coveralls, would invite everyone to "fill 'er up at the Esso sign" and enjoy "happy motoring."

As one of those broadcast pioneers, I recall the beginning of the decade when there were no instant replays, no highlights from out-of-town games, no long delays for in-period commercials, no board advertising and no colour TV. Who needed names on jerseys? We knew all these guys. And everyone stayed tuned for the three-star selections.

Any player who scored 20 goals in a 70-game season was a star in those days. It wasn't until the 1968–69 season, after the NHL had doubled in size, that three of hockey's best scorers—Phil Esposito, Bobby Hull, and Gordie Howe—surpassed the 100-point barrier. By then teams were playing 76 games. Leafs fans would wait another six years before Darryl Sittler became the first Leaf to reach the 100-point milestone. On February 7, 1976, Sittler would also become the first player in history to score 10 points in a game. Bill Hewitt and I called that game.

As a young lad, I had a passion for hockey. The stripes on the jacket reminded me of the stripes on hockey jerseys. I should have asked my Mom to stitch Leafs captain Syl Apps's number on my back—No. 10.

Before becoming the original author of the famous Hardy Boys series, my dad wrote exciting hockey fiction and radio and TV dramas for CBC. He enjoyed a two-decade career as a writer and director for the NFB. In 2017, he received a rare honour: induction into the Order of the North.

My junior coach, Lloyd Laporte, put together an amazing team in the late 1940s. The Inkerman Rockets, with no home rink, dominated junior hockey in the Ottawa Valley for a decade. In 1950–51, the Rockets played 20 playoff games leading up to the Memorial Cup— until we ran into Jean Beliveau and the Quebec Citadelles.

At St. Lawrence University in Canton, New York, I met my future wife, Joan Pellet (second from left), from Hillsdale, New Jersey, on the first day there. She'd never seen a hockey game. Joyce Thompson, who became a campus leader, was a sorority sister. Bill Meehan, from Arlington, Massachusetts, was my solid right winger. Joyce was smart enough to marry a doctor, not a hockey player.

Playing against Beliveau was a thrill but working with him on my Scotiabank Hockey College promotion was a bigger thrill. I've always called him "hockey's greatest ambassador."

The publicity director at St. Lawrence arranged for this photo to be on the cover of the 1955 NCAA Guide. Initially, the arena boards behind me were varnished, not painted.

In 2017, Bill Torrey and I were honoured as Legends of Appleton. Appleton Arena is where we played in the '50s. Torrey's managerial brilliance led to four consecutive Stanley Cups for the Islanders in the early '80s.

Sports Final with Brian McFarlane

MONDAY-FRIDAY 11:15 P.M.

I worked one summer as a cameraman at WRGB-TV in Schenectady, New York, and joined the station as the late night sportscaster soon after graduating from university as class president in 1955.

Shortly after this interview with the Islanders' John Tonelli, he was traded to the Calgary Flames. In 2020, Tonelli became the first Islander to have his number retired since Bryan Trottier (19) in 2001. Denis Potvin (5), Clark Gillies (9), Mike Bossy (22), Bobby Nystrom (23), and Billy Smith (31) had their numbers retired previously. They were all part of the teams that won four straight Stanley Cups from 1980–83.

With Dick Irvin in the studio at the Forum. At CFCF-TV in Montreal
I hired Dick, who had no experience as a sportscaster. But he caught on
fast and by the mid-'60s we were both with *Hockey Night in Canada* as
colour commentators. We were proud to wear those powder-blue jackets.

Initially, I planned to write only one book, to prove to my dad I could do it. But hockey research fascinated me and now I'm aiming at a hundred.

ABOVE: With Tim Ryan and Ted Lindsay on the NBC telecast team. We agreed that Scotty Connal, head of NBC Sports, was an amazing boss but our gig lasted only three seasons, 1972–75.

LEFT: Joan with Vladislav Tretiak, Russia's most famous goaltender. The last time I saw Vlad he gave me a bear hug that almost broke a few ribs. He was named to the Hockey Hall of Fame in 1989, the first Soviet player to be so honoured, even though he never played a game in the NHL.

Playing keep-away with Ted Lindsay. Our NBC team played media teams from around the NHL before each telecast.

Dave Schultz was a key factor in the Philadelphia Flyer's back-to-back Stanley Cup triumphs in 1974 and '75. He fought everybody. Still the all-time one-season NHL leader in penalty minutes with 472 in 1974–75, Schultz remembers being scared to fight in junior hockey. With the Flyers, he was scared of that one punch that would tarnish his reputation.

Ted Lindsay was part of Detroit's great Production Line with Gordie Howe and Sid Abel. He said, "Playing with you two isn't quite the same—but close."

With Stan Mikita, who rewrote the Blackhawks record book over the course of 22 seasons. He is the all-time franchise leader in points (1,467), assists (926), and games played. He is second in goals (541). These records led to a Hockey Hall of Fame berth and a statue on Madison Street.

Jacques Plante was not only one of the world's best goaltenders, he was an outstanding analyst and a popular intermission guest.

With Cyclone Taylor, then 90. During one intermission on NBC, Cyclone and I skated several laps arm in arm around the Pacific Coliseum in Vancouver. No other 90-year-old has done that, but now that I'm that age, if they asked, I'd do it.

Mickey Walker, 81 at the time, played on a line with me in some long-ago tournament. She was the world's oldest registered female hockey player. I could barely keep up with her.

For 10 years, we enjoyed operating a hands-on hockey museum, first at the Big Apple in Colborne, Ontario, then in Niagara Falls, and winding up in Clarington. Stephen Harper, then Prime Minister, attended our opening in Clarington with his son Ben and had me sign a hockey book for him.

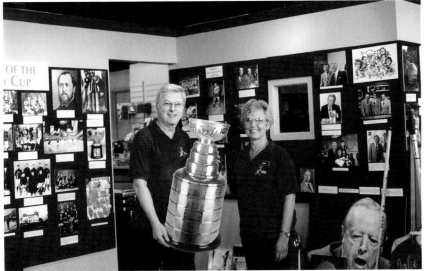

Joan and I hold the Stanley Cup for a photo op in our museum. Almost all of our visitors to the museum took photos of it, even though they knew it wasn't the real Stanley Cup.

In my Santa outfit with Gordie Howe. Santa asked, "Have you been a good boy, Gordon?" Howe replied, "Well, I've had a few penalties, Santa. But none of them were my fault."

Peter Puck has been a big part of my life for decades. I introduced him first on NBC and he was soon picked up by *Hockey Night in Canada*. We wrote three or four books together and Peter became the only published hockey puck in history.

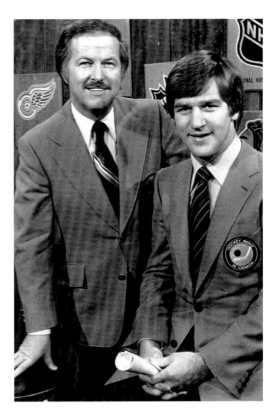

Bobby Orr joined us on *Hockey Night in Canada* as an analyst. But he didn't really enjoy the role. When I asked him to send me a photo for my hockey museum, he sent a dozen autographed photos, including the famous Stanley Cup–winning goal he scored while imitating one of the Wright brothers.

Dean of the Scotiabank College for 17 years. Thousands of young depositors enjoyed getting the free monthly hockey magazine and the chance to win a trip to an NHL game in Montreal or Toronto. One friend advised, "Don't take your idea to Scotiabank. They have no interest in hockey."

I first met Ralph Mellanby during my CBS days in 1960. Later, we worked together at CFCF-TV in Montreal. He went on to an amazing career as executive producer on *Hockey Night in Canada* and won Emmys for his work on Olympics coverage.

Speaking to a large group in London, Ontario. As a shy youngster, I later found it a challenge to speak in public. But I worked hard on my presentations and found it immensely satisfying if I earned a few laughs.

With Bill Hewitt in the gondola. We worked together for 17 years and never
shared a meal or had a beer together. A gentle man, Bill was reclusive and
greatly influenced by his father. He was an excellent play-by-play man
and followed his dad and his grandad into the Hockey Hall of Fame.

The log house we re-assembled from two deserted log homes in Quebec.

FACING TOP: Howie Meeker preceded Grapes as a commentator with strong opinions. He stressed team play and fundamentals and was hugely popular, although one Oldtimer teammate said to me, "You'd have to be in five places at once to please that guy."

FACING BOTTOM: Don Cherry ranks as one of the most fascinating hockey men I ever met. I knew he liked me and I liked him. I wish he'd had the chance to retire gracefully from *Coach's Corner*. He should be in the media section of the Hockey Hall of Fame. Other than Foster Hewitt, no broadcaster ever had a bigger impact than Grapes.

Joan and I on a cruise with Peter Puck sponsors.

I painted as a kid and won an art contest but gave it up for decades. Now my pond hockey acrylics sell well because they remind buyers how much fun it was to play shinny on an outdoor pond with no real rules, no painted lines, no time clock, no referees, and no parents barking instructions.

A Hall of Fame berth in 1995? Incredible. Daughter Lauren and husband Brad, daughter Brenda, and son Michael were there to make sure members of the selection committee didn't change their minds.

Both Joan and I have survived a Great Depression, a World War and other wars, the shock of being jobless and almost penniless, and the uncertainty that comes with moves from country to country and from city to city. But we've raised a fine family (Michael, Lauren, and Brenda). At the 90 milestone, we know this: we've always had each other's back.

In the early '60s, there were no curved sticks in the Leafs' stick rack, no player agents, no helmets, no talk of adding franchises or inserting college or European players into the mix. Backup goaltenders, like Zamboni drivers, were often no-name amateurs. In 1957–58, goalie Ed Chadwick played in all 70 Leaf games—the last Leaf netminder to perform without anyone to back him up.

The '60s were in full bloom, and still most NHL goalies were reluctant to follow Plante's lead and don facial protection. Hadn't one coach stomped on a losing goalie's mask, then tossed it aside in anger? Hadn't another hidden his goalie's mask? Goalies feared coaches like Imlach would question their courage if they hid behind a mask. So, they'd waffle, offer an excuse. "It's a bit hard to see the puck at my feet," they'd say. Or, "It gets too hot under that mask." In time, common sense prevailed, and all began to wear masks—all but holdout Worsley. "A few more pucks in the kisser won't matter that much to me," he'd say.

For four of the first seven seasons of the decade, the Montreal Canadiens finished atop the NHL standings. The Canadiens' success rankled the other clubs, especially the Leafs. The Leafs and their fans were weary of Montreal's dominance. They'd seen the Hab powerhouse wrap up five consecutive Stanley Cups from 1956 to 1960, and it disturbed them to think a long extension of the streak would highlight the '60s.

But under George "Punch" Imlach's no-nonsense approach, the Leafs were gaining strength. In 1959–60, toiling for the new man at the throttle, the Leafs won 35 games, lost 26, and tied 9. It was their first winning record in half a dozen years.

Imlach became a master at reclaiming other team's rejects, and when he landed veterans like Allan Stanley, Bert Olmstead, Red Kelly, and Johnny Bower, age became irrelevant. For the record, it was Billy Reay, the coach Imlach fired, who recommended that Bower—and Olmstead— be signed to Leafs contracts.

Horton was quick to test Imlach's sense of humour. A holdout at training camp in 1960, Horton signalled his willingness to resume contract discussions in an impish way. He sent Imlach a box of donuts—the stalest, mouldiest donuts he could muster. Horton was embarking on a career in the donut business, which would become a mammoth success story in Canadian business. Inside the box was a note: "Dear Punch. Do you think a man who can turn out a superior product like this needs to play hockey for a living?" A few days later, Horton was in camp, signed, smiling, rolling in donuts. The mouldy donuts he'd sent Imlach remained uneaten. Today, some nut would haul them out of a trash can and sell them on eBay.

The Leafs, especially Johnny Bower, breathed a sigh of relief when Rocket Richard, holder of 17 league records, announced his retirement in September 1961. They were glad to see the last of Richard. There'd be less stress on everybody in a Rocket-less future. Now they'd have to contend with only kid brother Henri, who was given a catchy nick-name—the "Pocket Rocket"—a fitting sobriquet for a player en route to a record 11 Stanley Cup triumphs.

The '60s were dominated by the Leafs and the Habs. The Leafs won four Stanley Cups in the decade, the Habs five and the Chicago Black Hawks one.

Those were the days, my friend.

CHAPTER 25

ALL ABOARD

When I joined *Hockey Night in Canada* in the mid-1960s, train travel was slowly giving way to plane travel. The former—while slower—was much more fun. Teams often travelled between cities on the same train, and even though the teams occupied separate Pullmans, players would bristle when they passed opposing players headed for the dining car. Just the sight of Eddie Shack ambling down the aisle was enough to bring a sneer to the faces of opponents.

Ted Lindsay said, "It's a wonder we didn't go at each other with knives and forks, plucked from a dining car table. If the Rocket and I passed each other, and we tried hard not to, we'd scowl and clench fists, not smile and shake hands or even embrace like many of today's young guys do. Even today, in my 90s, I grit my teeth even thinking about things like that.

"In those days, we'd talk among ourselves about pride and loyalty to our team and to our city, our passion for the game and how fortunate we were to be NHLers. My teammate Alex Delvecchio was a Red Wing for 24 years. Milt Schmidt and his Kraut linemates were loyal Bruins for as long as they played. Beliveau and the Richards—Maurice and Henri—wore the Habs logo with great pride throughout their careers. It was unthinkable that they would play anywhere but in Montreal.

Kids in English Canada idolized Apps, Kennedy, Armstrong, Bower, and Keon because they wore the Maple Leaf year after year."

What the fans didn't know anything about were the humiliating scenes on those speeding trains that terrified young players—the dreaded initiation rituals. When the shaving started, the panic started. But there was no place for rookies to hide.

Luckily, media newcomers never were victims of hazing, although Red Fisher was captured by the Canadiens one season and thoroughly indoctrinated. Even Foster Hewitt was targeted, according to former Leaf Billy Harris.

"On a train ride, we went to Hewitt's berth. Tim Horton slipped his big arms under Hewitt's body and pulled him from the berth. Well, Foster was terrified, speechless. Tim looked down at him and said with a grin, 'Well, Foster, I guess we'll save this initiation for another day.' And he returned Foster to the berth.

"I breathed a sigh of relief. I thought Foster was on the verge of a heart attack."

Not so fortunate was the Leafs' number one draft choice in 1975. The victim was Bruce Boudreau, who scored 68 goals and 165 points with the Toronto Marlboros in 1974–75. Those stats earned him no respect. His initiation was so humiliating, he almost quit the game he loved.

Boudreau says, "I still shudder when I think about it. It was horrible. The Leafs actually put me in the hospital after my rookie hazing. They tied my arms and legs and shaved me. Then they poured turpentine on my cuts. I admit I lay there bawling like a baby. Finally, the team trainer came along and took me to the hospital. I thought about quitting hockey right then."

Some of us in the media were tested in other bizarre ways.

During the 1966 playoffs—my first with *Hockey Night*—I was in Chicago at the old Bismarck Hotel. The Leafs contingent—upper-level guys—lured me and Ron Andrews, the NHL publicity director, into a poker game. I was a reluctant player because all the others at the table were older men with fat wallets.

During the game, every half hour or so, one of the men would leave the room and return some time later.

The player next to me saw my puzzled look and said, "There's a hooker in the room next door. We each take a turn with her for 10 bucks a pop. You're next and then Andrews."

I was in shock. I had made a vow in my youth never to have anything to do with hookers. Obviously, Andrews and I were the rookies being tested. Luckily, I had a few minutes to come up with a plan.

When my turn came, I put my cards down, pulled out a 10-dollar bill and went next door. There on the bed was a huge naked dark-skinned woman who scared the hell out of me.

She grabbed my 10 dollars and ordered me to get undressed.

I asked her if it was all right if I just stayed for a few minutes. Maybe talk about the weather. But not the Blackhawks. She'd think I meant birds.

"You can keep the 10 dollars," I assured her.

She shrugged and said, "Sure. I plan to."

A few minutes later, I returned to the poker game and was kidded.

"That was quick," someone said. "All of 10 minutes."

The next morning, I had breakfast with Ron Andrews and confessed my concerns and actions of the night before.

He began laughing.

"I did the same thing you did," he said. "Gave her 10 bucks and made small talk with her. But I stayed longer than you to avoid being kidded by those guys at the poker table."

"Do you think some of the others did what we did?" I asked him. "She would've made a hundred bucks without doing anything but talk."

"Not a chance," said Andrews.

The Bismarck was owned by the Wirtz family, owners of the Blackhawks, and movie star John Wayne stayed there occasionally. One night, Wayne was given the penthouse suite of Arthur Wirtz. Former Blackhawks coach Mike Keenan (a St. Lawrence grad) told me what happened next:

"Wirtz comes home from a business trip. He's tuckered out and decides to stay at the hotel. When he opens the door to his suite, he sees a stranger, a bald-headed man sitting on the bed with a drink in his hand.

"Wirtz rushes in and says angrily, 'Who the hell are you? And what the hell are you doing in my suite?'

"The stranger snarls back. 'Your suite? This is my suite. The manager gave it to me. Say, who the hell are you to barge in on me like this?'

"'Who am I?' Wirtz roars. 'I'm the owner of this hotel. Say, what the hell's your name?'

"The guy says, 'I'm John Wayne.'

"This obvious lie infuriates Wirtz. He grabs the stranger by the shirt and pushes him back on the bed. 'You are like hell John Wayne, you bald-headed old bugger,' he says, 'I'd sure as hell know John Wayne if I saw him. And you're not him.'

"The two big men begin wrestling around on the bed until the stranger yells, 'Wait a minute, wait a minute!' He reaches for a toupee on the nightstand and slaps it on his head. 'Now do you believe it's me?' he shouts.

"Wirtz stares at him. He starts to laugh. 'Yeah, now I believe you, John.' He grabs his big hand. 'Hey, Duke,' he says. 'Welcome to Chicago.'"

Thankfully, those dreaded initiations are gone from the game. Some happier memories of those good old days of Original Six hockey will never fade. Nor will memories of the days that followed, memories of colour TV, instant replays, a major expansion of the league, astonishing records, an invasion of European and American-born players, the brilliance of Orr and Gretzky and so many others, women goalies playing pro, a few slick owners who became felons. Even Clarence Campbell, the highly respected league president, was sentenced to jail for a day after being found guilty of a long-forgotten business scandal in Montreal.

I'm proud to say that not one hockey commentator of the day ever had to trade his powder-blue jacket for an orange jumpsuit. To which Eddie Shack snorted, "Shit, it's because you guys never got caught."

The game will always surprise us. Who would ever have imagined that Las Vegas, Nevada, would ice a team in the NHL? And become a Stanley Cup finalist in their initial season? Soon we'll be talking about other amazing events we've witnessed. And young fans who scan the record book will look back on the 2019–20 NHL season and ask, "What happened then?"

We'll say, "Be glad you missed it. There was a pandemic. It was a year like no other."

CHAPTER 26

SUCCESS AT SCOTIABANK

I'd been with *Hockey Night in Canada* for a short time when I decided to follow through on my plan to produce intermission features for the telecast. I formed Brian McFarlane Enterprises, hired the cameraman from my CFTO days—Jack Vandermay—and we became quite busy, working from our homes. Over the next couple of years, we produced dozens of intermission features: art fan Frank Mahovlich visiting the McMichael Canadian Art Collection; Halloween at Johnny Bower's house; Santa Claus (me) trying out with the Leafs, but, alas, rejected because he wore Detroit colours; a *Hockey Night in Canada* team actually playing six of the Leafs (and winning 1–0, thanks to some trick photography, since they actually outscored us about 20–1.) And a feature on what hockey would look like in the year 2000—which seemed eons away.

And I was well into writing and publishing by then, something I hadn't anticipated. I did plan to write one book, to prove to my dad I could do it. After *Fifty Years of Hockey* and *Clancy*, things began to snowball.

The Stanley Cup Story, a series of Hockey Annuals, *Hockey Quiz*, the Original Six series, three *It Happened in Hockey* books, *Sittler at Centre*, *Robinson on Defence*, a dozen Mitchell Brothers books, *Team Canada 1972*, a Peter Puck series—it never stopped. Strange, because I never planned for it to happen. Hell, I'm the fourth-best writer in my own family. There's my dad, my sister, Norah, and my daughter, Brenda, who has won awards for the stage plays she's written.

Even though I was dealing with publishers, helping a dozen go under, the idea of forming a hockey college for kids was always on my mind. After Imperial Oil decided to back away, I considered other destinations for the concept. I thought of taking it to the Bank of Nova Scotia, a MacLaren account, even though I know little about banking. Imperial Oil had approved it, then discarded it, and had no claim to it. I no longer worked at the agency. My only ties to MacLaren were through *Hockey Night in Canada*. I could go back and get MacLaren to approach the bank with a proposal. Or I could do it on my own. I chose the latter course.

I asked a businessman friend one day, "What if I took the idea of a hockey college for kids to Scotiabank?"

"It probably won't work," he advised me. "Scotiabank has no interest in hockey."

I showed him a proposal I'd worked on, specifically for Scotiabank.

He laughed. "That's not a very good proposal. Cheap paper. No glossy photos. The bank will want a pro forma proposal, and that takes a lot of detail, lots of preparation."

Detail? Pro forma? What's that all about?

I should have listened—he was a very smart man—but I ignored his advice, walked three blocks down the street from MacLaren Advertising to Scotiabank, where I met a man named Neil Speicher, the head of marketing. He greeted me warmly and said, "Brian, I was your dad's bank manager in Haileybury years ago. In fact, when your family moved south, I drove you and your dad around down here."

I was tempted to give him a flippant answer. "Are you sure? My dad never had any money."

I actually remembered the drive because I almost fell out of his car when—always inquisitive—I opened the back door when the car was going at top speed. My dad grabbed me by the shirt and yanked me back in.

After looking over my flimsy proposal, Speicher said, "I like it. It's short and simple."

"Maybe a little short on detail," I said.

He asked more about my hockey college idea and how it could be applicable to the bank. I told him most branch managers tolerate youngsters in a bank branch, but few of them show any personal interest in kids. I told him youngsters could easily be enticed into opening savings accounts at Scotiabank using hockey to bring them in. Once a boy or girl opened an account, they would automatically become a member of the Scotiabank Hockey College. Each member would be encouraged to stop by the branch once a month to pick up a special bulletin featuring stories and photos of NHL stars, including a centrefold of an NHL player. The stories would stress fair play, fitness, and respect for officials and parents. Other articles would be humorous in nature, provide tips on money management, and every month those who'd made a small deposit in their account would be eligible to win special prizes in a lucky draw, such as an all-expense-paid trip for the lucky winner and a parent to a Stanley Cup game.

I told Speicher that the payoff would be down the road. Kids who appreciated the treatment they got from Scotiabank today would be wage earners tomorrow—and in most cases they'd stick with Scotiabank.

It would be very good public relations. Speicher agreed.

With Speicher's help, I drafted another presentation, and the bank's top executives adopted it, with one condition: we had to keep the annual budget under $100,000. We estimated costs of magazines, costs of promotion, and all the other annual costs involved, and the figure came out to $104,000. I was rather frustrated because $15,000 of that was to be my salary. So, I said, "Look, take the other $4,000 off my fee."

That didn't sit well with Speicher because he said, "No, that wouldn't be fair. We'll find the four thousand somewhere. Let's start the program."

So, we did. For the next 17 years I was the dean of the Scotiabank Hockey College. I produced a magazine every month—writing it and even taking photos for it—that went to all the bank branches across Canada. The kids came in by the thousands and opened accounts. About 40 percent of them were girls. A centrefold of an NHL star, suitable for pinning on a bedroom wall, was hugely popular.

One of my articles was about a lad in Brantford, Ontario, who was gaining attention—Wayne Gretzky. Dave Hodge, years later, would recall, "You are the first person I heard mention Gretzky's name."

Len Woolsey, who succeeded Speicher as head of marketing, decided that Scotiabank should retain some high-profile hockey personalities to enhance the program. Gordie Howe and Jean Beliveau were retained, filmed some commercials at the Montreal Forum, and helped spread the word of the Hockey College. Those fellows didn't come cheap. Later on, we retained Howie Meeker and Peter Puck. I would ghost write columns for these celebrities every month.

One day the marketing people at the bank asked me to recommend another high-profile player, and I named Darryl Sittler. Sittler had just signed a new contract with the Leafs, and I knew he had a no-trade clause. He was everybody's hero at that time. I told the bank people, "If you get Sittler, you are getting a good one because he is not going to get you in any trouble. And he can't be traded away."

In no time Sittler became involved in a nasty dispute with his coach, Punch Imlach. One night before a game, he stripped the captain's *C* off his jersey, and owner Harold Ballard called him a cancer on the team. After months of feuding with Imlach, Sittler finally waived the no-trade agreement in his contract, and the Leafs dumped him off to Philadelphia, getting little in return. So much for my prediction that Sit would be around forever. You think something can't possibly happen and suddenly it does—especially in the hockey world.

Monthly meetings with the bank's marketing people supplied some interesting dialogue.

"Gentlemen," I said one day. "I've written an article for our bulletin about a youngster from Brantford who may become a great player when he's older. His name is Wayne Gretzky. I've got a photo of him here."

A bank executive raised his hand. "How do you spell 'Gretzky' in French?" he asked. "Remember, our bulletin is in our Quebec branches, too."

Was this guy kidding me?

"No problem," I answered. "The spelling is the same in both languages."

"But your photo of him is smaller than the size of our bulletin."

"Yes, well, a photo can be enlarged to fit any space. Don't worry about it."

The following month, I mentioned an article on Larry Robinson. The same man asked me, "Who's Larry Robinson?"

I'm not sure how far up the corporate ladder that fellow got. But I'm almost certain he never reached the top.

Some rather big names graduated from our Hockey College. NHLers like Steve Payne and former Blue Jays executive Gord Ash were members when they were kids.

I claim some credit for turning Scotiabank on to hockey. The bank recently spent $80 million for the naming rights to the former Rogers Centre in Toronto.

After 15 years of producing this program, Scotiabank earning many accolades (and millions in deposits), and after having to work with a manager of the program who didn't know a puck from a pineapple, my downhill slide began.

In time, new marketing people ignored the edict "If it ain't broke, don't fix it." One from Ireland wanted to make it a soccer college, and another wanted to ignore hockey altogether and make the promotion all about savings and money matters. In time, the name was changed to "Getting There," with the monthly bulletin covering a wide range of activities.

Soon after, I was called to a meeting at the bank where two young people I'd never seen before informed me the bank wanted me to step aside as dean of the Hockey College. They offered me a token role, a monthly column for one hundred dollars per month. "We'll do everything else internally from now on," I was told. "We'll focus more on money matters."

"You kids don't know anything about the history of this promotion, do you?"

"What's to know?" one of them asked.

"You should know that it was me who brought the idea of the Hockey College to the bank 17 years ago—in 1970. It's grown to be so popular that a couple hundred thousand young people—maybe more—are now depositors. It's almost certain that they'll remain depositors for years, perhaps a lifetime. That means millions of dollars flowing to the bank. Initially, I was paid $15,000 a year. I wrote the entire bulletin each month, even the columns for Howe, Beliveau, and Sittler, all of whom were paid much more than I. And I committed to several appearances each year at branch events all over the country."

"Sorry, we've only been with Scotiabank a few months."

I turned to leave.

"No, I won't write a column for you," I told them. "But now you know the Hockey College was my concept—when you two were just kids. And 40 percent of our members are girls. Bet you didn't know that, either."

"I'm sorry," one of them said. "We did not know any of this. We were told the bank created the program and hired you to write the bulletin."

"Well, now you know that's not true," I said. "Perhaps you should have done your homework. I'm sure the decision has been made at an upper level, and you're the messengers. And now I'm out of here."

One big plus from my 17 years at Scotiabank was the lasting friendship I made with Jean Beliveau. I truly doubt that there is any man in any of the world's sports who was more admired and respected than this great Canadian. How could I have known when I played against him in junior hockey that Beliveau and I would meet dozens of times in the distant future—at the Forum, at Hall of Fame events, and at Scotiabank—where he was affiliated with my Hockey College? His attitude then was so—Beliveau.

"Brian," he would say. "Scotiabank is paying me a lot of money—too much money—and there's not enough for me to do. You write my columns for the monthly bulletins, and the people at the top simply want to go fishing with me."

Always the gentleman, always the classiest person in the room—I loved Jean Beliveau. I was there the night Scotiabank honoured him with a dinner party in Toronto, where he was presented with a neatly wrapped gift. Curious, I asked him what the gift was. He smiled and said, "Brian, I do not need nor do I expect expensive gifts. But I did not expect this tonight." He opened a small box and showed me a pen. With the Scotiabank logo on it. Worth about $1.98.

He was an amazing ambassador for his game, his province, and his country. And my life became richer simply because he acknowledged me as a friend. It was a gift I will forever cherish.

In January 2018, I received a call from NPR, a prestigious network of U.S. radio stations. Would I be a guest on their show *Only a Game?*

Indeed, I would. My sister Norah is a big fan of the show, often praising the content.

"What's the subject matter?" I asked.

"The Scotiabank Hockey College."

I was surprised. I don't even have the Scotiabank Hockey College listed on my bio.

I taped the interview at a campus radio station in Fort Myers, Florida, with a young woman named Karen who was located in Boston, and it went almost an hour. I managed to get Karen to talk about other matters: my dad and the Hardy Boys, playing with the Flying Fathers and the NHL Oldtimers. But she kept coming back to Scotiabank. I think she was most impressed when I mentioned the strict $100,000 budget we had for the introduction of the Hockey College in 1970, compared to the multi-millions Scotiabank pours into hockey today, including the $80 million mentioned for the naming rights to the home of the Leafs. Neil Speicher retired shortly after we introduced the Scotiabank Hockey College. He was battling a crippling illness, but he was pleased when his associates threw a retirement party for him at the King Edward Hotel. I was invited and was shocked and saddened at the scene I witnessed. A small hotel room, a few chairs and table with nothing on the table. No food, no beer, no wine, no gifts. Six or seven colleagues wandered in, and one carried a bottle of scotch and some plastic cups. The party began with each attendee sipping from plastic cups. Some, like me, didn't even drink scotch. There were a few words of praise for Speicher's many years of service to the bank, a few "remember whens," and in 20 minutes the party was pretty much over. The men wandered off, and Speicher and I were left alone. His look said it all. I thought he was about to cry.

"Let's get out of this damn room, Neil," I said. "Let's go down to the bar and get our drink of choice."

We did and had more than one.

But I was seething. Speicher was a good man, a loyal Scotiabank man for decades. He deserved a much better send-off than that. He was dead a year later.

I would feel a similar sting when I was bumped from *Hockey Night*. There was no send-off party at all. Not a phone call or a thank you note for 25 years of service. Perhaps I'd been a pariah on the show all that time and never even realized it.

Perhaps, by coincidence, Scotiabank felt much the same way. I went from dean to undesirable.

But I walked away with my head up.

Years later, in 2019, I received an email from Winnipeg:

> Brian, my name is John Spina. This email is in regard to the *Scotiabank Hockey College News* of the 1970s and early 1980s. As a youngster, I would often accompany my parents to the local Scotiabank, where I would pick up a free copy of the *Hockey College News*. I remember thoroughly enjoying those magazines. I don't think I ever realized how valuable those magazines were. There was advice from Gordie Howe advising kids how to play with the perfect length of hockey stick. There was your monthly column "Stickhandling Through Life," where you taught the value

of learning from your mistakes to become a better person. And there was Peter Puck. My list goes on.

I wonder if you have ever given thought to writing a book about the Scotiabank Hockey College. About the solid values the program taught.

My reply? "No, John. I don't think that will ever happen."

CHAPTER 27

AN AMATEUR AMONG EX-PROS

God help me, I thought, as I warmed up before my first game with the NHL (Ontario) Oldtimers. The rink was in a small town north of Toronto, and I was nervous. I was the only amateur ever invited to play for the former pros. Who wouldn't be nervous? It was a fundraising game, one of 30 or 40 the Oldtimers played each season, and the rink was full. They played games in the Maritimes one season—in at least one U.S. city and even in Germany—and I went along.

What bothered me on my debut was seeing a wave of green uniforms warming up at the other end of the rink. They were young guys in their 30s and 40s, and obviously in good shape. They whirled around their net—20 or 25 of them, looking confident—not a stumblebum among them. All anxious to show the NHL Oldtimers, like Bob Goldham, Norm Ullman, Andy Bathgate, and Sid Smith, they were no creampuffs.

What a night to break in, I thought. *The mob of young Greenshirts will surely give us a sound beating.*

The game began, and things suddenly looked different. The Greenshirts still looked young and strong and skated well. But they had trouble getting the puck. The old pros wouldn't let them have it. We popped in a couple of goals before I took my first shift on right wing, which went well, as I recall. I came back to the bench, and nobody scowled at me. Nobody snickered. In fact, they said a few encouraging words. I began to relax.

Danny Lewicki and Peter Conacher scored two more, and I realized the Greenshirts' goalie might be in over his head. I heard Ivan Irwin say, "Guys, let's not make it a rout. Give them a chance to score one or two."

Let them score? Why not? The opposing players had family and friends in the crowd, sons and daughters rooting for them. If a Greenshirt could skate around Bob Goldham or Murray Henderson and beat goalie Ivan Walmsley, he'd be a hero in his household and get a standing O when he stopped into Tim's for coffee the next morning.

My wife came to see me play that night, anxiously hoping I'd fit in—as I was. But she saw little of No. 12 and missed my goal.

Joan was escorted by the other wives to a party room over the rink's north end. There were windows overlooking the ice. There was a good view of the game action. And it was warm up there.

But she was told to sit down with her back to the windows and ignore the game.

"We've seen these old buggers play hockey a thousand times," she was told. "We've brought a couple of bottles of wine and snacks, and we're here to talk."

On the ice, our lead stretched to 8–0, and the Greenshirts still hadn't scored. Coach Art Smith (Sid's brother) tapped Goldham on the back.

"Goldie, you've blocked about eight of their shots. Let 'em go around you and pop in a couple."

Goldie gave him an earful. "Art, this is hockey. If they can skate around me and score—good. But I'm not going to just let them skate around me."

And he didn't. But a few of the others were more generous. The Greenshirts popped in two or three, and the crowd cheered wildly.

The Oldtimers won easily, retired to the party room after the game to meet a hundred locals who sought autographs and a chance to reminisce with them. Coach Smith made a nice little speech, and an hour later we all headed home 20 or 30 bucks richer.

The same procedure followed every weekend. Another town, another game, another win. Year after year for 15 or 20 seasons, the faces changing from time to time. Rene Robert joined us after retiring from Buffalo, and Ron Ellis and Frank Mahovlich from the Leafs. I played on a line with each, although I didn't click with the Big M. After I mishandled a few of his passes, he said to me on a faceoff, "Which team are you playing for, McFarlane?"

Norm Ullman was the niftiest, and quietest, centreman I ever played with. Passes always on your stick. Always in position for a return pass, He loved to play and he's probably still playing somewhere. Ullman is the most anonymous 490-goal scorer in NHL history but thankfully, a Hockey Hall of Fame inductee in 1982.

But most are gone. Ivan Walmsley, Bob Goldham (one of my best friends), Wally Stanowski, John "Goose" McCormack, Bo Elik, Aggie Kukulowicz, Ike Hildebrand, Murray Henderson, Danny Lewicki, Hugh Bolton, Keith McCreary, Sid Smith, Cal Gardner, Gus Bodnar, Harry Pidhirny (who once said he really enjoyed playing on a line with me), Andy Bathgate, Harry Howell, Harry Watson, and Jackie Hamilton. Hamilton played in the league as a skinny 17-year-old, a fleet 140-pound centre. With the Oldtimers, he was a slow-moving 240 pounds. But smart. And an entertainer. He told me once how he won a few faceoffs in the NHL. "I'd get a mouthful of water from the bench and hold it in one cheek. When the puck was dropped, I'd squirt some at the opposing centre. He'd get distracted, and I'd win the draw."

As a centre, I'd never thought of doing that. A good thing, too. It would have earned me a punch in the mouth.

Everybody loved Goose. He played in the NHL with Montreal, Toronto, and Chicago, and with some minor league teams as well. He was once banished to the minors by Conn Smythe for getting married in mid-season.

At the Oldtimers' Sunday morning workout, I get feedback from a lot of guys who'd spent time in the minors—some of them felt they spent too much of their careers there—and you get a feel for what it was like back then. The stinking bus, the violent games in rundown rinks. Guys with limited skills striving to move up the ladder to a better league, to a bigger paycheque, hopefully in the NHL. It didn't matter what team. When NHL scouts were at a game, a guy might smack a smaller opponent into the boards, using stick, elbows, and fists. He'd do anything to make an impression. There were brutal, nasty buggers on every team, the NHL a destination as far away as Pluto. But everyone was striving to get there, leaving bruised and broken bodies in their wake.

After the game—a rush to the shower before the hot water runs out, then on to the local bar—the Blue Line, the Penalty Box, the Time Out. Blaring country music—Waylon Jennings, Tammy Wynette, George Jones, and others—greeting all who entered.

The first draft beer after a game was frothy and cold. Perfect. The second almost as good. Three or four pitchers of it on the tables.

After an hour, having rehashed the game, depression moves in.

You sit, pondering your future.

Why am I here? In this city, this league? I expected a lot more than this. In junior, I topped the charts. I should be up there—at least in the AHL. You shrug. You sit there with your mates, listening to the sad songs from the jukebox. You feel so down, almost on the verge of tears, when George Jones sings, "He Stopped Loving Her Today."

Basketball—not hockey—on the TV. There's a girl back home you'd like to call. But it's late, and she has to get to work in the morning. Why would she even want to hear from you? It will be weeks before you're home again, maybe months if your team is in the playoff hunt.

There's a watering hole like this in every hockey town. You feel a wave of loneliness. The hockey groupies sit in a corner, laughing loudly, casting glances your way.

One of them, heavier than any player on the club, struggles out of her chair, passes you as she heads for the restroom.

"You played good tonight, darlin'."

"Thanks."

"You look sad. Come over and join us?"

"Yeah. Maybe later."

Your younger mates are listening. "We'll go." *Hell,* they're thinking, *we may get lucky.*

Lucky? They might get more than they bargained for. Something a doctor might have to treat.

That's how it would be after most games on the road.

Back in the Oldtimers' dressing room, I say to Goose, "Forget the minors, John. You played in Montreal with the Rocket. In his heyday. How great was that? What was he like?"

"His opponents hated the Rocket. But I liked him. He was a good man, a quiet man. And a fierce competitor, as you all know. You saw him play."

"Yeah, but just in his last season—1960. The Habs won their fifth Stanley Cup in a row. Then he packed it in."

There was the night our Oldtimers played against him and a team of former Habs greats at the Gardens.

I certainly remembered. In the dressing room before the game, one of our coaches—either Joe Primeau or King Clancy—said, "Remember, fellows, the crowd will want to see the Rocket score a goal against us. So, let's make sure he scores one."

I turned to Goose and whispered. "Goose, it's the Rocket. Doesn't he just, well, score?"

Goose laughed.

"Not anymore. He's old and fat, and he's on his last legs. So, we'll give him a goal, and everybody will give him an ovation."

And that's what happened. When the Rocket lobbed one in, the Gardens exploded in applause and cheering. Fifteen thousand Leaf fans saluting one of their favourite "enemies" from the past.

Another game, another season, this time at the Gardens against the Red Wings. I'm out there checking Gordie Howe, for God's sake. Watching him make a fool of me. Thousands of people laughing at the mismatch.

Referee Red Storey had already singled me out, giving me a 30-second penalty for "impersonating Foster Hewitt."

Damn that Storey. This is one of the biggest moments in my life, and he sends me to the box the moment he sees me.

Later, I hear Ted Lindsay shouting, "Get that McFarlane. Don't let him score."

But I did make a rush, and when the defence pair for Detroit opened up, I slipped through and scored a goal. I was so surprised I forgot to raise my arms in the air—celebrating.

And when I looked over for a nod of approval from my wife, her seat was empty. The other wives had whisked her away.

But I have video proof of that goal—as if anybody cares.

At the Oldtimers' Sunday morning workout, I tell the boys I'm working on a story about Wilf Paiement's father, Wilf Sr.

"We had a long talk at the Gardens last night," I say. "Did you know Wilf Sr. was once the world arm-wrestling champion?"

Howie Menard reacts. "Old Wilf is in town? What a man! My brother is a big, big man, as strong as an ox. He arm-wrestled old Wilf one day in Timmins, and my brother's arm was flat on the table within seconds."

Monsieur Paiement told me he was super strong. And when he ran a lumber camp one year in Quebec, his workers threatened to kill him and his family in a dispute over pay raises.

"Paiement, they'll find your bodies in the lake," the ringleader—a man named Dumont—threatened.

"Were you frightened?" I ask.

"Of course not. I grabbed Dumont by the neck and felt the bones snap," Wilf Sr. said. "He went to hospital for weeks and then died. But I was never charged. Fourteen of them who attacked me that day went to the hospital."

I hesitated to shake hands with Monsieur Paiement when we parted, fearing he'd break my fingers. But I did. His hands were soft.

Bobby Lalonde came out recently. I thought of the afternoons we televised minor hockey games in Montreal. With Dick Irvin and me calling the play—along with Red Storey—and Lalonde was the best player in the league. He was about 12 years old then.

He was in Vancouver when the Canucks mistreated defenceman Mike Robitaille.

"A real sad story," he told me. "Mike was badly injured, and the coach and others thought he was faking it. He was forced to play, and he was in agony much of the time. He went down one night, and he couldn't get up. He pleaded with a player on the opposing team to help him, Don Awrey.

"Help me, Donny. Help me."

But what could poor Awrey do? There's a sort of unwritten rule you don't help a player on the other team.

Eventually, Robitaille sued the Canucks for negligence and won his case. He was awarded $600,000, I believe it was, by the court. Big money then.

During his recovery he battled depression, he felt ostracized by his teammates, he felt union head Al Eagleson gave him little time or support. In a clinic, he recalled sitting in a sandbox like a two-year-old. And he developed agoraphobia, which meant he couldn't leave his house without breaking into a sweat.

"My wife, Isabel, was the only person who knew my suffering and supported me," he told me one day. Robitaille and I are friends.

I give Robitaille credit. He survived, got better, and landed a job on the Sabres' broadcast team. Became a huge presence in Buffalo. A popular guy. I helped roast him one night a couple of years ago. Isabel was there, and was everything he said she was.

But he still suffers pain from those long-ago injuries, according to a recent email.

I played Oldtimers hockey with Bobby Lalonde for almost 20 years and was constantly amazed at how well he handled the puck.

He had great hands, but how did he survive all those years in the NHL at five-foot-five?

I made great friends with all the Oldtimers. When I opened my hockey museum in Niagara Falls, they rented a bus and came over to spend the day, signing autographs. They donated items to the museum. Museum visitors were thrilled to meet them. No one was charged for a signature.

One of my favourite Oldtimers was Wally Stanowski, who, at a spry 96 years, was the oldest living Leaf. At our annual dinner for retired NHLers and friends, one of us read a lengthy list of NHLers who had died during the past few months. The room was hushed when Stanowski hollered, "Hey, why don't you just read the list of those of us who are still around? It wouldn't take so long!" Stanowski's cackle rose above all the other laughter.

If there was one member of the NHL Oldtimers who earned the utmost respect from every player on the club, it was defenceman Bob Goldham. I was thrilled to be on the ice with him and thrilled to share a broadcast booth with him—for about the same number of years. He was a gentleman in the Joe Primeau tradition. He was perhaps the first former player who began to make enquiries in writing to the NHL and the National Hockey League Players' Association (NHLPA) about pensions and other issues. Carl Brewer and others followed suit, and in time millions of dollars owed to the players were finally pried from the NHL coffers. But Goldham was the first to pry into the relationship between players and owners.

Early on the morning of September 7, 1991, Goldham's wife, Eleanor, called to say he had passed away from a heart attack. He was 69. I sat sipping coffee at my kitchen table, tears flowing freely, as I recalled all the goodness and class in my friend and colleague.

The *New York Times* noted Goldham's passing with these words: "Goldham, known for his shot blocking talents, was instrumental in Toronto's improbable Stanley Cup championship in 1942. Goldham scored the winning goal in game six and set up the winner in game seven to help the Leafs achieve an unmatched feat: coming back to win the Cup after trailing three games to none."

A few days later, I stood nervously in the pulpit of Armour Heights Presbyterian Church to deliver his eulogy.

Why me? Dozens of his former NHL mates from Detroit and Toronto were sitting directly in front.

At a crowded reception after the service at the Goldham home on Brooke Avenue, Bob's daughter Barbara explained the choice.

"My dad loved you," she said, leaving me speechless. "He loved working with you and being a best buddy with you."

Barbara also said, "My dad adored my mom. Their marriage was the happiest one I've ever seen."

My knees wobbled. I wanted him back, wanted to give him a manly hug and tell him I loved him, too. Here's one reason he won my respect and admiration.

One season, *Hockey Night in Canada* planned to replace me with Goldham in the broadcast booth. He called me to say, "Brian, I will turn down the offer. I'd never take a job from a friend."

I told him, "Bob, take the job. Broadcasters have ups and downs, like hockey players. Here today, gone tomorrow. I will survive."

As it turned out, there was a place for both of us that season. But I'll never forget that thoughtful gesture.

It's a hockey mystery why Goldham never received a Hockey Hall of Fame induction. That's not just my opinion. Ask goalie Glenn Hall to name the greatest defenceman to ever play in front of him, and he'd say "Bob Goldham."

Bob and I had a mutual friend in Gordon Alcott, a Georgetown, Ontario, native who founded the Little NHL in 1936. Alcott was my insurance man. There's an arena named after him in Georgetown. Alcott set goals for himself. He'd hand you a card that read, *I'M GOING TO BEAT HULL!*

If Bobby Hull scored 50 goals, Alcott would set his goal at 51 insurance policies.

Alcott arranged a trip to Maple Leaf Gardens for his kids one night, and Goldham recalled "sitting on a box in the back of a pickup truck" for the journey.

He became the first Little NHLer to make the NHL.

In 2015, Goldham was posthumously inducted into Canada's Sports Hall of Fame. In there with Gretzky, Messier, Mahovlich, and Morenz.

After I was inducted as a media member into the Hockey Hall of Fame in 1995, my Oldtimers mates presented me with an expensive clock at our monthly luncheon. And while I was never a pro, they treated me like one. What good fortune it was for me to be one of them for a couple of decades. On the ice with them, I always felt I represented the thousands of players who were NHL wannabes, all the guys who "came close" to playing pro. Guys, I played for you.

Of perhaps the 50 to 60 old-timers who played with our touring team over the years, one was still lacing them up after all the others were retired or deceased. Peter Conacher, the last of the breed and a man greatly admired, was still playing Sunday morning games after his 85th birthday.

CHAPTER 28

THE PERILS OF PUBLISHING

My sister Norah and I are close. She writes under the name Norah A. Perez, and I am immensely proud of her accomplishments. She has just published *The Slave Raffle*—her first ebook after a dozen novels published in the traditional way, and it is her best. One of her novels with a Civil War background sold at least 60 thousand copies in the U.S., where she lives.

Chris Ondaatje (brother of Michael), a Bay Street financier, enticed me with a book deal when I met him by accident on a busy Toronto street one day in the mid-1960s. He told me he'd started a publishing company—Pagurian Press.

"I'd like you to write a book for me," he said. "A history of the NHL. We'll call it *Fifty Years of Hockey*."

"I can do that," I told him. I told Ondaatje I'd set three goals for myself—to write a book (to prove to my dad I could do it), to write a popular song, and to paint a painting. In time, I was able to do all three.

Ondaatje was smart. He offered me a share of profits instead of a royalty. I don't recall getting any kind of advance. With no experience and no agent to advise me, I accepted.

Not a good idea. As my pal Ray Bradley would say, "Who's the dummy?" It was me, not Ondaatje.

In 2003, Ondaatje was knighted by Queen Elizabeth when she named her birthday honours. I remember thinking, *Ondaatje a knight? That's a huge honour*—but still a surprise to me.

I thought it might be because the Queen loved the hockey books I'd written for Ondaatje. Perhaps she'd like an autographed copy? But no, it wasn't for that. She never wrote or called. Perhaps it was because Ondaatje competed for Canada in the bobsled event at the 1964 Olympics. No again. While Canada's number one team scored a gold medal, Ondaatje's number two sled came in 14th out of 17 competitors. It must have been because he explored the Nile and had written books in addition to becoming a successful financier and philanthropist. And because he had English roots. I thought of calling the Queen and volunteering to become Sir Chris's assistant. We could go and slay some dragons together.

But Ondaatje wasn't the most famous individual given a knighthood by the Queen that year. Movie star Roger Moore was, after taking over the role of the suave 007 made familiar by Sean Connery. Moore played Her Majesty's most famous secret agent, James Bond, in seven films.

I not only churned out that book for Pagurian, which sold well, but also tackled the life story of King Clancy at almost the same time—for ECW. There I earned royalties. And a friendship with publisher Jack David that has survived more than half a century.

The solid reviews of *Fifty Years* and *Clancy* convinced me to begin another hockey book a year later—*The Stanley Cup*—and the cycle was underway. One or two books per year for the next couple of decades. At one time, the late Jack McClelland volunteered to act as my agent, urging me to write six books per year under the banner Great Canadian Hockey Stories.

I thought two books per year was an accomplishment. Six books? Probably impossible. Now I'm closing in on 100 books. When I surpass that total, my head will not balloon. My dad, my sister, and my daughter Brenda have all won awards for their creative writing. I'm the fourth-best writer in my own family. But remember, I did win an essay contest when I was 12.

I liked McClelland. My dad had written books for him, including *McGonigle Scores!*, a hockey novel *Toronto Telegram* columnist Ted Reeve called, "the finest piece of hockey fiction around."

McClelland was a legend then and would always be a big name in Canadian publishing, a pioneer. He'd published all the big-name Canadian authors—Atwood, Berton, Richler, Cohen. And Les McFarlane. McClelland and I went our separate ways, both somewhat reluctantly. He passed away on June 14, 2004.

Over the years, I suspect I've helped put a dozen publishers into bankruptcy and left three or four agents wondering why they even bothered with me as a client.

At some time back then, the famous author William Stevenson (*A Man Called Intrepid*) called me.

"Brian, I was intrigued by your book *Fifty Years of Hockey*. I was impressed when I learned it sold 50 thousand copies. I hope your royalties reflected such good sales."

I gulped. "Mr. Stevenson, I didn't receive much in royalties. I agreed to a share of the net profits. That wasn't a good idea. I never did that again."

"That's unfortunate," he said. "But that book became *One Hundred Years of Hockey*. It must have made you a lot of money."

"Not really," I told him. "But Scotty Bowman gave me a good quote about the book. He said, 'If it's not in this book, it didn't happen,' and Grapes said he and Blue loved it. I think Blue read it to Grapes when he went to bed each night."

We talked some more, and the call ended.

I was pleased he didn't admonish me with the words, "Well, there's one born every minute."

In 1976, Stevenson authored a bestseller, *90 Minutes at Entebbe*. The book was about a secret international incident—Operation Entebbe—at Entebbe Airport in Uganda, where Israeli commandos succeeded in rescuing the passengers of an airliner hi-jacked by a Palestinian. The "instant book," written in a week in a New York hotel room, was on sale within weeks of the event it described.

Now, with the game of hockey flourishing, with new NHL franchises costing $600 million U.S., but with book publishing in decline, I'm careful to ask a publisher what they want in a book.

"You want my novel *The Hockey Guy*?" I asked two or three publishers. "A couple of reviewers said, 'This book must be published.'"

"Nah, hockey novels don't sell."

"You want *Hockey Ha Ha*? The game's funniest stories?"

"Nah."

"What do you want?"

My current editor, Michael Holmes, said, "Write about the events you've witnessed in hockey for over half a century. You've been writing about the people you encountered during your journalism and broadcasting days. Make this book your own story."

"I can do that," I told him. "But I don't like writing about myself."

"So? Do it anyway. You may get rich and famous."

"Too late for that. I'm getting old and senile."

Michael Holmes was a curious editor. He asked lots more questions that day.

"Didn't you skate alongside Cyclone Taylor in your NBC days in the early '70s?"

"Yes, in Vancouver. Cyclone was 90 years old at the time. Viewers had never seen a 90-year-old gliding around the ice before—and talking non-stop. Cyclone wrote glowingly of that day and those few moments in his memoir. Now I'm closing in on that 90 milestone myself. I was still playing old-timers' hockey at 84 in Florida with former NHLers like Don Awrey and Bob Murdoch."

"And you played against Wayne Gretzky?"

"Yes again. He was 12 years old at the time. I was over 40, playing with a team of NHL Oldtimers. I recall it vividly. Wayne going around Andy Bathgate, his tiny legs churning, to score a goal or two. I think Andy might have said, 'Go, kid!' Then, maybe not. I met Walter

Gretzky after the game, and I even recall Wayne's coach's name—Ron St. Amand. Why don't you ask me if I outscored him in that game?"

"Did you?"

"No. But whenever I meet Walter, I remind him of that day, and I always mention Ron St. Amand." (Walter died as this book was going to print. But I was able to squeeze in a "Farewell, Walter" line. You were beloved, Walter. You were Canada's "Hockey Dad.")

"You played right wing for Mario Lemieux?"

"Yes, at a rinky-dink rink in the Catskills one summer day. He set me up for a goal against John Vanbiesbrouck. Larry Robinson played, and he was a witness. How lucky was that? I'd like to say Mario pleaded with the Penguins to sign me to a contract after that goal. You may scoff, but remember how he took Warren Young, an obscure 28-year-old winger, and set him up for 40 goals one season? I think he simply forgot."

"You were named an honorary bishop after whipping in three goals playing with the Flying Fathers—a famous team of Catholic priests?"

"Correct. In Moncton. Father Les Costello, the former Leaf, called me. He said, 'Come with us. You've got three kids, so maybe you're not Catholic, but you're a father.' After I scored my three goals, Father Les said, 'Bishop, I know why you scored. The goalie you faced didn't have a prayer.'"

Father Les was a funny man and a great man. I loved the guy. He scored a goal for the Leafs in the Stanley Cup Final and then gave up his $7,500 contract to earn fifty bucks a month in the priesthood. No NHL hockey player had ever done that. He helped found the Flying Fathers team and helped raise about four million for various charities. There should be a niche in the Hockey Hall of Fame for men like Les. He told me once he was the priest who married Shania Twain's parents and the priest who buried them. Years earlier, three of us representing *Hockey Night in Canada*—Jack Dennett, Dan Kelly, and me—were added to a media team to play against the Flying Fathers in Sault Ste. Marie. Dennett hadn't been on skates in 20 years. Father

Les nudged him in the ribs with a sharp elbow and told him, "Jack, you aren't worth a shit out here tonight."

Dennett turned to me in shock. "You should have heard what that priest just said to me."

I said, "That's Father Les, Jack. He'll say anything. He grew up with miners. Sometimes, he forgets and uses their salty language."

With the Flying Fathers, he would arrange for a woman holding a baby to turn up at a game looking for the child's father. She'd point at Father Les, who'd try to hide behind the other players.

Father Les told me about the Flying Fathers playing games in Germany, then visiting the Vatican, where they met the Holy Father.

"Yeah, it was in 1972 we had the opportunity to visit Pope Paul the Sixth. The Holy Father came right down and talked to us: Father McKee, Father Scanlon, Father Lavallee, and myself. And I presented him with a hockey stick. And when he looked at it rather quizzically, I laughed and said, 'If you don't know what to do with it, you can always stir spaghetti with it.' And that's a true story. While they were all congregating there, I went up and sat in the Pope's chair. When I sat down a kind of a hush came over the congregation. All I wanted to do was give him a little blessing, but nobody there thought it was at all funny. The Swiss guards came rushing over and muttered, 'Hey! Holy place, Father. Get out of here!'

"I guess I set the Canadian church back about 200 years. There won't be a Canadian pope for a little while, anyhow.

"And that's a true story, too."

I had a marvellous time with this unique group of priests.

They not only put on an entertaining show during every game, but also took time to sign autographs and visit hospitals. At a reception after a game at Maple Leaf Gardens one day—our Oldtimers versus the Flying Fathers—Father Les looked me in the eye and recited a poem.

> Tiger, Tiger burning bright,
> In the forests of the night;
> What immortal hand or eye,
> Could frame thy fearful symmetry?

"Who wrote that, McFarlane?"

"Blake, Father."

"Hey, listen to that, guys. I'm so impressed. Most dumb hockey players don't know that. And the poet's full name, McFarlane?"

"Hector (Toe) Blake, Father. Coach of the Montreal Canadiens."

"You smartass. Get out of here."

I didn't get a chance to tell him the poem might have been about Tiger Williams.

Father Les Costello died at 74 doing what he loved—playing hockey.

He died on the ice with the Flying Fathers. He was fatally injured when he struck his head on the ice (I never saw the Fathers wear helmets) during the warm-up before an exhibition game at Kincardine, Ontario. A sad day for all who knew him.

I know the Hockey Hall of Fame tries hard to recognize the greats of the game. But someday perhaps the Hall will find a way to recognize those who've made mammoth contributions other than famous players, builders, officials, and media members. The Flying Fathers come to mind; Doug Moore, the man who invented Jet Ice; the Turofsky brothers, who took great photos of game action; outstanding team doctors or PR types or filmmakers; men and women who've devoted decades to minor hockey in their community. Maybe even Stompin' Tom and his "Hockey Song."

It's just a thought.

CHAPTER 29

QUESTION PERIOD

My editor, Michael Holmes, had more questions for me and some of them were about Bobby Hull.

"You mentioned earlier that Bobby Hull turned on you in a New York restaurant one night. Why was he so angry?"

"I told Bobby I wished I'd seen him play with Hedberg and Nilsson—Winnipeg's big line in the WHA. And he turned red and growled, 'Whatta ya mean you never saw me play in the WHA? You had plenty of chances.' He turned away, saying, 'I don't want anything to do with you.'"

"How did that scene end?"

"With four or five bottles of red wine in front of Bobby. Empty, of course. He gets angry when he's thirsty. I think red wine in a dry mouth turns him from a Hull to a hellion. It's a temporary thing. He apologized the next morning."

I met him recently at the media luncheon during the Hockey Hall of Fame inductions. We sat and chatted, and I'd heard—now that he's an ambassador for the Chicago Blackhawks—that he was off the wine—now that's a good thing. But bad for the wine industry. Then when the waitress began clearing the tables to close up, Hull got edgy. "Hey, miss," he shouted. "Bring me another glass, please. No, make that a bottle of wine. Tell them it's for Bobby Hull."

The waitress ignored him.

He shouted louder. "Miss, bring me a bottle of white wine. Now! Tell them it's for Bobby Hull."

She didn't even turn her head.

So much for abstinence.

Hull loved the night life. He was aware that time chipped away at celebrity and his "Golden Jet" years would vanish before he knew it. He didn't want to miss any of the fun. He spent a lot of time fighting his inner demons. And he never shied away from controversy.

People still love him. A young fellow from Calgary wrote me recently, asking if I'd write scripts for a five-minute radio show he was backing financially. When he bragged, "I've got Bobby Hull as my executive producer," I almost swallowed my gum. And my dentures. Told him I'd have to think about it. But I was dubious. What I thought about was how much he was paying Hull to be a so-called executive producer. I bowed out, thinking Hull had never produced much of anything— except some good kids—without his skates on.

Because I'm sensitive to my friendship with the rest of the Hull family—particularly brother Garry and his wife, Lois, I always try to find some good things to say about Bobby Hull. One or two things should be said. He signed more autographs for more kids than any player I ever met. And every pro player should thank him for doing what Howe and the Rocket should have done before him—demand more money for their services. Both Howe and Richard must have known they were the two brightest stars in hockey for a long time. Why were they content to take whatever management offered—thousands of dollars below what players in other pro sports were earning? I saw a Richard contract one day, and he signed for $12,500—so little I think the contract must have been a fake. The Rocket and Howe kept all the other players back. Hull came along and said, "To hell with that," and he fought for twice the money. "I want what I think I'm worth." And he didn't need an agent to make demands for him. Other players followed suit, and salaries began to shoot upward. They shot up again when he jumped to the WHA, giving that wobbly league some stature.

Another thing I commend Hull for. When he wound up for his famous slapshot in a game, he'd often pull back if an opposing player fell in front of it. He feared severely damaging an eye or a jaw if the puck struck the blocker.

At a sports banquet one night, I asked him if he minded if I told a joke about him. He said, "You can tell as many jokes as you like about me." He's really good that way. Really good.

I told the audience that Bobby was in divorce court, and the judge said, "Mr. Hull, I'm going to give your wife $3,000 per month."

Hull said, "That's great, your honour. I'll try to chip in a few bucks myself."

I said, "Bobby's been with so many women, they just named him an honorary evangelist."

He has a good sense of humour, like his brother Dennis. Dennis can earn a hundred grand a year telling funny stories at sports banquets. As for Bobby, he's quick with a quip. At a golf banquet, I told the story of how my wife came home from a visit to her new doctor. She said to me, "Dr. Phil says a woman in my age bracket should be making love 15 times a month."

I said, "Great. Put me down for three."

It got a laugh. But a bigger laugh followed.

Hull was sitting in the back. He stood up and shouted, "Brian, I'll take the other 12."

Hull's quip doubled the laughs. Mind you, knowing Hull, he may not have been joking. My wife was a beauty then—and still is at 88. (Guys, always go for the brownie points.) And when I told Dennis Hull about Bobby's quip, Dennis said, "Hell, I'm surprised Bobby could do the math."

"Have you had other confrontations with former players? Didn't Bob Pulford suggest you were full of shit?" asked Michael Holmes.

"Pulford didn't really say that. I'm sure he thought it. He did shout at me, blasting me for some shots I took at Al Eagleson, his good friend and my former lawyer. Eagleson's also a convicted felon. Pully bellowed at me, 'Brian, Eagleson never did anything wrong. I was in the meetings. It was all bullshit!' I told Pully, 'No, what you're saying is bullshit. If he never did anything wrong, why did he plead guilty to the charges against him in a Boston courtroom? Why did he serve jail time?'"

But that's Pully, defending his boyhood pal. Pully probably thinks O.J. was a victim, unjustly accused.

I don't understand Pulford. He can be charming when he wants to be. He was making a fortune as GM of the Blackhawks, but he'd still go in the team dressing room and scrounge for cigarettes from the players' pockets while they were on the ice.

Johnny Bower said Pully did the same thing—scrounged smokes from the guys—when he played for the Leafs. But Bower was smart. He'd have me—if I was around, or some sportswriter—hang on to his smokes until practice was over. There's another change since my early days. Nobody smokes anymore. Not even Guy Lafleur, who out-puffed everybody.

"And weren't you the announcer—the only one—who ever stepped on the ice with a microphone in the middle of a Stanley Cup playoff game?"

"That's me. During an NBC game in 1974. At Madison Square Garden. Barry Ashbee, a Flyer player, was badly injured. I was at rinkside with a microphone when they opened the gate for the stretcher bearers. I walked out with them and talked to linesman Matt Pavelich about the incident. Brad Park said from the Ranger bench, 'Brian, you're not supposed to be out here,' I said, 'Brad, I know. But I'm not stopping now.' Clarence Campbell admonished me a few days later, when I met him back in New York. I passed him in the corridor at Madison Square Garden."

"Hello, Mr. Campbell."

"Hello, Brian."

He walked another 10 paces and turned.

"Brian!"

"Yes, sir?"

"Stay off the ice!"

"Yes, sir."

Perhaps I thought if I could get on the ice for one playoff game, I'd get my name on the Cup. Didn't happen. You have to play in one game.

I wanted to ask Mr. Campbell, "How come half a dozen photographers jumped on the ice that day to snap photos? You didn't tell them to stay off the ice."

"Was Ashbee okay?" Michael Holmes asked me.

"No, his eye was badly damaged. Never played another game. For the Flyers to lose Ashbee was such a shock. One day he noticed red spots all over his body. About two days later, he addressed the team and told his mates he had leukemia. First an eye, then leukemia. Devastating news. A month to the day that he told them, he died. Barry Ashbee was such a character guy. Every Flyers fan shed a bucket of tears the day he passed away. Just as they did a few years later, when goaltender Pelle Lindbergh crashed his sports car at high speed and did not survive. I went to Philadelphia to cover that tragedy for *Hockey Night in Canada* as well. Coach Mike Keenan cried on camera telling me about it."

Lindbergh was a great young goalie. He led the NHL with 40 victories during the 1984–85 season and won the Vezina Trophy, the first European goaltender to do so. He was a First Team All-Star and was the first goalie to bring a water bottle on ice with him during NHL games. Lindbergh suffered from severe dehydration. His opponents, players, and coaches bitched about the practice at first, but now all the NHL goaltenders have a water bottle handy.

The two Ds—drinking and driving—ended Lindbergh's career on November 10, 1985. Lindbergh lost control of his customized sports car in the early-morning hours and struck a wall, critically injuring himself and severely injuring his two passengers. He died on November 11 after a five-hour operation to harvest his heart and other organs for transplant. His family—and his gorgeous fiancée—were heartbroken.

"Did you enjoy working for NBC?"

"Loved it. I thought they'd be cold and aloof. Instead, they were warm and welcoming. Scotty Connal, the head of NBC sports, was responsible for that. He formed a team of NBC announcers and crew, and we'd play media teams in the cities we visited for the *Game of the Week*. So, Tim Ryan and I formed a line with Ted Lindsay. I'm sure

Lindsay felt right at home, like he was back on the ice with Gordie Howe and Sid Abel again."

And with NBC the three of us were told to go to a Chrysler dealer and pick out a car of our choice to drive each season. That never happened with *Hockey Night in Canada* when Ford was a sponsor. Aside from the perks, the best part of our three years with NBC was the show of respect we were given. Scotty said, "We hired you three because we think you're the best." He never threatened to fire us if we got an agent (we didn't) or said anything controversial (we did). Or offended an owner (we probably did). He never called us "utility" announcers. He was on our side. He played defence on our NBC team and he was good.

His 32-year career at NBC was highlighted by his work on news as well as sports. He made the crucial decision to show Lee Harvey Oswald's prison transfer live on air, a move that gave NBC the only live coverage of Oswald's assassination. When he supervised our hockey telecasts, he suggested painting the bottom rink board yellow for better viewing of the puck.

My boss at *Hockey Night in Canada* called me in one day and said, "I hear you've been saying nice things about the NBC guys."

I said, "That's right, I have."

"Well, we're nice, too," he growled.

Of course. Why hadn't I thought of that?

Actually, most of them were nice.

CHAPTER 30

SHACK AND BALLARD

Michael Holmes was curious about some of my other relationships with hockey personalities.

"Didn't Eddie Shack harass you for years, all because of a song you wrote about him—'Clear the Track, Here Comes Shack'? Is there more to that story?"

"Yes. First, Eddie gave me permission to write the song. I remember his exact words, 'I don't give a shit what you do with it.' Then when it went to number one on the charts ahead of the Beatles, he kept asking me for royalties—and for free records. Then he squealed to Leafs owner Harold Ballard about me being a cheap son of a bitch And I'm the guy who always made sure he got plenty of attention on our hockey telecasts. He called me a cheap bastard at banquets. When I'd heard enough, I gave him an earful at the airport in Vancouver. A bunch of us were headed for a Howie Meeker roast on Vancouver Island. And Shackie had been on my case throughout the flight. You know his act. Big cowboy hat, dancing around the carousel, too much wine. When we landed, I called him over, looked him in the eye, and from my gut spewed the vilest language possible. I called him a *bleep, bleep, bleep*— and every dirty word I could think of. I'm surprised he didn't punch me in the mouth. Knock me into the bags on the carousel. Bob Goldham came over to me and said, 'I guess Shackie knows how you feel about him now.'"

Yeah, I was surprised he didn't wallop me—the things I called him.

At the roast the next evening, I gave him a grand introduction.

And I feel badly about the friction between us over the years. We both mellowed and were getting along when suddenly he passed.

I have another airport story involving Shack. The Leafs were flying back from a game in New York one day, and former president Richard Nixon was waiting in the same lounge. George Armstrong urged Shack to go over and say hello. Shack did, introducing himself. President Nixon shook his hand and said, "I know who you are and I know about the Leafs."

Shack came back and said to Army, "Chief, who in hell did you say that guy is?"

Shack played with our Oldtimers after he retired, but he never quite fit in. We never knew when he'd show up or not—and this after the group booking us had advertised his appearance. In the warm-up before one game, he barrelled into me from behind, and I ached from head to foot for the rest of the night. Was it accidental? I didn't think so.

Here's another Shack story, and this comes from Darryl Sittler. The Leafs were flying somewhere, and sitting in the seat ahead of Shack was a bald-headed man. Shackie says, "Watch this," and he puts his fingers in his water glass and then goes *"Ker-Choo!"* He flicks the water all over the bald head in front of him, and the guy almost jumps out of his seat belt. The poor man thinks he's covered in snot, and Shackie roars with laughter. *Har, har, har.*

At first I smiled at the story. But on reflection I deem it not at all funny.

Shackie annoyed me one day when I was selling hockey books at an event. Shack stopped by my table, picked up a book, and walked off with it. "Hey, Eddie," I shouted, "It's a 20-dollar book. Not a free case of Molson's."

He pretended he didn't hear me.

Then he became an author. I found myself hoping to catch him at a book-signing event. I vowed to grab one of his books and run off with it.

I'd hear his big laugh and his shout: "You little bastard. You got even with me."

Months later, just as I wrote the above, came news in a Howard Berger blog that that Shack had entered palliative care in his struggle with throat cancer. A few days later, he passed away. I was jolted by the news, surprisingly so because I had always considered Shack my nemesis. I suddenly felt bad about the things I'd said and written about him. I never considered he might pre-decease me. I said to myself, "Now it's too late to get a message to the guy. To tell him how colourful he was, how he deserved to be called 'The Great Entertainer.' How I fully expected we'd both be around to sit down over a beer one day and laugh about our silly confrontations in the past. Maybe even become friends."

Now it won't happen. It was good to see and hear how many fans credited Shackie for entertaining millions in his prime. It's time to admit there must have been a lot of "good stuff" going on under that big Stetson. Otherwise, why would a class guy like Red Kelly have him as a friend?

"You mentioned Harold Ballard, the owner who once barred you from his building. Did coach Punch Imlach applaud Ballard's decision to throw you out?"

He probably cheered. Rushed over to slap a big lock on the door as it closed behind me. Imlach never forgave me for taking Sittler's side in the feud they had going. And for me accusing him of tearing apart a pretty good Leaf team when Ballard made an idiotic decision to bring Punch back after he was fired in Buffalo. Why would he bring back a manager-coach so obviously out of touch with the modern game—a has-been. Pushed out the door in Buffalo, a coach with a bad ticker. Former Leaf Dave Hutchison told me of the time the players put Imlach's photo on a dart board and tossed darts at it. And how, when Imlach's car wouldn't start at the airport after a return flight from Montreal, Leafs players drove past him dangling battery cables from their own cars.

Punch and I almost started out with the Buffalo Sabres together. When the NHL expanded to include Buffalo and Vancouver, I was interviewed by the team owners—the Knox brothers—and was offered the job in Buffalo doing play-by-play. I accepted when Chuck Burr, the PR director who wanted me to join the Sabres, told me he was leaving, and I could have the PR job as well. That made the position even more attractive.

So, I talked it over with my family on the weekend, called Pittsburgh and Chicago to turn down similar opportunities there, and phoned Burr back on Monday morning.

"Chuck, I accept your offer. I can't wait to get started with the Sabres."

"Hang on," he said. "Sorry to tell you this, but we're going with our second choice, Ted Darling."

It was a huge blow. I'd just bowed out of similar positions with two other NHL teams because of the Buffalo offer and I was ticked.

"Chuck, you're a son of a bitch," I said before hanging up.

My wife and I went on a pub crawl that night, something we never do, to soothe the pain. Months later, I was told that Punch Imlach had killed the Buffalo offer to me when he heard about it. That made me feel better. I would not have liked working for the Sabres with Imlach calling the shots. But I liked the owners of the Sabres, the Knox brothers. And was proud to sit next to Seymour Knox III at a recent banquet.

When Ballard, Imlach, and Clancy were the Big Thinkers with the Leafs, two of them thought my words and opinions were traitorous. But Clancy, an Ottawa guy like myself, liked me. And I was accustomed to Ballard threatening to ban me from his rink. He did it half a dozen times. A lot of other media guys got similar treatment. But I always found a way to get back in.

"But one time he made it stick?"

Yes, I was not allowed in his building. But he couldn't stop me from working outside. On one occasion I hosted a new season of *Hockey Night in Canada* while standing on the sidewalk outside Maple Leaf Gardens. A guy in the crowd shouted, "You're going to get bloody cold working out here in January." Producer Ralph Mellanby was there. We chatted on the phone the other day, and he mentioned that season opener. He likes to tell that story.

Most people don't know I worked for Ballard in public relations for about nine months. He was another boss I thought I could get along with, but failed. One day I argued with him about his policy of no women in the press box. I told him he should reconsider, that women were on the move, that the Gardens might even be picketed.

He growled at me, before turning away. "Forget about it, McFarlane. No fucking women in the press box."

Another time I asked if we could accommodate six mentally handicapped children in a small space near the press box. They were rabid Leafs fans, and I was assured they'd be well-supervised and well-behaved.

Ballard gave me a look. "Are you crazy? I don't want any idiots falling out on the ice."

Ruby Richman, a basketball promoter, called me one day about renting the Gardens. Could he speak to Ballard?

I went to Ballard and told him of Richman's call. "What should I do?"

"Call him back," Ballard said. "Tell him I'm in New York or somewhere. He's Jewish you know. Those Jewish guys will always talk you into something you'll regret."

"The fans always treated you well, didn't they?" Michael asked.

I never knew how they felt about me. Not after one shouted at me early in my career, "McFarlane, you're the reason I come to the games. I can't stand listening to you at home." I gave him a friendly wave, using all five fingers. But his comment hurt. Made me wonder what I was doing wrong, why some fans didn't like me. And when I'd do an interview with analysts like Gary Dornhoefer on the catwalk over their heads, a few fans would shout, "Jump, McFarlane, jump!" But I never jumped. If I had, I'd have jumped down the throat of the guy with the biggest mouth. Dornhoefer was upset at the guys who urged me to jump. But a week later he was shocked to hear them shouting, "Jump, Dornhoefer, jump!"

"But the players never griped about your comments, did they?"

"Not to my face. They may have worried I'd do something similar to what broadcaster Richard Garneau did to Jacques Lemaire on a French telecast."

"Oh. What was that?"

The Habs played in Minnesota one night, and Garneau was a bit harsh commenting on Lemaire's play. Lemaire accosted him the next morning and told him he was not happy about it.

Garneau said, "How did you find out, Jacques?"

"My family always listens. They tell me."

"Jacques, I promise you it won't happen for the next game against St. Louis."

"That's good. My family will listen."

Lemaire took a lot of shifts in the next game. Garneau did not mention his name even once.

Michael Holmes had a final question.

"You said earlier in this book you'd finish a story you started about Bob Murdoch."

Yes. Well, Murdoch told me in Florida about his first training camp with the Montreal Canadiens.

"Brian, in my day at camp, the Habs would suit up and play in tough scrimmages right off the bat.

"So on my first shift, I bumped into John Ferguson in the corner and I knocked him down. Suddenly, Fergie jumped me from behind and dropped his gloves and beat the shit out of me. and we each got five minutes for fighting. Well, he got five minutes for fighting, I got five minutes for receiving. We went to the penalty box and he's cursing me. 'You fucking rookie, I'll cut your eyes out when we get back out there.'

"Well, geez, it was the fastest five minutes of my life. I'm thinking, I've got to challenge him again or I'll get no respect at all. So we get back on the ice and I go over and give him a little bump—just a nudge to let him know I'm not terrified of him. Well, he drops his gloves and proceeds to kick the shit out of me again. So we're sent to the box for another five minutes.

"Here I am, in my first scrimmage. I've been on the ice for all of 30 seconds and Fergie's still fuming and screaming at me. I remember thinking, *Look, I've got a college degree. I could be teaching school somewhere out west for 25 grand a year. This professional hockey is a horrible profession. It stinks.*

"And that was the start of my life in pro hockey."

CHAPTER 31

MY BIGGEST HOCKEY STORY NEVER AIRED

Let me tell you about an interesting meeting of former NHL stars that took place at the Ramada Hotel in Toronto on the night of December 11, 1990. Carl Brewer, with whom I played hockey on Sunday mornings, invited me along. "It'll be really interesting," he promised, and Brewer was true to his word.

I was astonished to see Gordie and Colleen Howe in the room. And Bobby Hull and Bobby Orr. There was Andy Bathgate, Norm Ullman, Frank Mahovlich, Eddie Shack and his wife, Norma, Lori Horton (Tim's widow), Eddie Litzenberger, Billy Harris, Harry Howell, Murray Henderson, Paul Henderson, Ivan Irwin, and dozens of others.

Oh my god, half of those names are no longer with us.

I looked around for other media members, and there were none. Brewer had given me first dibs on what would be forthcoming. He had agreed to let me tape the proceedings, so I reached for my recorder.

Brewer called the meeting to order and spoke softly for about five minutes about his efforts to find answers to questions he had about his NHL pension plan. "For months," he said, "despite all my efforts, I really couldn't find out anything. I talked to other guys and found we were all in the same boat. We couldn't get any answers (about our pensions) and we couldn't get any co-operation. Earlier, my friend Bob

Baun informed me of a $45 million surplus in the pension fund. Then in 1987 or thereabouts, there was another surplus in the fund," he said.

"So, I went out and got some legal advice from Mark Zigler, a Toronto-based lawyer specializing in pensions. Then I contacted Ed Garvey, who has done some interesting work in the NFL. Recently, he got the NFL players a $29-million benefit and put it into the NFL pension. The NFL owners had taken what I call a contribution holiday, which the courts found to be illegal. That $29 million meant that every NFL player received a third more on his pension, and those who were currently disabled had their pensions doubled."

Brewer's lawyer friend Zigler spoke and told of his frustration in attempting to get information on pension matters.

"Al Eagleson, head of the NHLPA, basically told us to go away," he said. "The books on the NHLPA, Hockey Canada, and the NHL were closed to us. The pension issues also included international hockey revenues, and there was some question if monies from that source ever went into the pension," he said.

"At about that time, I ran into Ritch Winter, a lawyer out of Edmonton, Alberta. A remarkable man, a good friend, he's a player agent as well. Here's Ritch."

"I have been an attorney representing players for a long time. I met a player named Dave Lewis, and he became my first client. David had $100,000 stolen from him by his then-agent, and this agent eventually landed in jail for three or four months, thanks to the efforts of Dave and his wife. So, my introduction to the hockey business wasn't very glamorous," said Winter.

"I said to myself that this is incredible that such a thing could happen. Let's get in touch with the players' union and try and get some help. There should be some regulations in place to try and protect these young men against the kind of things that happened to Dave Lewis. Well, I called Alan Eagleson several times, hoping to get some protection for the young players. Eagleson didn't want to have anything to do with me.

"Five years later, we were still talking about the problems that faced the players that I represented. Ron Salcer (a fellow agent) and I found

Eagleson and the players' association to be the only impediment holding us back. We couldn't get any information from them about salaries; we couldn't get any assistance from them at all," said Winter.

"Everywhere we turned, the union, which is supposedly in existence to help players, was turning against them and providing no assistance. A lot of hockey agents said, 'That's just the way it is in hockey.'

"I think most of you know the results of it. We took some great strides forward despite the atrocious behaviour of the NHLPA. At one stage, the Calgary Flames sent a petition demanding the information that they were entitled by law to receive. No response.

"Finally, at the annual meetings in Florida, the players woke up to the fact that they had some rights. A lot of them began to stand up to their union leader. They wanted information. They got salaries disclosed for the first time in NHL history, despite the fact the union had been against it for 15 years.

"In 1985, some $24 million—and this is not an exaggerated figure—in surplus money was transferred to the league's pension plan from the Manufacturers Life Insurance Co. What they did, just before that money was transferred, was to amend the plan to give the clubs an interest in that money. Before that, league president Clarence Campbell agreed the surplus belonged to the players.

"They did allocate a relatively small portion—4 million of that 24 million—to improve your pensions, and you got a lovely letter from Al Eagleson and John Zeigler saying, 'Congratulations, your pension has been improved.'

"Well, what happened to the rest? Twelve million of it went to improve benefits. Not to you, not for the people on whom this surplus was earned for service up to 1982. It went to pay for the super-pension for players who were active in 1986 and onwards and who managed to get 400 games under their belt. If they did they would get payment equivalent to $250,000 at age 55. Well, that surplus earned on your money went to pay for their pensions. The clubs should be paying for that out of their own pockets. They shouldn't be funding it out of that surplus," continued Winter.

"What happened to the additional eight million? Well, the clubs have been using that to reduce their contributions every year. They're taking what Carl called a contribution holiday.

"It is really outrageous that there is all this extra money around, and your pensions keep losing their value every year because of inflation. Improvements to your pensions are negligible. Meanwhile, all of this money is sitting there and is being used by the NHL for other purposes. It seems to me, like other employees who get pushed around, that your only recourse is to the courts. Hopefully, as a group, because there is great strength in numbers. You can get some kind of satisfaction from a court case as to who owns this surplus after all. Certainly, you will let the people who have reclaimed this surplus know that you mean business and that your pensions are very important to you."

Since a lawsuit against the league was almost a certainty, this was a historic meeting, and I was the only media person in the room. And I had my tape recorder running—discreetly—throughout. What a story!

But I was scheduled to leave for Saskatoon, Saskatchewan, that week to tape a feature for *Hockey Night in Canada*. What to do?

I phoned my new boss, Ron Harrison, and told him of my "scoop," and how we should break the story on *Inside Hockey* the following Saturday. I had everything on tape—loud and clear. He said he would discuss with others and get back to me. Meanwhile, he said, "Don't go to Saskatoon, I'll have Ron MacLean do that story."

To cover all the bases, I suggested he put Eagleson on camera to rebut any facts he disagreed with and give his side of things. Then we'd have a great feature.

It was two days before Harrison got back to me with the decision—no dice. "The story's too hot—too controversial. I can't get approval."

To me, it was a gutless decision—and terribly disappointing. I lost a lot of respect for *Hockey Night in Canada* that day. And even more when I asked Harrison about the fee I stood to lose ($1,000) for *not* going to Saskatoon. He said, "Sorry, that fee went to Ron MacLean."

Pissed off? You bet. I should have sold my story to one of the newspapers. And the rest of the story? In October 1992, a judge ruled in favour of the players and said the NHL clubs must reimburse pension surplus money that the league had improperly used since 1982. The NHL appealed the decision to the Supreme Court, which dismissed the appeal in 1994.

The NHL eventually reached a settlement with the players to pay $40 million from surplus pension funds. That lawsuit ultimately led to criminal charges against Eagleson, who served six months in prison for fraud and theft.

Hall of Famer Red Kelly said of Carl Brewer: "Once he had his teeth into it, he wouldn't give up. He just kept going. A lot of players didn't think he knew what he was doing, but he stuck with it and he was proven right."

CHAPTER 32

DINNER IN NEW YORK

For 33 years, dinner in New York became a special occasion for the McFarlanes. And almost every year we dined at the famous Waldorf Astoria. But we were never alone. We were joined in the main ballroom by up to a thousand hockey fans, a majority of them Canadians who live and work in Manhattan.

We were there for the annual Canadian Society of New York's tribute to a famous hockey player or coach or manager. Yeah, Hockey Night on Broadway.

And I was there as master of ceremonies, thanks to dinner chairman Paul Levesque, a transplanted Montrealer.

He made it clear in the beginning, in 1983, that none of the big names at the head table would be paid a fee. Or the emcee or the anthem singer (Michael Burgess loved to attend). The celebrity and his wife would be invited to a weekend at the Waldorf—all expenses paid—and few invitees ever turned him down.

Well, Phil Esposito did—once he heard the committee had decided to bring Vladislav Tretiak in from Moscow as the honouree, along with Ken Dryden, two of the biggest stars from the 1972 Team Canada series. Esposito never liked Tretiak. He told Levesque, "I won't come if that fucking communist is there."

Come on, Phil—Tretiak was a charming guest. (Ironically, a few months later, Esposito's daughter married a Russian player on the Tampa Bay Lightning.)

Permit me another aside about Tretiak. In 2018 we're at the annual Hockey Hall of Fame inductions. Each year a few of us meet for a late-night coffee in a shop en route to the exits. In a corner of the shop, I see several men around a table. And one of them, his back to me, is Tretiak, now head of Russian hockey.

I say to Joan, "I should go over there and say hello. But I'm afraid Tretiak will not remember me. And the others may not want to be interrupted."

She says, "Go."

Before I reach their table, they look up. Tretiak turns and looks over his shoulder. His face lights up, he leaps from his chair, takes two steps toward me, and crushes me with a Russian bear hug.

"Vlad, you remember me?" I gasp.

"Of course," he bellows. "Dinner. New York. Chicago you interview me on TV. I never forget."

It made my night. And I almost didn't intrude.

At the hockey dinner in New York, each passing year it became difficult to snare Bobby Orr or Wayne Gretzky.

But look at the list of those who did agree to attend, beginning with NHL president Clarence Campbell in 1983: Jean Beliveau, Gordie Howe, Rocket Richard, Glenn Hall, Red Kelly, Bobby Hull, Denis Potvin, Pat LaFontaine, Marcel Dionne, Frank Mahovlich, Rod Gilbert, Bryan Trottier, Al Arbour and Bill Torrey, Scotty Bowman, Mike Bossy, Mario Lemieux, Glen Sather, Brendan Shanahan, Larry Robinson, Henri Richard, Yvan Cournoyer, Bob Gainey, Mark Messier, Scott Stevens, and Adam Graves.

By year 30, some young guns began to nudge Paul Levesque aside and found a new emcee, which was fine with me. My jokes had become older than Bob Hope's. Thoughtfully, they invited my wife and me back as special guests and honoured Levesque for his great work over the years.

They also scored a coup in getting Gretzky to attend the following year—for the first dinner I missed. But it was a costly decision. I learned they donated a fee in the neighbourhood of $60,000 to Wayne's foundation for his one-night stand.

That ended the tradition of bringing hockey superstars to the Waldorf—and their family members and even some friends. All three of Bobby Hull's brothers showed up with their wives when Bobby was saluted. And brother Dennis was always a willing, popular entertainer.

Once honoured, the celebrity players could come back the next year if they chose—and many did. The Kellys and the Mahovliches seldom missed it.

The players and their wives loved the excursion to the Big Apple. Shopping and a Broadway show and a rather exclusive reception the evening before the dinner, where Tim Ryan (my co-host in the early years) and I would pull amazing stories from the players who showed up.

I recall Frank Mahovlich telling the group: "When I was a rookie with the Leafs, Rocket Richard was winding down his career—one of the greatest right wingers in the game. I played left wing and I was determined to not let him make me look foolish. So when the puck came to him I reached out and grabbed him. He turned and growled, 'Hey, kid, let go of me!' What did I do? I said, 'Yes, sir, Mr. Richard.' I let go, and he flew away with the puck."

In 1979—when the Habs won the Cup—Guy Lafleur regaled us with the tale of how he stole the coveted trophy and brought it home to Thurso, Quebec, his hometown. And how all the neighbours came around to kiss the Cup and have photos taken with it. And how his son filled it with water from the garden hose. And how the Cup custodians were going crazy in Montreal looking for it. And how he sneaked it back to the Forum and dumped it off and drove away—really fast.

There were so many good tales from those dinners. And a few that had you shaking your head.

Eddie Shack (Red Kelly's guest) in the bar after the event, saying to Andra Kelly—a real lady: "Andra, you were a hoochy-koochy figure skater before you met Red. Did you fool around a lot?"

Andra on Eddie: "He lives close to us in Toronto, and every once in a while I'll look out my kitchen window, and Eddie's there, waving to me. He'll shout, 'Andra, can Leonard come out and play?'"

Red on Shack: "Eddie came in with his little dog Fou Fou one day. He got down on his knees and said, 'Red, I have a confession to make. I stole a goal away from you once. The scorer gave me the goal, but you scored it, and I took it. It's been on my whatchamacallit ever since.'

"'You mean on your conscience, Eddie?'

"'Yeah, that's it.'

"'Well, I don't remember that goal, Eddie.'

"'Good.'

"Then he lay down on the floor and went to sleep. I got a blanket to put over him, but when I got close, Fou Fou snarled at me through her little teeth, and I put the blanket back."

Oh, and how about this one, with apologies to Bobby Hull, who seems to be occupying a lot of space in this book.

We're in Jacqueline's, a fancy restaurant, with Hull and his wife; Jean Beliveau and his wife, Elise; Red Fisher and his wife; and host Paul Levesque and a lady friend.

The talk is all about Guy Lafleur, and Hull turns to me. He's upset. "You media guys dumped on Guy Lafleur all the time. His chain-smoking, his drinking, this and that. You guys were unfair to Guy."

"Wait a minute, Bobby," I protested. "I never dumped on Lafleur. Not on camera or in my writing. But I was upset with the smoking, the drinking, some of the other things he did, like the high-speed driving. I didn't dump on him but I didn't care much for his lifestyle when he was young."

"Hah!" Hull snorted. "I suppose you didn't like my lifestyle, then."

"Not particularly," I blurted out before really thinking. Oops! The words flew out as I felt my wife's knee hit mine under the table.

"We'd better be going soon," she said.

Well, we stayed because Mrs. Beliveau held up a finger pointed at Hull. "Listen to me, Bob-bee," she said. "There were many reasons to criticize Guy's lifestyle. And not too many jumped on him for it. In fact, many people were quick to overlook his indiscretions."

I thought she was about to utter, "Yours, too, Bob-bee."

In 1994, Prime Minister Jean Chrétien offered Jean Beliveau the post of governor general of Canada. I cheered the decision. But Beliveau declined in order to be with his daughter and two grandchildren, Mylene and Magalie, who needed him. Their father, a Quebec policeman, committed suicide when the girls were five and three. I had not known of that tragedy.

I say Jean Beliveau would have been a perfect choice for governor general. I often called him the most respected hockey player in the history of our game.

As for Bobby Hull, I must pause for a moment and give my next few paragraphs some serious thought before continuing. Am I breaking some unwritten code here—some rule that suggests writers like me should not reveal the many personal problems of famous NHL stars like Guy Lafleur and Bobby Hull? Or the late Steve Durbano and the late Bob Probert? Should we simply ignore the transgressions of wife abusers, drug abusers, alcoholics, and lawbreakers in our game because they have big names?

For too long we turned a blind eye to the misdeeds of Alan Eagleson, who stole from the young men who trusted him most. Canadians chose to ignore the accusations of Carl Brewer and others. To many, theft, fraud, and criminal behaviour became less important than a Team Canada victory over the Soviets.

Despite his one-finger salute to the Soviets in 1972—and accusations of his bullying and intimidation—Eagleson was a serious candidate to become NHL commissioner, perhaps even prime minister.

Players hesitated to debate with the Eagle because he would mock them, ridicule them, and harm their careers—especially non-clients. It took Brewer and an American writer, the late Russ Conway—both friends of mine—to bring Eagleson to his knees and send him off disgraced and even to jail.

Remember, he was tried and convicted in a U.S. courtroom while the RCMP was still "investigating." Brewer was right when he said to the Boston judge, "Your honour, this would not have happened in Canada." Indicating that Eagleson had clout. And many friends in high places.

I have no qualms about writing about Eagleson's greed and grounding—even though he once acted as my lawyer. But Hull?

I've explained why I hesitate before writing about Bobby Hull, who I watched break into the NHL and retire as one of the greatest players ever. We've been to Hull family reunions and several Hull parties, few of which have included Bobby. Do I risk those friendships if I write negatively about him? No Hull family member has asked me not to. But my wife reminds me that blood is always thicker than water. But I also feel strongly that Hull crossed the line at times in his personal life and should be held accountable. It is difficult for me—really difficult— to turn on him when I think of him as the Golden Jet, the muscular superstar with the physique of Adonis, the scoring champ who signed every kid's autograph book, who had the guts to revolutionize the game by thumbing his nose at the Blackhawks, and giving a patchwork, disorganized new league authenticity and credibility. With me, he has always been co-operative, even allowing me to make him the butt of my jokes at banquets. But I'm aware of his demons, too. Emotional outbursts that are at odds with his normal behaviour. Eruptions of anger, and, yes, potential violence. Curiously, anger seldom seen on the ice in games he played where tempers often fray. Growing up in our era, spousal abuse and sexual harassment were common. But secretive topics, seldom discussed. A battered woman with a black eye and wearing sunglasses simply "ran into a door." While most people frowned on spousal abuse—or chose to ignore it—others excused it, saying, "Aw, the guy just lost his temper" or "I bet she provoked him." Hull's fans and supporters may feel in his marriages that he was often provoked. But here's a statement uttered by his first wife, Joanne McKay, following an incident that occurred while the couple vacationed in Hawaii in 1966.

"I looked the worst after that Hawaii incident. I took a real beating there. [Bobby] just picked me up, threw me over his shoulder, threw me in the room, and just proceeded to knock the heck out of me. He took my shoe — with a steel heel — and proceeded to hit me in the head. I was covered with blood. And I can remember him holding me over the balcony and I thought this is the end, I'm going."

McKay claimed she suffered four more years of physical abuse before filing for divorce in 1970.

The two would get back together in the mid-1970s (Hull was with the Winnipeg Jets then), but, according to McKay, he threatened her with a loaded shotgun one day, causing her to flee the marriage.

Hull would marry Deborah, his third wife, in 1984. He was arrested in a parking garage two years later and charged with domestic assault and battery against his wife. He was intoxicated, and his wife beaten. He was belligerent and lashed out at the arresting officers during the arrest.

In court, Hull pleaded guilty of swinging at an officer and was fined a mere $150—plus six months of court supervision.

That was a long time ago, and perhaps Hull has changed. But we don't know that. And should it make a difference? Are the Hawks so enthralled with their "ambassador" that they consider spousal assault a minor character flaw, an "indiscretion"?

And how do some of the former greats who starred for Chicago feel about Hull's role—one that they might have assumed themselves but for him? They can lead an exemplary life, be amazing representatives for the team and the organization, and still never be considered for the role of an official "ambassador." That's Hull's role.

As one Chicago writer said in 2014, "If the Blackhawks truly want to be known as an organization that holds its core values and principles above all else, it will do the necessary deed of cutting ties with the wife-beater it has been harboring for over twenty years. Hull has gotten away scot-free thus far."

To not condemn is to condone. And that is why I write as I do.

Don Wittman, the late highly respected CBC sports commentator, and his friend Ray Bradley, a top Molson executive, were dining with their wives at a Winnipeg golf club one day. In the main dining room, there was a wedding reception underway. Hull's son and his bride were being feted. Hull's former wife Joanne McKay had flown in from Vancouver with her husband.

"We heard a big commotion," said Bradley, "and there was Bobby in a fight with his former wife's husband. It was a shocking sight."

I'll end this chapter with a more pleasant story about Hull.

Ron Hull, Bobby's brother who lives outside Windsor, Ontario, stops by our country place one day. He's visiting brother Garry in Cobourg, Ontario, and they are off on a fishing trip the following day. We've invited Garry and Lois, long-time friends, to dinner, and Ron is a welcome addition. Bobby's name seldom comes up when we meet, but it does this night.

Ron says, "Whenever people speak negatively about Bobby, I think of a morning in Chicago when a young fan at the morning skate was seeking autographs. One Chicago player rudely ordered him aside as he left the dressing room.

"'Get outta here, ch—'

"Bobby was told of the comment and asked if the kid was still around.

"'Yeah, he's standing over there. He's on the verge of tears.'

"Bobby went over to the youngster, took him by the hand, and brought him into the Blackhawks' dressing room. In a few minutes, the young fan was back at rinkside, a monster smile on his face. He was clutching a stick signed by most of the Blackhawks."

CHAPTER 33

ALL ABOUT GRAPES

I know you'll want to know what I think of Don Cherry and his amazing success on *Hockey Night in Canada*. I was with him for much of his ride and saw him go from coach of the year to a coach out of work to *Coach's Corner*, where he revolutionized hockey broadcasting—and quite possibly still would be, but for a final slip of the lip.

In his *Hockey Night* debut at age 46—during the 1980 playoffs—he made us laugh talking about one of his former coaches, Joe Crozier. "I went to Cro and told him he was playin' six defencemen. 'It's too many, Cro. We gotta go with four.' So he goes to four, and I don't play for the next 60 games."

Now, let me confess how disappointed I was when *Hockey Night* needed a replacement for Dave Hodge on *Coach's Corner*, and I lost out to newcomer Ron MacLean. I'd done a handful of *Coach's Corner*s with Grapes and I know he liked me and liked working with me, because he told me so. We'd established a good rapport. He liked that I would get right to him, in order to maximize his time on camera. That was fine with me.

With host Dave Hodge gone (to Vancouver after his famous pencil flip that cost him his job), Don Wallace, our executive producer, took me aside one Friday and said, "Take the weekend to think about your future roles with us. We can use you in a number of ways. As a colour man, as a host, even on *Coach's Corner* during the intermissions."

I met Wallace on Monday morning and told him I'd like to do a bit of everything, but I really wanted to work with Grapes on *Coach's Corner*. He surprised me by saying, "That job has just been given to Ron MacLean. I just got off the phone with him. I'm moving him to Toronto."

Son of a bitch. I felt misled. Wallace had given me first dibs on the positions that were open, then changed his mind overnight.

Wallace and I had clashed earlier. He took me aside at one of our seminars and lectured me about my "negative attitude." And how it might be rubbing off on the young announcers. I told him I didn't know we had any young announcers. I also said, "Don, if I have a negative attitude, it's because of the treatment we receive, and it begins with your boss and mine—Ted Hough."

"Gee, Brian," he said, seemingly surprised. "Ted Hough's been great to me. He's been like a father to me."

"That's because you're on his side of the fence, Don. But he doesn't show any respect for the announcers. We never get a contract on time. We earn a fraction of what Blue Jays announcers are paid. He calls us 'the software—easily replaced.' We are secretly graded from one to 10 on each telecast—like school children. He threatens to fire us if we get an agent to represent us. Or if we work for radio stations or other broadcasters or in commercials. He threatened to fire me once for 'perambulating' when he heard my voice on CHUM radio. He has an A team and a B team at playoff time, and the A team gets double the number of games and double the pay. No wonder some of us have negative attitudes. When I was with NBC, my boss there, Scotty Connal, loved my positive attitude. Scotty played hockey with us, he drank beer with us, he applauded our work, he even arranged for Chrysler—one of our sponsors—to loan us a new car each year. He owned a condo in Hilton Head and he told me, 'You and your wife can stay there anytime as my guests.' And we did. I know he liked me and respected me. And I loved him."

Wallace stared at me, then said, "Well, I guess you're never going to change." Obviously miffed, he walked away.

I didn't get a chance to tell him how Hough treated Bill Watters. Because of the lateness of another contract, I asked Watters if he would be my agent and help in moving things along. He agreed and made an appointment with Hough. Hough got wind of Watters's role with me and called me at home. It was dinner hour. My wife was at Ryerson, studying for a fitness degree (at age 44), and I was cooking dinner for the kids.

Hough was angry. He said, "I understand Bill Watters wants to meet with me tomorrow. I thought it might be about international hockey. But no, it's to discuss your contract."

"Yes, he does want to see you. The contract is way overdue."

"Listen, I want you to know I don't deal with third parties. You no longer work for us until you get rid of your agent."

"Ted, I've got something on the stove. Let me call you back in five minutes."

I paced up and down, thinking of what I should say—how to save my job.

I called Hough back and said calmly. "Ted, you say you don't deal with third parties. But didn't Ralph Mellanby have Gerry Patterson (Guy Lafleur's agent) negotiate his contract with you?"

Silence.

"And didn't Howie Meeker use the same Gerry Patterson to negotiate his contract with you?"

More silence.

Then Hough said, "All right, point made. I'll meet with Watters tomorrow. Goodbye."

The following day, Watters called. He was not happy about their meeting.

"Brian, I've met with all the general managers in the NHL, and some of them are real bastards when it comes to contracts. But I've never met one like your boss. We fought and argued, and if I'm not out of your life by the end of this phone call, you'll never work for *Hockey Night in Canada (HNIC)* again. Hough was adamant."

I said, "I hear you, Bill. You did your best. Let me handle it."

A few days later, I capitulated and signed a contract—on Hough's terms.

Ron MacLean moved in and replaced Dave Hodge. We all missed Hodge, who was at the height of his popularity. But looking back, Wallace made a good choice. I mean it. MacLean soon became hugely popular—the face of the telecast, although his first season had some predictable bumps.

Like Hodge, and like me, MacLean did his homework, and his passion for the game shone through. Luckily, he didn't have to negotiate his deal with Hough, but with the CBC. Big changes had been made. He quickly developed into a quick-witted outstanding host and overall good guy—a hockey guy. He even refereed games. He was the new Brian Williams at the CBC. And I believe his starting salary was $40,000.

In my day, it was a struggle—even after 20 seasons—to make $25,000 a year on *HNIC*. In quick time, MacLean and Cherry (with endorsements that were denied the pioneers like me) were earning by 2019, I'm guessing here, upwards of a million a year. Good for them.

As for my attitude toward young people, I pride myself in always finding time to encourage and enlighten young people in the TV sports business—especially the on-air aspirants. But the kids who were around me then are wise old veterans now—good men like Doug Beeforth, Rick Briggs-Jude, John Shannon (what amazing success he has enjoyed—until recently when he disappeared—after switching from the production side to the on-camera role), Joel Darling, and one or two others will tell you I was there for them when they started out. And they were always there for me.

As for Grapes, I consider Don Cherry a friend. He has always supported me in my broadcasting and publishing ventures and even in the bars, on occasion. And I support him. When he first began getting popular on *Hockey Night in Canada*, I approached him with an idea. "You should write a book, Grapes, and I can help you with that. I'll be your ghost writer."

He frowned and said, "Gee, it's a little too late for that. I've already told Stan Fischler he could work with me on a book."

Stan Fischler, an American writer, works out of New York. I thought it odd that Grapes would agree to work with an American. Grapes is always so Canadian. He was always bitching about European players taking jobs from Canadians. But I guess—no, I'm sure—it simply didn't occur to him that an American writer was taking a Canadian writer's job. To be fair, Fischler is a successful chronicler of hockey and has a following. But he showed he was no fan of mine when he once said of me, "On TV, McFarlane is about as bright as a three-watt bulb."

Ouch! I didn't know Fischler at the time. But I knew he wasn't much of a hockey guy if he named Aldo Guidolin as the greatest coach of all time. Sure the Fischler comment hurt. There was a kind of unwritten rule back then that those of us in the same profession didn't go around stabbing one another in the back. And I confess it was immature of me, petty even, to get back at Fischler, but I did—and I'm not proud of it—on a nationwide NBC telecast. In the 1975 playoffs, Buffalo played Philadelphia, and both teams struggled through the first 20 minutes of a game. There were no goals scored, and the play was scrambly.

In the intermission, Phil Esposito—his Bruins had been eliminated—was my guest. I surprised him by saying, "Phil, that first period would put you to sleep faster than a Stan Fischler hockey book." Esposito's mouth split into a big grin, his eyes flashed, and he pointed a finger at me. "Hey, that's a good one," he said.

Older and wiser now, I should not have said that on air. It was petty and unprofessional. Don Cherry told me that when he was writing his book *Grapes* with Fischler as ghost writer, he ran into a few problems. "Rose and I worked hard on that book," he said. "We wrote every word out in longhand. Then we'd send the copy to Fischler, and it would come back looking a whole lot different. For example, I never liked Denis Potvin of the Islanders, and Fischler liked him. So, instead of me saying nasty things about Potvin, the copy would read like I liked the guy. Rose and I finally figured we should send our stuff right to the editor."

There was no mic or camera in sight so I said to Grapes, "Don't stand for that bullshit. Tell your ghost writer to rewrite it to your liking. It's your book. And tell your publisher, too."

As for not liking guys, Grapes is probably not happy with my boyhood pal, Frank Chiarelli. Father of Peter Chiarelli, for a time the GM with the Edmonton Oilers. Now in his late 80s—about Cherry's age—Frank Chiarelli was a four-time All-American at RPI in the early '50s, while I was playing for St. Lawrence University. We clashed on the ice several times over four seasons, and both teams soared to the top in the East. Chiarelli and his coach, Ned Harkness, led RPI to an NCAA championship in 1954. You'll laugh at this. In the middle of a game against RPI in my senior year, there was a delay for some reason. Chiarelli and I had a chance to talk in the faceoff circle.

After the game, someone asked me what we chatted about. I said, "I'll be getting married a few months after graduation. I asked Chiarelli to consider being my best man."

"And?"

"He said he'd have to get permission from his priest."

The priest said no. Come on, how much would that have hurt the Catholic church? But that's how it was in the '50s.

Recently, Frank Chiarelli wrote a self-published book titled *Sour Grapes and Sweet Success*. It's about two famous hockey personalities—Don Cherry and Sam Pollock. Chiarelli has high praise for one person in the book and is highly critical of the other. You figure it out.

No, I'll spell it out. Cherry knows how to take a few swipes—on and off the ice. Chiarelli says Grapes is at the end of the hockey spectrum. The wrong end. He says that Grapes couldn't play, couldn't coach, and can't broadcast. Above all, he was no brawler. Brawlers have penalty minutes to show for their work; he had practically none.

I'm going to disagree, Frank. The guy was a pro for 20 some years, so he could play. He had 100 or more penalty minutes in four of his first five years in the AHL and he won two coach of the year awards—one in the AHL and another in the NHL with Boston. He was a really popular NHL coach and as a broadcaster he had a bigger following on TV than any of the rest of us.

Chiarelli says Ralph Mellanby is "the guy who rammed Don Cherry in to the pulpit of *Coach's Corner*."

Well, that's true enough.

"It doesn't matter," he carries on, "that there is no content on *Coach's Corner*—the subject matter is so trite that, in effect, there is no content—it is just those easy Canadians—they would sit through anything, even nothing.

"He [Mellanby] was aided by the ineptitude of the CBC bureaucrats who hired Cherry in the first place. He had collaborators who partnered in the foul deed. They were all thirteen Sports Directors since day one of CBC sports."

Not true, Frank. Mellanby hired Cherry. The CBC had little say in it. Mellanby felt Cherry was a natural for TV. When he offered Grapes $100 a game for that 1980 playoff series, Cherry said, "Make it $150 a game and promise me I won't have to wear one of those blue jackets, and I'm in."

That's how Cherry got started. Somehow I get the feeling that Chiarelli and Cherry won't be having a few pops together anytime soon. But if they did get together over a few beers, I'll wager Chiarelli would discover that Cherry is really good company off camera, and they actually have much in common. I mean, they're both opinionated old hockey guys.

I have pleasant memories of working with Grapes. Interviewing him on TV was fun. On a trip to Montreal, he'd join me for a tour of the museum or an art gallery (he liked sailing ships). I took him to a used bookstore one afternoon, and he bought enough books for two bags. I bought none. When I publish a book, Cherry is always there with a nice quote about the contents. "Two thumbs up from me and Blue." That means a lot to me. It would to any writer. And to the publisher.

I wonder, after reading this book, if his thumbs will go up or down.

About Cherry's dismissal from *Hockey Night in Canada*. When you Google all the articles and comments, it appears to be a 50/50 mix of those for and those against. Trevor Whiffen, a long-time friend, lawyer, and business partner of Cherry's, says, "Grapes is disappointed on a lot of fronts. He's disappointed that some people he counted on—friends and allies in the media—turned on him at a time of need and didn't give him support and in fact went out of their way to distance themselves from him." Whiffen is the governor of the OHL's London Knights. "Don is an extremely loyal person. Anybody that values loyalty expects loyalty. Don is always disappointed when those around him don't reciprocate."

Dave Hodge, who worked with Cherry on *Coach's Corner* before Ron MacLean but was not a big fan, made a point. "The day Don Cherry decided he should speak to and for Canadians on any subject at all should have been the day that somebody told him he couldn't, because he was an ex-coach hired to comment on matters related to a telecast called *Hockey Night in Canada*."

Perhaps Mellanby should have delivered that message years ago. Grapes always listened to Mellanby. Bobby Orr's words carry a lot of weight, and he sticks by the man who calls him the greatest hockey player in the world. "He got fired on Remembrance Day. That is just wrong," said Orr. "The whole thing is unbelievable. Don Cherry is a good man. We all know what he was saying. He was saying we should buy a poppy. All of us. You can take it any way you want, but I have known him a long time and I know he is not a bigot or a racist. He is the most honest and generous guy there is. He's very good to the veterans, the police, the firefighters, minor hockey players, and fans. They all know what he meant, and I know what he meant. What they've done to him up there is disgraceful, it really is. Freedom of speech doesn't matter. Don is hurt, but he's going to be fine. He's getting some nice calls from his friends here in Boston. He is getting some wonderful support."

"I think he's meant a lot to the game and provided a lot," said Leaf captain John Tavares. "It's obviously disappointing, what happened and the result. I think everyone would wish something like this didn't happen."

I had a good relationship with Grapes over many seasons. Three or four times, on his way to Kingston to visit his mother, he would veer off Highway 401 and drive a few miles to visit us at our log home. He would pound on our door and gripe about it later. "How come you're never home when I call?" he beefed.

"I guess my wife saw you coming, Grapes. She had just enough time to hide the car, lock the door, and pull down the blinds."

The truth is, I wished I'd been there. Having a couple of pops with Grapes on my front deck would have made my day.

CHAPTER 34

BOWER THE BEST

I was invited to two of Johnny Bower's birthday parties, including his final one, in December 2017. It was his 90th, and it came a few weeks before his death. It was an honour to be asked to say a few words about the hockey icon, the humble ex-goalie who's high on my list as one of the most popular and most respected players in a full century of NHL play. Right up there with the late Jean Beliveau. A couple of years ago, we golfed and dined with the Bowers in Florida, along with Ted Lindsay and his wife, Joanne.

A few years earlier, Nancy Bower invited the McFarlanes to Bower's 80th birthday party in the west end of Toronto. Well, she said it was his 80th. It was a surprise party for a guy who, I pointed out, was older than artificial ice, a chap who was Lord Stanley's favourite netminder. And it was a real treat when former Leaf captain George Armstrong showed up. Army didn't attend many functions, of any kind. But Bower was his roommate for years, and they were very close.

I enjoyed Armstrong, always have—a very funny guy. At Harry Watson's wake, I asked him to tell me a story from his younger days. He came back with, "When I was a kid, my parents sent me to a summer camp. And you know what the cooks did at summer camps in those days? They put saltpetre in our food. You know what saltpetre does to you, eh? Well it didn't affect me—until last year."

At Bower's party, I notice Armstrong talking to several of the players' wives. They burst out laughing. On the drive home, I ask my wife what he said to them. "George is so funny," she told me. "He was telling us that he doesn't like social events, he doesn't like signing autographs. He talked about one guy who came up to him and asked him to sign his cap. He grunted, 'Oh, all right.' And he signed. The guy then asked him to sign his shirt. George scrawled his name on his shirt. The guy asked George to sign a book. George stared at him for a moment and said, 'I'll bet you'd like me to sign your ass.'"

The guy grinned and said, "Would you?"

George said, "Drop your drawers and turn around."

The man obliged.

George took a big black Magic Marker and wrote across the guy's bare butt: *Johnny Bower.*

I interviewed George on *Hockey Night in Canada* many years ago during Christmas week, when society wasn't as politically correct as it is today. He was half Ojibwa. On national TV, I asked him what he bought his wife for Christmas.

"I bought the squaw a new pair of moccasins," he replied.

"But your wife has Scottish roots," I mentioned.

"That's right. I'm Indian, and she's a Scot. No wonder our kids are wild and tight."

Things said then wouldn't fly today.

At his party, Bower told me he enjoyed watching western movies on TV when he roomed with Army on road trips. "But sometimes George would get up and shut off the TV in the middle of a movie. You know those scenes where the wagon train would be surrounded by Indians circling on horseback, and the white settlers would be picking them off one by one with rifle fire. Well, George would jump up and say, 'That's enough. I'm not going to see my people take another beating from the white man.' And *click*, off would go the TV. He'd jump in front of me if I tried to turn it back on," said Bower.

"And I guess everybody in the world has heard about the time I came into the Leafs' dressing room after a practice and tried to put my dentures in. But they wouldn't fit. I looked across the room, and Army was grinning at me. 'Army, you so and so. These aren't my teeth. You've switched them.' By then all the players were laughing. I said to him, 'Where the heck did you get these teeth?' He said, 'You know I live right next door to an undertaker.'"

On *Hockey Night in Canada* one night I called Armstrong "Chief," and a fan wrote in accusing me of being a racist. Everyone called George Chief, and I was amazed when this viewer wrote a stream of letters to my boss condemning me and demanding that I be fired. To his credit, *Hockey Night in Canada* executive Frank Selke Jr. tried to placate the fan with several explanatory letters, but the man refused to see any viewpoint but his own. When I told Army about the exchange of mail he just laughed. "I want people to call me Chief," he said. "I'm Chief Shoot-the-Puck."

Without Armstrong and Bower, the Leafs would not have won four Stanley Cups in the '60s. Army was the leader, the captain, and Bower provided sensational goaltending. At one point, Punch Imlach called Bower "the most amazing athlete in the world."

When Bower started out, he certainly didn't look like a future four-time Stanley Cup winner and a Hockey Hall of Famer. The only boy in a family of nine, he had no hand-me-down skates. A family friend and former pro gave him his first pair. His dad cut bent branches from trees to whittle them into hockey sticks. And his first goal pads were cut from discarded kids' mattresses.

But he progressed through minor and junior hockey only to take a detour and enlist in the Canadian army as a teenager. Records indicate he was only 15. Future teammates simply didn't believe he was old enough to have served in the Second World War. He was hospitalized overseas with arthritis, which kept him from being involved in the raid on Dieppe. More than nine hundred Canadians, many from Bower's South Saskatchewan Regiment, were killed there. And almost two thousand captured. And 119 planes shot down, the most aircraft losses on one day during the entire war.

After his army stint Bower played some minor hockey, then joined the Cleveland Barons of the American Hockey League, where he set an abundance of records.

"You know what?" he told me once. "I'm the only goalie who ever showed up for a pro training camp lugging a pair of regular skates. The Cleveland trainer was shocked. 'Where'd you get these?' he asked. I told him an old pro back home, a forward, tossed them to me when he retired. I'd been wearing them for years. 'Well, I'm going to toss them, too,' he said. 'Into the garbage bin. I'll find you some goal skates to wear.' And he did. It saved me being laughed out of the dressing room."

No NHL team seemed to notice or care when Bower earned raves for his play, although the Rangers brought him up for a season. But they had young Gump Worsley on the roster and showered him with a lot of publicity. I guess they figured he'd be a better long-term bet than Bower. And he was certainly the more colourful of the two.

The Rangers sent Bower to their minor league club in Vancouver, but he soon found his way back to Cleveland, where he excelled for several more seasons. The Leafs finally woke up and brought him aboard in 1958–59. He was well into his 30s by then, and even Bower didn't think he'd be much help to a last place team. And Punch Imlach didn't want to pay him much—around $12,000 per season.

I asked Gordie Howe about Bower once, and he quipped, "I think I was in grade school when Bower was in the league." Bower recalls fishing with Howe one day somewhere in Saskatchewan. "Gordie caught a good-sized fish, and we cooked it over an open fire. Then Gordie ate the whole thing. Left me the tail and some fins."

After a stellar season, George Armstrong ordered his roomie to demand a $10,000 raise from Imlach. They met one morning before practice, and Imlach exploded when he heard Bower's request. "Get out of here!" he thundered. "And you better be dressed and ready for practice in half an hour, or I'll fine you 25 bucks."

In the room, Army asked Bower about the meeting. "You get your raise?"

"No, I didn't. And I didn't want to get fined, either."

"You crazy white man. Go back and get what you're worth."

In a second meeting, King Clancy, Imlach's assistant, intervened. "You'd best not get Imlach angry," Clancy advised. "You don't want to be riding those busses in the American league again, do you? Will you take a $5,000 raise?"

Bower thought of those long bus rides. "Yeah, I'll take the $5,000," he said.

He filled a big hole, and blossoming stars like Dave Keon and Frank Mahovlich filled others. Punch Imlach, a snapper of whips as a coach, drove the Leafs, and in the '60s they won four Stanley Cups. After one Cup win, Bower was so elated he tossed his goal stick high in the air. While his teammates rushed to embrace him, the stick came tumbling down, struck him on the head, and cut him for eight stitches.

Rocket Richard of the Canadiens gave him the most trouble. "That bugger scored more goals on me than any other player. And he would rub it in. He scored a goal on me one night and said to me, 'Hey, Johnny, look out for number two.' I wondered what he meant, when suddenly he whipped another one in. 'Hey, Johnny, that's number two. Be careful of number tree.' And, by golly, a few minutes later he fired a third goal past me—number tree. He laughed as he skated past my net. I was so happy when the Rocket retired. I figure it gave me another few years in the NHL"

Jean Beliveau was not as lucky as the Rocket. "Johnny Bower gave me the most trouble of all the netminders I faced. I had a long reach and I liked to fake the goalies, to deke them. But he would never fall for my fakes, and he had a great poke check."

One day I wrote: "Johnny Bower is one of the most humble, most beloved players I ever met. He is a Canadian icon. People everywhere in Canada want to meet him, hear his words, and seek his autograph. He is a treasure, a joy to be around."

Now words like that come in the past tense.

But even an icon like Bower, when he scouted for the Leafs after his playing days, couldn't find much job security. He was at his desk in the Leafs' front office one morning when Harold Ballard walked in.

"Hi, Johnny, how's my boy?"

"I'm good, Mr. Ballard."

"When's all this scouting you're doing going to pay off for us?"

"Well, Mr. Ballard. You never know. It's not like the old days. There's a draft each year, and you have to get lucky."

"Lucky! Never mind that. I want results. You scouts said Lanny McDonald was a good draft choice. He's been with us three seasons now and hasn't done squat. How come?"

"Well, Mr. Ballard, some young players take a couple of seasons to find themselves. Lanny's comin' along."

"No, he's not. I should fire you for sticking up for him. In fact, I will fire you. Right now. Pick up your stuff and get out of here."

Ballard walked away.

Bower was in shock. He'd just been fired. He didn't see that coming.

The door opened, and George Armstrong walked in.

"What's the matter, John?"

"Matter? I've just been fired. That's what's the matter. I'm sick about it."

"What?"

"Yeah, Mr. Ballard just fired me. He told me to collect my stuff and get out."

"Wait a minute," Armstrong said. "I'll tell you what to do. Leave your stuff. But go home and relax. Come in tomorrow morning like nothing has happened. Harold will forget all about this."

"You think?"

"Do as I say. Just go home."

Bower went home. He showed up the next day and was at his desk when Mr. Ballard marched in. He gave Bower a wave and entered his office.

Bower breathed a sigh of relief. Armstrong was right. He decided he hadn't been fired after all.

"How do you figure that?" Bower asked. "I listened to Army and kept my job. If I hadn't listened, I'd have been down on the unemployment line."

Those were the days.

I told some of my Bower stories at his 90th birthday party, in a room packed with well-wishers, family, and special friends.

On the ride home, we recalled the time the Bowers stayed overnight at our log home in the country—after a golf tournament—with their granddaughter. And what a delight they were.

Hundreds of tributes followed Bower's passing on December 26, 2018. One that stood out was from NHL commissioner Gary Bettman:

> There is so much to appreciate in Johnny Bower's accomplishments on the ice, including the four Stanley Cups and membership in the Hockey Hall of Fame. And yet there is so much more to say about the man who served his sport, his country, his community with so much distinction. Johnny Bower enriched us all by sharing the pure joy he felt for the game he played and the men who he played it with and against him. It was a personal privilege to know him, a delight to be in his presence, and an honour to celebrate him as one of the 100 greatest players in history. Johnny Bower was a bright light in our sport, a light that will shine forever. As the NHL grieves his loss, we send heartfelt condolences and comfort to his wife, Nancy, his family, and his countless friends inside and outside the game.

Countless friends, indeed. And a bright light that will shine forever. A delight to be in his presence. Well said, Commissioner Bettman. I like Bettman and the manner in which he's grown the NHL into a legitimate Big Four sport. He meets a thousand people or more every year and never forgets a name.

Johnny Bower wasn't the only Ballard employee who worried about job security. When I worked for Ballard for several months in public relations, I was told by one of his underlings that Ballard was closing down my department. Department? I didn't know it was a department. It was an office and a desk, and Ballard didn't listen to any of my suggestions, anyway. I marched around the Gardens looking for Ballard. Wanted an explanation. I couldn't find him anywhere.

It was the day before I planned to take my family on vacation out west. I'd promised my kids they'd see a big chunk of Canada. We drove off the next morning and were in a campsite in Kenora a few days later when I told my wife, "I'm not going back to the Gardens. I don't think I have a job there anymore."

"Did you quit?

"No."

"Were you fired?"

"I'm not sure. Maybe."

"Doesn't matter," she said. "You're a broadcaster, not a PR person. It was never going to work out working for Mr. Ballard. Go back to what you do best."

CHAPTER 35

ORR ON THE LINE

The phone rings, and my wife picks up. She says to me calmly, "Bobby Orr is on the line."

What? Bobby Orr? Calling me from Boston? What a surprise. I can't recall when one of hockey's greatest stars called me at home. Maybe Carl Brewer a couple of times. And Frank Mahovlich once to offer me a pair of free tickets to a Leafs game.

We chat and make small talk for a minute or two. Then he tells me the reason for his call. Weeks earlier I had emailed Bobby's son Darren (who works for Bobby) with a request. I had finished my novel *The Hockey Guy*, about a fictional player who gets to play for the Bruins alongside Bobby Orr. I asked Darren to tell Bobby about the book and how a New York publisher would be interested in publishing it if Bobby would support it. Initially, Darren wrote back, "Bobby has no interest in hockey books."

I sent another email off with an admonition, "Darren, that was a rather curt response. You say Bobby has no interest in books, and yet he just published a book. If you tell Bobby how you responded to me, he'll probably say, 'Darren, that's no way to reply to Mr. McFarlane.'"

So Bobby takes time to call me personally and explain. "I can't really support your book," he says. "I hope you understand. Besides, I've heard there are some F-bombs in it."

"Yes, a few," I said. "There are hockey guys talking, and they use the F-bomb."

I'm tempted to add, "You've heard enough of them in your career. And I know from my referee friends you've uttered a few, too." But no, I did not really expect him to support my novel. I know how cautious he is about lending his name to any project. And he should be.

I tell him how impressed I am that he took the time to call me and I appreciate his concerns. No problem, the novel may never get published, anyway. But when the call ended, I got to thinking about Orr and his impact on the game. He was a really astonishing player, and in his post-hockey career one of the most respected people in the sport. What made Orr's mind-boggling accomplishments truly remarkable was that he played for most of his career on wonky knees, knees that had required numerous operations. I've had three knee operations. Goalie Mike Palmateer has had 30. Orr must have had a dozen—most before arthroscopic surgery made the outcome of such procedures so much more successful.

And while his scoring titles have been well publicized, and never duplicated or surpassed, one of his most amazing records has hardly been talked about at all. It's Orr's career plus-minus rating of plus 597. To the uninitiated and the casual fan, it means he was on the ice for 1,188 even-strength Boston goals and on for only 591 goals against. In his all-too-brief career, he won three Hart Trophies (MVP), two Art Ross Trophies (scoring champ), two Conn Smythe Trophies (playoff MVP), and eight consecutive Norris Trophies as best defenceman. He was awarded the Lou Marsh Trophy as Canadian athlete of the year and *Sports Illustrated*'s annual award to the athlete of the year. How can anyone top that?

In 1976, he was named the MVP of the Canada Cup tournament— his only appearance in the international spotlight. No wonder both Harry Sinden and Don Cherry, who seldom agree on anything, call Orr "the greatest player in hockey history."

While I saw Orr play as a junior with Oshawa and marvelled at his talent, I also witnessed Wayne Gretzky perform, beginning at age

12. Personally, I find it difficult to put Orr ahead of Gretzky on my "Greatest Player Ever" list. Orr is obviously the greatest defenceman ever, and Gretzky the most scintillating forward. So, in my opinion, they are tied at the top of the list. I simply can't choose one over the other. But that's just my list. Yours may differ.

I think of Michael J. Fox, the Canadian actor, telling me of meeting Bobby Orr one day. "To my surprise, I couldn't speak," he said. "Brian, I've met the greatest stars and world leaders. I chatted with them, but with Bobby, my mouth flew open, and no words came out. I mean, it was BOBBY ORR."

The call from Orr prompted me to think of a pleasant day at a long-ago golf tournament north of Toronto. Orr, the "celebrity guest," was assigned to our foursome, and he treated us like he'd known us for a lifetime. He was limping a bit that day, and when we finished the round somebody drove him off in a golf cart, while the rest of us gathered together off the 18th green and talked about him.

"Wasn't he great company?" someone said.

"That was the greatest day I've ever had on the golf course," said another. "All because of Bobby. He kept telling me, 'Come on, bud, we need a solid drive from you,' and 'Great putt, pal.' Things like that. I'll never forget it."

I asked Bobby for a favour that day. I told him I was opening a small hockey museum in Niagara Falls and I needed an autographed photo of him to put on display. Orr said, "No problem. Leave it with me." A week later, I received by mail a dozen photos, including the famous one of his Stanley Cup winning goal in 1970—a really large photo. All autographed. Was I thrilled? You bet I was. Cost a bundle in postage to send them. I sent him a note of thanks. But I thank him again—all these years later. That gesture, along with Stan Musial coming off the diamond to do a third interview with me, were the two most thoughtful player gestures a grateful broadcaster ever received.

I knew of his generous nature from a mutual friend, the late Russ Conway, the Hall of Fame journalist from the Lawrence *Eagle-Tribune*. Conway was nominated for a Pulitzer Prize for his expose of

Alan Eagleson. (A lot of aging Canadian journalists are still embarrassed that Conway beat them all to the story.) Conway's diligent work helped send Eagleson to prison. His research and articles were a big factor in the conviction of the former executive director of the NHLPA for fraud.

Conway told me a story about Orr one day:

"When Bobby was at the peak of his game, I was on my way to a Bruins morning skate. But it was one of those days when everything was going badly. My car wouldn't start, I slipped on a patch of ice, and I found some letters I forgot to mail. So when I get to the Boston Garden, Bobby Orr slaps me on the shoulder and says, 'Russ, how's everything?'

"I say, 'Everything's horse bleep' or something similar, because I'm having a lousy day.

"Bobby laughs and says, 'I've got a cure for that. Meet me after practice.'

"So, of course, I meet him after practice.

"He takes me into the Bruins' dressing room, and the trainer loads him up with a lot of pucks and sticks and team souvenirs. He throws all this stuff in the trunk of his car, tells me to hop in, and we drive off. He doesn't say a word as we drive away.

"Now he pulls off the highway and drives into the parking lot of a major hospital. Then he turns and wags a finger at me. 'Not a word of this trip gets in your newspaper. A deal?'

"'If you say so. It's a deal.'

"In the hospital he says hello to everyone he meets as he makes his way to the children's ward. There, he goes from room to room, from bed to bed. Keep in mind these are sick kids—cancer patients and others with major health problems. But they all know Bobby Orr, and how their faces light up when he kibitzes with them and hands out his hockey souvenirs—photos for all, a stick here, and a puck there. And I've got a big lump in my throat watching all this.

"It's another hour before we're out of there. And the lump in my throat has doubled in size by the time we reach the parking lot.

"He starts the Caddie, and we drive away, neither of us talking, both of us moved by the experience. Finally, he turns to me and grins. He says, 'Well, Russ, how's your day now?'"

Don Cherry is right. There are so many Bobby Orr stories, and it would take volumes to tell them all. As for me, it was a privilege to work with Orr on *Hockey Night in Canada* when he joined us as a guest analyst on our show from time to time. While he never felt really comfortable in our world, we were thrilled to have him with us for a season or two.

And it was an added thrill for me to be in the broadcast booth at the Boston Garden on Bobby Orr Night. It was January 7, 1979. The game was a meaningless exhibition contest against the Soviets, which really ticked off Cherry, and I have no recollection of the game itself. But the opening ceremonies—they will stay with me forever. The ovation Bobby Orr received that night from the Boston fans was simply incredible. It seemed to go on forever.

"Bobb-ee! Bobb-ee! Bobb-ee!"

I remember the pinstriped suit he wore that night. During the ceremony, Johnny Bucyk handed Orr his No. 4 jersey. The arena exploded in cheers as he pulled it on. Then a large banner with his number on it and the years he served the Bruins—1966 to 1976—not nearly long enough—was raised to the rafters. Some speeches were curtailed because of the lengthy ovation, which lasted about 11 minutes. I wondered what the visiting Soviet players were thinking when the ovation went on and on. A few of them may have played against Orr in the Canada Cup series. The others could only gawk and marvel at the well-deserved adulation he received that night. Such a night would never have happened for one of them—in Moscow or anywhere else. Their eyes were popping, while ours were filled with tears.

That was the year Orr was named the greatest athlete in Boston sports history, ahead of legends like Ted Williams, Bill Russell, and Bob Cousy. Imagine a Canadian kid beating out American titans of sport like those three men. Another poll had the name Orr at number 31 on the greatest athletes of the 20th century. That's pretty heady stuff for a humble crewcut kid from Parry Sound.

Then there was that day in Chicago—again I was fortunate to be there—when Orr announced he was retiring from hockey. Shame on the Bruins for letting this icon go to the Blackhawks. Orr should have remained a Bruin forever. If Eagleson convinced him to sign with his old pal Bill Wirtz, then shame on him, too. Eagleson never told Orr that Boston was willing to give him part ownership in the team—as much as 18.5 percent if he'd stay. Advising him to sign with Chicago was so wrong, so unethical, and so preposterous that he was kept in the dark. We'd all like to know the facts, the real story behind that deal.

In Chicago, on November 8, 1978, we were there with our cameras for the press conference when Orr called it a career. He'd struggled through a few games with the Hawks over two seasons. Do you know he played in a mere 36 NHL games in his final three seasons? Everyone in the packed room was crying. It was a very emotional parting. Others have retired—Howe, Guy Lafleur, Ron Ellis, Ted Lindsay—only to come back months later. With Orr, we all knew that it was final. And we were all choked up. One year later, Orr was ushered into the Hockey Hall of Fame. No waiting period for him. Nor should there have been. At age 30 he became the youngest member of that elite group.

Bobby Orr left an indelible mark on the game of hockey. It's a shame the kids playing today didn't get to see him perform. When my grandsons—and great-grandson—ask me, "Who was Bobby Orr?" I try to take them back to the late '60s and early '70s. They can hardly believe there were only six teams when he arrived in the NHL as an 18-year-old. I tell them that Bobby Orr was the most exciting player in hockey, one of the best I ever saw. Even as a junior he was phenomenal. He played for the Oshawa Generals as a 14-year-old—that's too young for any kid to be playing junior—but Orr played and excelled against young men four and five years older. He was a phenom even then.

Before Orr, hockey people—and I was one of them—thought it impossible for a defenceman to win the Art Ross Trophy, awarded annually to the highest scorer in the game. He changed that thought in a hurry. In his rookie season, he won the Calder Trophy, and by his third season he set a goal-scoring record for a defenceman with 21. In

1969–70, he stunned us all by finishing on top of the scoring race with 120 points. That was 21 more points than his teammate Phil Esposito, one of the greatest scorers in history. No defenceman had ever come close to that kind of production. It was unthinkable. Then, five years later, he won the Art Ross Trophy for a second time, this time with 135 points. In between, he finished second in scoring three times and third once (all four times behind Esposito).

Many outstanding defencemen have come along since Orr retired, but none have quite been in his class. My opinion.

I asked Grapes about Orr one day. He said, "Bobby was supernatural. Terry O'Reilly came up with a good idea. He said they should pass Bobby around from team to team. That would keep things even. I told O'Reilly to keep his ideas to himself."

At an event in Kitchener, Ontario, I asked Hall of Famer Milt Schmidt to tell me more. "Well, Bobby was the type of person who never wanted any publicity. He wanted his teammates to get the attention. He was swamped with requests for his time. Here's the kind of guy he was. When I managed the Bruins, we were playing up in Montreal one night late in the season. Tommy Williams was with us at the time, and Tommy had a bonus coming if he could score one more goal. But he wasn't getting many chances, and now it's the second-last game of the season. It looked to me like he was never going to get that goal. Now Orr scores a goal and the PA announcer says, 'Boston goal by Orr.' Bobby skates over and tells the timekeeper and the referee that he didn't score the goal, Tommy Williams scored it. Well, who's going to argue with Orr? What bothered me was that Tommy Williams was sitting on the bench when that goal was scored.

"After the game, I went up to Orr and I said, 'For Chrissakes, Bobby, if you're going to do something like that, would you please wait until your teammate is on the ice.' He just laughed."

I can see Orr squirming and saying, "Come on, Milt, no need to tell stories like that."

Orr wore No. 2 during his four years with the Oshawa Generals and, in late November 2008, the Oshawa club finally retired his number. He was teary-eyed and told the crowd, "To be honoured in this fashion is something I'll never forget."

Wren Blair, then 83, the man who discovered Orr, was there, beaming with pride. And Don Cherry quipped, "Sure, Bobby was a good player. But remember, he had a great coach."

I'll wager Bobby is still saying to journalists like Conway as he rushes off to do good works, "Not a word of this gets in the paper—a deal?"

An afterthought: On August 11, 2018, my wife and I were in my old hometown of Whitby—in a hall, celebrating the life of our friend Cliff Meta, who passed away suddenly a few weeks earlier. We were seated next to a couple—Jill and Tom Maxwell, who knew the young Bobby Orr. Jill had been a nurse in the Parry Sound hospital, and Tom had been a coach on a local hockey team—one that had a pint-sized, crew-cut kid named Bobby Orr on the roster.

Jill said, "Bobby came into the hospital one day with an injury of some sort, and once he was treated, I told him I was going to marry the coach of his team—Tom Maxwell.

"He looked surprised, then said, 'But nurse, you can't marry him. He's too old for you.'

"I asked Bobby how old he thought Tom was. And he said, 'I dunno. But he's old.'

"And I told Bobby that Tom was 24, and I was 21, and I was going to marry him."

Tom was listening and chuckled. He said, "Even at that young age, Bobby showed a lot of leadership. We'd go into a restaurant as a team, and Bobby would be in front. All the other kids would file in behind him."

Jill added, "Bobby was always good about mentioning people like Tom, who had some influence on him when he was very young, long before he became the greatest player in the game."

There's a story I hesitate to insert here. It shows another side of Bobby. But it shows he's human, like all of us. I'm sure if he reads it, he'll say, "Yeah, that happened, and I regret it." If he's upset, all I can say is, "Sorry, Bobby."

Following a game in Chicago against the Vancouver Canucks, a number of players from both teams went to a popular bar, the Rusty Scupper. One of the Canucks was Hilliard Graves, a tough but small-ish winger.

"Bobby was calling out some of the Canucks for not putting out," says Graves. "Then he yapped at me. He said if he ever came back, he was going to get me. He was really mad. But so was I. I said if he tried it, I'd take his knees right off. He reached out and punched me in the chest, knocked me right off my bar stool. I threw him to the floor, but he jumped up and punched me under the eye. I nailed him twice, one on the nose and one on the eye, and he went down. A few moments later, I see him standing at the door to the men's room, and he calls me over. Bobby was almost in tears, really upset. 'I'm really glad you hit me,' he said. 'I deserved it. I've been acting crazy lately. I don't know what the hell's wrong with me. I'm so frustrated. I've been looking for something, I don't know what.'"

It's obvious he knew that the end of his career was looming. And he was having a hard time dealing with it. Who wouldn't? With that talent? Not yet 30.

And there's a final question I can't get out of my head. Did Bobby really take out a full-page ad in the newspaper supporting Donald Trump?

Oh, Bobby.

But there's his pal Derek Sanderson moving into the picture like a referee, getting between Bobby and the non-Trumpers who blasted him.

"Why can't we [Bobby and I] state an opinion without being cut to shreds?" growls Derek. "I grew up during the Vietnam War. We were allowed to protest back then. Bobby stated a political preference. It was totally within his right to take out that newspaper ad. I thought the reaction was over the top. He didn't kill any babies."

Which prompts the question: Why do either of you take sides publicly when you are both Canadians, non-voters and non-citizens?

Perhaps Stu Cowan, writing about Orr's stance in the *Montreal Gazette*, said it best for a multitude of Orr fans who were disturbed:

Learning that one of my boyhood heroes supports and so fully endorses a narcissistic president who doesn't try to hide his racism, is a pathological liar, calls the media "the enemy of the people," boasts about groping women, puts children in cages, refuses to listen to scientists and doctors as the COVID-19 pandemic gets worse and looks to divide rather than bring people together, it hit me like an open-ice bodycheck.

CHAPTER 36

THE PERILOUS ADVENTURES OF PETER PUCK

The Imp of the Ice. That's what we called Peter Puck, the talking hockey puck, when he came bouncing into our lives in 1973 on the NBC hockey telecasts. Ted Lindsay, Tim Ryan, and I were in Atlanta to televise a Flames-versus-Leafs game. This was long before the Flames packed up and headed for Calgary, where hockey support was not a wild guess but a guarantee.

Scotty Connal, our visionary NBC boss, invited a number of media people from the southern states to Atlanta for the weekend. All expenses paid. Many of them had never seen an NHL game. It was hoped they'd be attracted to the sport and write positive columns about it.

In Atlanta, the game they witnessed was lacklustre. The Leafs humiliated the Flames 8–0 in a boring tilt. When Leaf rearguard Mike Pelyk's name surfaced as the star of the contest, it wasn't as though our southern guests had just witnessed Bobby Orr at his best.

Wined and dined, the reporters returned to their workplaces unimpressed. Most of them forgot about hockey.

But not all. Some did write about a high-energy newcomer they'd seen on our telecast intermission—Peter Puck. Peter was an animated rubber rascal who explained the fundamentals of hockey better than the announcers could.

I had the pleasure of assisting in the creation of Peter Puck, then introducing Peter to the network's nationwide audience.

That was the beginning of a decades-long relationship between us.

Peter was developed by world-class animators at the Hanna-Barbera studios in Hollywood. Bill Hanna and Joe Barbera were master animators. But they knew as much about hockey as the Flintstones. They sought my help, but the name Peter Puck came off the lips of Barbera.

When I met with Barbera in Los Angeles, he recalled a conversation with Scotty Connal.

"When Scotty asked me for an animated character for the NBC games, I said, 'Sure, Scotty, we'll give you Peter Puck.' The name was a natural."

Connal and Barbera asked me to get involved, to go to Hollywood and supply Hanna-Barbera with some of my hockey books and literature about the game: offsides and icing, what the referees do, the history of the Stanley Cup—that sort of thing.

I said, "Why not? No charge."

My wife said to me, "You should learn to stop saying those last two words."

Hanna-Barbera produced nine episodes, each of about four minutes in duration, for a total of 44 minutes—and a star was born. When I introduced Peter on the NBC telecasts, I soon became known as Peter Puck's father. And the fan mail began pouring in.

"Dear Peter: Does it hurt when the players smack you on your bottom?"

"Dear Peter: Do you have a girlfriend? If not, may I be your girl?"

And this one, in jest, from Dave Gardner, then with the Montreal Canadiens: "Dear Peter: How can I score goals when I sit on the Montreal bench and don't get much ice time?"

Apparently, Canadiens GM Sam Pollock didn't think Gardner's letter was funny. He was traded a few days later.

I kept many of the letters. Most were from young fans and they included colourful artwork created by the senders. Perhaps the letters would become a Peter Puck book one day. Why not?

The book idea surfaced in the off-season. The book, published by Methuen in Toronto, was called *Peter Puck: Love That Hockey Game!* It's a collector's item now—costing up to a couple hundred bucks on the internet. The storyline followed closely the content of the TV episodes. At the Hanna-Barbera studios, I selected specific frames from the original 35-millimetre films. Presto—Peter's first book. And no need for expensive artwork.

Methuen printed 50 thousand books, and I soon found myself on the *Today* show talking about Peter.

One of those books—signed by the author—went into the hands of Leafs owner Harold Ballard. I thought he'd be pleased.

He caught up with me at Maple Leaf Gardens a day or two later. "I'm going to sue that fucking publisher of yours for $50,000," he bellowed.

He waved his copy in front of me and jabbed at the photo on the back with his finger. The photo showed Peter Puck emerging from Leaf forward Bill Flett's long beard. "Look at this! Flett's wearing his Leafs jersey in the photo, with my logo on it. Your publisher's not going to get away with that."

I knew I was in trouble. But I was also quite familiar with Ballard's bombast.

"But Harold," I said. "That was my idea to have Flett in the photo. I told them to crop it so the Leafs logo wouldn't show. I guess they forgot. Anyway, I'm to blame, not the publisher. I guess you'll have to sue me for the 50 grand."

He gave me a look, mumbled something, and walked away. Nobody got sued.

By then Peter was appearing on *Hockey Night in Canada* as well as NBC, and new episodes would become a priority. Plus the need for a solid marketing plan. In Canada, the T. Eaton Company had already shown interest in Peter Puck merchandise, and along with Peter (in costume) I made a few personal appearances in select Eaton's outlets. The response was excellent. Peter appeared in the famous Eaton's catalogue and was second in popularity to Mr. Claus in the annual Eaton's Santa Claus parade in Toronto, watched nationwide.

By then I'd bought the marketing rights to Peter, negotiating first the Canadian rights and later the world rights. I partnered with a guy I trusted and he botched a major deal and walked away, leaving me with a debt of a quarter million. We paid it off in a year, thanks mainly to insurance on a ton of Peter Puck books that were destroyed by accident while in storage. I retained a sports marketing company to handle these rights and make Peter a star. The company made deals but were forgetful when it came to paying royalties. There was a divorce. Peter Puck appeared again (a comeback) on *Hockey Night in Canada*—a new-look Peter—for three seasons. According to Scott Moore, a top CBC network executive at the time, Peter was second in popularity on the show to Don Cherry on *Coach's Corner*. The CBC paid one dollar for the rights (it was never paid), which included clauses committing the network to consult with us and get approvals from us on all things Peter. The CBC totally ignored these edicts and did pretty much as they wanted.

And when Rogers acquired TV hockey rights in a monster deal a few months later, Peter Puck was left behind. He's not welcome anymore.

Stay tuned, hockey fans. Peter may bounce back again as the world reshapes itself after COVID-19. He and Penny Puck can mentor and entertain a new generation of hockey kids and their parents as they skate back into the hockey spotlight.

CHAPTER 37

MELLANBY AND ME

I'm holding a hockey book in my hand. On the cover there's a photo of former *Hockey Night in Canada* executive producer Ralph Mellanby. It's his book, *Walking with Legends*. On the cover photo, Mellanby is flanked by Don Cherry, who is wearing a solid dark suit. That can't be right. Oh, I get it. It's a very old photo. Or an old suit. Maybe both. Mellanby gets the credit—or the blame—for siccing Cherry and his dog Blue on an unsuspecting hockey nation. Also on the cover, on Mellanby's left, is a young Wayne Gretzky, even more nattily attired than Grapes. When it comes to legends, Mellanby picked two of the biggest names in hockey for the photo op.

I know he's going to be saying things about me inside the book. Of course I'm curious. We've had our disagreements over the half century I've known him, and I wonder what he'll say about our relationship. I hope he remembers it was me who first recommended him to Ted Hough, head of *Hockey Night in Canada*, back in the mid-'60s. Hough and I disagreed often, but he listened to me then. He took my advice and hired Mellanby, the real beginning of a rather amazing career. And we shared some good times on the NBC telecasts for three seasons in the '70s, so why worry about Mellanby's opinions? He may still be pissed that I never went to see his son Scott play when he was in minor hockey with the Don Mills Flyers. Dave Hodge never went, either. I had enough trouble getting to my own son's games.

I recall Hodge saying of Scott, half kidding, "Can you imagine if that little son of a bitch makes the NHL." We laughed at the time, thinking there's no way. But Scott Mellanby exceeded all expectations and played solid NHL hockey for more than 20 seasons. He played in more than 1,400 NHL games and scored 364 goals—close to Hall of Fame stats. Nobody calls him a little son of a bitch anymore. Scott's earned a ton of respect, both as a player and in management.

When Mellanby took me aside before a regional telecast one Wednesday night and told me he'd just won an Emmy for his work for one of the U.S. networks, I said, "Great, Ralph. Congratulations. I'll mention it on the telecast."

"No, no," he replied. "Not tonight. Mention it on Saturday night. That's a national telecast."

Mellanby will chuckle if he reads this. He'll say, "Yeah, I did say that."

Looking back, it made sense. Go for the big Saturday night audience. Tiger Williams knew that. When asked to be Dave Hodge's guest on a Wednesday night, a regional game, he declined. "Invite me back on Saturday, Davey. My old buddies in Swift Current will all be watching then."

I open Mellanby's book, and there's an intro by Grapes. Grapes writes, "If it hadn't been for Ralph, my television career would have been over before it began. The CBC wanted to fire me a month into [my first] season [some stuffy CBC executives thought Grapes should go to announcing school, learn how to speak proper English]. Ralph said, 'If he goes, I go.'"

Grapes has often said, "Ralph laid his job on the line for me. He's the best."

Mellanby's ego sometimes rubbed people the wrong way. But he should be proud of what he did for *HNIC* and the U.S networks he joined for big events like the Olympics. I feel it's okay to think you are good at what you do if you really are good. You think Guy Lafleur, Darryl Sittler, and Bobby Orr didn't know they were exceptional players?

I'm sure Mellanby's cover boy companion—Grapes—has quite an ego, too. He told me and others more than once, "I can't go back to coaching because I'm too great on TV."

But Ralph can be self-deprecating. I said, "Ralph, you've got two amazing kids. Your daughter's a whiz in the TV world. And Scott's NHL stats are tremendous."

He laughed and said, "Yeah, but when I tell them anything today, they yawn and say, 'Dad, we've heard all your bullshit.'"

Ralph Mellanby has been a huge contributor to hockey. Someday he may be a nominee for the Hockey Hall of Fame, the first non-on-air broadcaster to be inducted to the media section. And why not throw in an Order of Canada at the same time. Even if Mellanby nods and says, "Well, why not? It's about time. Maybe Scott should come in with me?"

Over the years, he certainly endorsed his announcers for honours, like the Sports Media Canada annual awards. He pushed for Hodge and Irvin and for me to win it.

I read on.

His first chapter is devoted to a famous father-son duo—Foster and Bill Hewitt. Mellanby says he spruced up Foster's image. The powder-blue jackets he insisted we wear (all but Cherry) made us all look good. But Foster looked particularly good, and he wore it everywhere. It was Mellanby who persuaded Foster to recreate his first radio broadcast in 1923. He put Foster in a phone booth to simulate the sound of a 1923 microphone in an enclosed space (Foster's small booth at rinkside in Mutual Street Arena was a glass-enclosed one)—and it worked.

Years later, a young researcher came up to me. "Mr. McFarlane, I was in the CBC archives yesterday and I came across the most amazing broadcast. Foster Hewitt calling his very first game. I can't believe they have a recording of it."

I smiled. "Sorry to disappoint you, young man," I told him. "That's Ralph Mellanby's work. It's a simulation of Foster's first broadcast."

Now I come to chapter 2 in the Mellanby book, and it's all about me. A surprise. I come ahead of Danny Gallivan, Dick Irvin, Dave Hodge,

Ron MacLean? (So there, guys.) Gallivan should have come first. He preceded all but Foster Hewitt.

Mellanby and I first met when I was working for CBS in 1960, and we did NHL games from the four U.S. cities. Mellanby was a floor director with a TV station in Detroit. We met again a few months later when we joined a start-from-scratch TV station in Montreal—CFCF-TV. I was the sports director, and Mellanby was a floor director who quickly became a director and producer. And, in time, executive producer of *Hockey Night in Canada*. I'll pass along a few snippets about me from Mellanby's book:

> [Brian] had the same vision for the show [*Hockey Night in Canada*] as I did. Because he was educated and had vision, [he] was the right partner for us to achieve our mutual ambitions.

So far, so good.

> Brian could do play-by-play, colour commentary and work on the panel during intermissions on both radio and television. He could write, and he had great ideas for the show. I often used Brian for voice-overs or to host "Showdown in the NHL." Anytime we did a special, Brian was my first choice to be part of the show. I also feel he could have been a great producer, had he elected to try his hand at that. People used to jokingly call him "Brian McMapleLeaf." But I didn't think that was fair. He wasn't a Leaf guy, he was a *Hockey Night in Canada* guy. Brian was an unbiased pro who later went on to host Montreal Canadiens games and also found his way to Winnipeg, Calgary and Edmonton broadcasts.

I'd be a fool to complain about any of those words. But honestly, I would have been a lousy producer. And nobody calls me McMapleLeaf anymore.

R. M. He was a great public speaker at *Hockey Night in Canada* functions. Whenever we got a request for a speaker, we would always get Brian to do it. And throw a few bucks his way.

Sorry, Ralph, here's where we differ. I didn't think anybody but you at *HNIC* knew I did speaking engagements. Over the years I did a handful for *HNIC*, but I booked 30 to 40 engagements a year on my own—for much bigger fees than a few bucks. At the *Hockey Night in Canada* annual Christmas parties, Cherry and MacLean were always invited to get up and entertain. I confess I was disappointed. I'd learned how to make people laugh. I might have even won Ted Hough over with a couple of quips. Back to Mellanby's book.

Brian's biggest strength, however, was also his downfall. He would take up causes, and in doing so, he brought a lot to the show that I liked. But occasionally he'd go too far and I'd have to reel him in.

Did I really go too far when I said on a Leafs-versus-Bruins playoff telecast from the Boston Garden in 1968: "The Leafs' Forbes Kennedy is in trouble now. He came off the bench and triggered a brawl. Then he struck George Ashley, the linesman, and knocked him on his butt. That means he faces a fine or a possible suspension"? It was a fair comment. Not for a second did I think it wasn't. But it upset some people. NHL president Clarence Campbell beefed, "Who is McFarlane to tell me what punishment Kennedy deserves?"

Well, under the NHL rules, Mr. Campbell—your rules—Kennedy had obviously earned a fine or a suspension. Why wouldn't I say so?

But my comment, while accurate, infuriated Leafs manager-coach Punch Imlach even more than Campbell or the 10–0 defeat handed to the Leafs by the Bruins that night—the night the Bruins fans attempted to assault defenceman Pat Quinn in the penalty box after his devastating hit on Bobby Orr.

Back in Toronto, King Clancy collared me. "Brian, Punch wants to see you. He says your comments got Kennedy fined and suspended. He wants you fired for what you said. We looked at the tapes, and Punch is certain Kennedy never touched the linesman."

I said, "King, I don't work for Punch. I've got a phone. Tell him to call me. And tell him a few million people saw Kennedy punch Ashley and knock him flat. We all know Punch sent Kennedy out to start a brawl. So who's more responsible for getting him suspended: me or Punch?"

Imlach didn't call, and I didn't speak to him. Two nights later, the Bruins eliminated the Leafs in four straight playoff games, and Imlach was fired by Stafford Smythe a few minutes after the final whistle. Driving home after the Leafs' season-ending loss, I heard about Imlach's dismissal on the radio. I turned to my wife and said, "Good news. Punch was about to get me fired, and he gets fired, instead."

I might have added, "That's the end of a dreadful era. Punch should never have been rehired in the first place. Everyone in hockey knew the game had passed him by. He went from one of the most admired managers in hockey in the '60s to one of the most hated in his second go-round. Ballard was an imbecile to rehire him."

In his book, Mellanby says:

> Nowadays, nobody thinks twice about broadcasters voicing their opinion, but back then it wasn't done. The owners and the league didn't get it. They didn't understand that broadcasters had to say what they thought. And that's what I wanted from my talent.

Mellanby was executive producer of *HNIC* for the first year of expansion—1968. The NHL went from 6 teams to 12. We were in St. Louis for a playoff game—the Blues versus the North Stars. Dan Kelly, Dick Irvin, and I were the announcers.

A young Scotty Bowman approached Ralph before the game and said, "I guess we're not good enough for the number one announcer—Danny Gallivan."

Ralph told Scotty, "We're making history, Scotty. Using our young guys—just like you are."

> Brian continued to be something of a rebel, always speaking his mind. He'd say something derogatory about the Maple Leafs and owner Harold Ballard would call me.
> "I want McFarlane off the show!" Ballard would scream.

Believe me, I knew how sensitive Ballard was to anything but praise for his often lacklustre team. I recall the Sittler line being bottled up by Bobby Clarke's line for an embarrassing stretch of time one night. I said, "The Sittler line is having a lot of trouble breaking out because of Clarke's strong checking." Anybody could see that was true. But Ballard collared me after the game and in front of 40 people shouted, "Any more of your fucking pro-Philadelphia comments, and you'll never get in my building again."

I said, "Harold, let's find a quiet place to talk about this."

"No, no talking," he roared. "Stop all your bullshit about the Flyers."

> [Bill] Hewitt's departure came and went, and it was as if nobody cared. I never understood why. We weren't inundated with letters. Nobody asked about him. He just faded away.

Faded away? So did Ward Cornell. So did Brian McFarlane. Jack Dennett. Howie Meeker. That was a common occurrence with *HNIC* talent. When Ward Cornell was let go, Ted Hough almost bragged to a journalist that nobody cared. "Ward was just part of the 'software'— easily replaced." Dornhoefer was quietly dismissed. Mickey Redmond left for Detroit, and John Davidson—two of our best walked away. Meeker was hugely popular and was suddenly gone. There was no hue and cry, never a going-away party. Redmond, accustomed to a top NHL salary, was shocked at the miserly announcer's fees. He once said, "Why don't they pay us all a fair salary and be done with it."

Look at the recent flood of dismissals and departures.

Former goalie Glenn Healy was the first big name sent packing by Rogers as part of the cost-cutting plan. Healy accepted the decision like a pro, telling internet scribe Howard Berger, "I said at the time there is no pity party for this guy. I obviously don't like the fact that so many good, dedicated people have lost their jobs since then, but change is inevitable. It used to be we'd sit glued to our TVs for three hours during *Hockey Night In Canada*. Now, kids are waiting for alerts on their mobile devices.

"As for me, I had the chance to work with the best people in the world—on the air and behind the scenes. Every Saturday, people saw me and listened to my views on the No. 1 hockey program of all time. How could I possibly allow that to be diminished by grousing over the business decision to let me go? I worked games with Bob Cole. *BOB COLE*, for heaven's sake. I'd be standing between the benches; the whistle would blow and I'd say nothing because I was listening to him like the TV viewers. 'Oh yeah, I better chime in here,' I'd remind myself. It was the greatest time in my post-playing career. All I take with me are those special memories."

A classy guy, Healey. I know those feelings. Almost every time I worked an NHL game—no matter where—I pinched myself and thought I was one lucky broadcaster. And reminded myself to try to do each game to the best of my ability, never dreaming the gig would last for 25 years.

And Glenn, I wish I'd handled my departure as well as you did yours.

If Ralph Mellanby had stayed with *Hockey Night* I believe my career might have lasted another few years. Mellanby would have fought to keep me. Didn't happen. I was gone like Gomer.

Nobody noticed my absence. People shrugged and went on with their business.

A thank you note perhaps, for 25 years of service, would have been appreciated. I've been to two or three games in the past 25 years. Only once was I invited back by *HNIC*.

That game was in November 1995, when Bill Torrey and I were inducted into the Hall of Fame, and we both dropped ceremonial pucks to open a game at the Gardens. How many old announcers ever get to do that? And I got royal treatment from Bob Cole and Harry Neale in the gondola that night for a final time. Not a bad way to leave. I still have one of those famous powder-blue jackets to remind me of those days. And no, I wasn't asked to turn in the jacket when I just "faded away" in 1990.

I'll move on, but not before I give you a final comment on the Forbes Kennedy suspension. Many years after the fiasco between the Leafs and the Bruins, I met up with Forbes at a golf tournament in the Maritimes. I told him how I'd infuriated Clarence Campbell and Punch Imlach with my comments during his last NHL game. And how Imlach claimed Kennedy had never even touched the linesman. He simply fell over.

"Did you hit him, Forbes?" I asked.

His eyes gleamed in remembrance. "Oh, I hit him a good one," he said. "Flush in the face."

CHAPTER 38

THE HOCKEY MUSEUM

In 2006, I was looking for a new home for the Brian McFarlane Hockey Museum. We had been operating the museum successfully in Niagara Falls for several years, which meant many hours of commuting on weekends from our home in north Toronto. Prior to that, the museum was part of the Big Apple theme park in Colborne, Ontario. We had a travel museum as well and were booked into the Canadian National Exhibition (CNE) in Toronto and at other events.

The Peter Puck Theatre—with seating for 10—was a favourite with the youngsters. And a shootout for young and old, with hockey cards as prizes, was also popular. I have a memory of my 90-plus-year-old mother-in-law sliding a puck through a hole between the wooden goalie's legs, then raising her stick high and doing a little jig.

Our guest books were filled with positive comments from museum visitors.

I was showing two lads around the Falls museum one day when I looked out the window and saw a man waiting on a bench.

"Is that your father?" I asked the boys.

"Yep."

"Wait here a minute."

I walked outside and escorted the father into the museum. "No charge," I told him. "I want you to be here with your boys."

He came back a week later and handed me Hall of Fame goalie Terry Sawchuk's used goal stick, signed by all of the Red Wings of 1960.

"That was nice of you to let me in free last week," he told me. "Here's a little donation to the museum."

When a new hotel was approved for development in Niagara Falls, on our Victoria Avenue site, we had to relocate.

Where to go next? We were wooed by owners of a hockey arena in mid-Toronto and the city of North Bay, Ontario. The latter's lakeside site was enticing. Then came a call from Clarington, Ontario, mayor John Mutton. Could we meet in his office there?

On the drive to Clarington, I said to my wife, "This is a wild goose chase. There's no way Clarington can afford to purchase and sustain a hockey museum."

At our meeting, Mayor Mutton thought otherwise. He made us an offer we couldn't refuse. He wanted to keep the McFarlane name on the project. He wanted the museum to be "The Official Home of Peter Puck." The municipality would build a million-dollar extension to the Garnet B. Rickard arena to house the museum.

It all sounded too good to be true. And it was.

I told Mutton I had promises of support from the Hockey Hall of Fame, NHL commissioner Gary Bettman, and players like Darryl Sittler, Pat LaFontaine, and Wayne Gretzky. Not to mention all my NHL Oldtimers mates. My wife told him how successful our gift shop had been in our previous location. And how profitable our travel museum had been. He said, "This will be your legacy to hockey. Your museum will be in Clarington long after all of us are gone."

We accepted the mayor's offer. Initially, all went well. The arena extension was underway; a market study had been conducted indicating 25 thousand visitors a year would enter the museum.

But two things happened that caused us concern. Mayor Mutton was charged with spousal assault as he was working toward re-election.

Eventually, he was acquitted, but too late to keep his job. The new mayor, a man named Abernethy, was opposed to the museum project. That was Mutton's "baby."

The McFarlanes were no longer being consulted on museum matters. And the community became alarmed—as we did—when council approved a half-million-dollar expenditure to a Montreal firm to lay out and design the museum. I said to my wife, "What a foolish, costly decision. Our friends at the Hockey Hall of Fame would have been happy to do it—gratis. And they know hockey. The Montreal group has an abysmal knowledge of the game."

The museum—now called Total Hockey—opened in fall 2006 with great fanfare. People came from miles around and began lining up as early as 5 a.m. My wife had suggested I contact Prime Minister Stephen Harper—a hockey fan—and I did. He and his son, Ben, attended, and the prime minister signed autographs endlessly—as did my NHL Oldtimers friends. Michael Burgess sang the anthem.

But, even then, the museum was doomed. There was no signage on the outside of the building or on Highway 401 indicating the museum's location. The photo captions were tiny, even though I'd insisted they be large. The gift shop was a disaster, filled with items that did not sell. My wife shook her head in disbelief.

The mayor did not attend and could not wait to close the museum down a few months later. Local newspapers griped about all the expense involved. One bright spot was the hiring of Kevin Shea, a respected journalist, to curate and manage the museum. But he was brought in too late to save the museum.

I expressed my thoughts on the closing of Total Hockey in a letter to the newspapers in the community:

> My reaction to the closing of Total Hockey is one of sorrow and regret. I enjoyed working with the good people of Clarington and made many new friends in the Municipality. I was hopeful that Total Hockey would be something of a legacy, my gift to the game of hockey.

Yes, I am disappointed. But the termination does not surprise me.

Total Hockey could not survive for a number of reasons, some of them political.

I had hoped that the hockey museum in Clarington would become a mirror image of the hockey museum my wife and I ran successfully for several years in Niagara Falls. The Niagara Falls museum had no debts and its guest books were filled with positive comments. Hockey fans loved it. It worked.

Former Mayor John Mutton and Council expected that my museum would be even more successful in Clarington. A costly market study indicated that it would. Regrettably, this did not become a reality.

Initially, I had reservations about moving my hockey museum to Clarington. But the former Mayor was very persuasive, Council liked the idea of another tourist attraction—a unique one—and approved the purchase at "a fair price." We did not sell the Municipality "a bill of goods" as one local critic suggested.

The hockey museum was never meant to be a money-maker. Nor was it meant to be a drain on the public purse. It was expected to be a break-even tourist attraction.

Now that Total Hockey is about to hear the final whistle, some observations might be appropriate.

The Municipality made one major error in planning the project. That was to retain a Montreal firm at great expense ($500,000) to head up the project. The McFarlanes were not consulted on the choice and would have opposed it. We would have accepted an offer of help from experts at the Hockey Hall of Fame—people with expertise who had been helpful to us in the past.

The result was a museum that was less attractive, less friendly, less "hands on" than it was in its previous location. In a word—it was sparse. Where I would place forty photos on a wall, the Montreal group would place six. Many excellent displays and artifacts were "held back"—never to be seen. The museum was reportedly "the official home of Peter Puck," yet on opening day I saw no evidence of Peter—not on the screen in the "Peter Puck Theatre" or in costume. I asked the theatre custodian, "Why aren't the Peter Puck tapes being played?" He said, "Well, we're not playing them on opening day."

"You mean there's a better day to play them?" I asked.

The McFarlanes strongly recommended that the gift shop be the key to Total Hockey's financial success. In Niagara Falls, the ratio of gift shop sales to admissions was about 8:1. It never approached that level in Clarington.

Government grants—which sustain a much larger hockey museum in Kirkland Lake—were not sought.

I would later learn that the Anne Murray Centre in Nova Scotia received a Federal grant of $560,000. And Anne was worth millions.

Bev Oda, the then heritage minister who lived within minutes of the hockey museum, was busy doling out dozens of grants to other groups but the Clarington group ignored my advice to seek grants.

Because here was no signage—some transients actually thought Total Hockey was a sporting goods store.

Mayor Abernethy was never a fan of Total Hockey and even campaigned against it.

I regret that Total Hockey has been labelled a financial failure. It needn't have been. Better financial planning, more signage, more sponsors, a well-stocked gift shop, and a spinoff touring museum would have resulted in a better bottom line. Our previous (touring) museum was booked into the CNE, shopping malls and fall fairs and was an excellent revenue producer.

Clearly, the money overspent on layout and design was simply impossible to recoup.

Months ago, I suggested that the museum contact dozens of hockey stars, past and present, and request donations of signed photos, sticks and other artifacts. Many of them told me personally they would be pleased to donate. A collection started then might have grown into a million-dollar memorabilia collection by now.

One positive note. The Grand Opening of Total Hockey was a huge success. There was a feeling of great pride in the Municipality on that cold day. There was much positive feedback.

Prime Minister Harper's presence in Clarington with his son, Ben, that day was historic. He signed countless autographs and his appearance brought national attention to the Museum and the Municipality. However, the true test of Total Hockey was in the reception it received from the public. Alas, the visitations, predicted to be in the 25,000 range per year, fell far below that figure.

What should be done? Before the artifacts are sold or auctioned off, I suggest efforts should be made to interest Western Canada in a hockey museum. Calgary, Banff, Edmonton or Winnipeg might be interested in re-establishing Total Hockey. Wayne Gretzky or Mark Messier might be persuaded to buy Total Hockey and donate it to the Province of Alberta in their name—a province where they enjoyed so much success.

Hockey Canada, based in Calgary, might be approached. There's nothing like Total Hockey out West. Why not give it a shot?

Thank you, Clarington, for your interest and support. I enjoyed being part of the challenge. I regret the wasteful expenditures involved.

Finally, I respect Council's decision to close down Total Hockey, even if it leaves my friend Peter Puck homeless.

Life, like hockey, has as many joys and triumphs as it has trials and disappointments. Life goes on, Total Hockey does not. And that saddens me.

The museum artifacts were placed in storage in Clarington and remained there for years. One day, a man from Edmonton, Garry Meyer (we'd met on the speaking circuit years earlier), called to say he wanted to purchase the museum and re-establish it in Edmonton. He'd made an offer of $50,000 to buy it—and his offer was about to be approved—a bargain price. I told Meyer I had first dibs on buying it back from Clarington and was tempted—but felt I might be too old to start over. Meyer came to our house and stayed overnight, and we bonded. I believed him when he said he wanted to keep the integrity of the museum intact and wanted to move it west. He even wanted to keep my name on it. "That's not necessary, Garry," I told him.

Clarington officials were relieved when I called to say I was not interested in repurchasing the artifacts and suggested they accept Meyer's offer.

They did and even agreed to pay all expenses in shipping the museum to Edmonton. "Man, they must have been anxious to get rid of it." I told Meyer. "Wow, did you get a bargain."

Did it ever open in Edmonton? Not yet.

I would have found a new home for it within a year.

CHAPTER 39

OUR SPEAKER TONIGHT

When I was a young broadcaster, I never envisioned myself standing before hundreds of people in a ballroom (especially not the Waldorf Astoria ballroom) and introducing the head table guests as the evening's master of ceremonies. Or, on other occasions, being part of the dais as a guest myself—and being introduced as the keynote speaker. I suppose back then I was aware that there were events that required speakers and emcees, but those were roles that skilled spokespersons filled. In Schenectady, I was surprised when a service club invited me to speak to its members. And I was a dismal failure. A few stupid jokes; an ill-prepared address about hockey, a game my audience knew nothing about; a 25-dollar payment (an overpayment for what I delivered); followed by a determination to do much better next time. If there was a next time.

Once I was established in Toronto, there were plenty of "next times," and I smartened up. Whether I was asked to be an emcee or a speaker, I called on my old Boy Scout motto: "Be prepared." I brought my tape recorder to each event (a cassette, not the old Wollensak), recorded my presentation, and critiqued it afterwards. If a joke failed to get a laugh—and many did—I tossed it out and sought a better joke. If I heard a good line on a TV talk show, I'd write it down, perhaps adapt it to a hockey situation and try it out.

I learned how to survey a room when I got to an event. A bunch of beer-swilling men heard a different presentation than a ballroom filled with men and women in fancy attire. In Saskatoon one year, I looked out over the crowd of well-dressed men and women attending a sports celebrity dinner and cautioned myself. "Be careful, this is a classy group," I told myself. "Remember the advice a veteran speaker once gave you: 'When in doubt, throw it out.'" Meaning remarks or jokes that might be the least bit offensive.

It happened that Team Canada hero Phil Esposito was the featured speaker that night, and while I gave him a grand introduction, Phil hadn't gauged his audience like the rest of us at the head table. He was entertaining and told funny stories, but his last minute at the microphone had everyone holding their breath.

"Folks, let me tell you about Gerry Cheevers, our goalie in Boston," he said. "Gerry let in seven goals one night, and Harry Sinden, our manager, was pissed. He came into our locker room and said, 'Cheevers, you must have felt like an asshole when that seventh goal went in.'"

There was a slight murmur around the room at the word "asshole," but Esposito carried on.

"And Cheevers took a puff on his cigarette and said, 'No, coach, I didn't feel like an asshole. I felt more like a queer.' Harry said, 'What do you mean?' Cheevers smiled and said, 'Wouldn't you feel like a queer if 15 thousand people are calling you a f— c—?'"

Esposito's comment sucked the air out of the room. Women gasped, some men laughed nervously, other men were left open mouthed. Head table guests turned to one another. "Did Phil really just say all that?"

"Yes, he did."

Esposito finally noted the crowd's reaction, pulled the microphone close, threw up both hands, and uttered a final line: "Hey, folks, that's what Cheevers said."

To this day, I'll wager that the people in that ballroom, whenever the talk turns to public speaking, will say, "Let me tell you how Phil Esposito shocked us to the core at a dinner here years ago."

Esposito was different. A Toronto promoter offered him a good fee to speak at an event one year. Esposito was living in Tampa Bay, Florida, at the time. When he got to the airport to pick up his flight tickets, he found he'd be sitting in a centre seat. He called the promoter. "I'm not coming to your friggin' dinner. I hate centre seats."

The promoter pleaded. "Phil, I'm sorry. But you're Phil Esposito. Just ask someone to switch seats with you."

"No, I won't do that. I'm not coming to Toronto."

And he hung up.

As an emcee, you have to be aware that the unpredictable can happen. For one major dinner in Toronto, I was told that one of the speakers would be Paul Henderson. I prepared a glowing introduction for the Team Canada star only to find out a few minutes before I got up that the speaker was another Paul Henderson—the former president of the International Sailing Federation. In Oshawa one night, I prepared to introduce a well-known civic official with a joke about marriage. But the joke only worked if he was happily married. Always check, Brian. I asked about his status and was told, "Oh, don't say that. That marriage is totally on the rocks."

The most difficult role I had as emcee was in Niagara Falls one year. I could feel the banquet falling apart from under me. The local committee invited 14 head table guests—all speakers—with Dennis Hull as keynote speaker, plus Red Storey, who thought he was the keynote, plus two professional comedians who flew in from Las Vegas to draw laughs. We didn't need more laughs. Hull and Storey would provide plenty of those. It was entertainment overkill, and I had to deal with it.

I approached the guys from Las Vegas.

"How much time do you need?"

"Our routine runs 45 minutes to an hour."

"That's too long. You'll have to cut it to 20 minutes. You've got at least 14 speakers ahead of you."

"Twenty minutes. We flew all the way here for 20 minutes?"

I said to myself, "Yeah. And you're probably getting five grand each. Be grateful."

Then Dennis Hull approached me. "Brian, I've got to lead off. I have another appointment tonight and I can't stay."

"Geez, Dennis. They've got you down as the last to speak."

Hull solved the problem. He grabbed a microphone, called for attention and went into his routine, got a big hand, and left by the side door. Meanwhile the clock was ticking. We try to get these things over by 10 o'clock. But that wasn't going to happen. The Las Vegas pair fidgeted, anxious to perform. And Red Storey kept looking at his watch. *When the hell is Brian going to call on me? It's past my bedtime.*

I tried to hurry along. Got the Vegas guys into their routine. They were nothing special. A waste of time and money. It must have been after 11 p.m. by the time I nudged Storey and got him up. He was his usual self—energetic, funny, popular. A veteran of a thousand appearances.

An event I thought might not end until dawn was over before midnight. All in all, a success. Nerve-wracking, but not quite the disaster I anticipated.

I mentioned the annual Canadian Society of New York hockey dinner as a particular favourite—and one of the few in which no fees were paid to high-profile hockey stars. The lure was New York itself.

One year, superstars Bobby Hull, Gordie Howe, and Rocket Richard were there together. Richard was the honoured guest. Dennis Hull was often a guest speaker, and he enjoyed a great second career as a stand-up comic. He always got laughs with lines like: "It's nice to see so many established NHL stars at the head table tonight. It's nice to see Gordie and the Rocket here, too."

I was surprised the selection committee never named two of my favourites to the "honoured guest" list—Johnny Bower and Ted Lindsay, although Lindsay was asked to come and help celebrate Gordie Howe's

"Night at the Waldorf." I always felt the selection committee had a slight bias in favour of the Montreal Canadiens because most of their Hall of Famers were honoured—with the exception of Doug Harvey.

Over the years as a speaker, I became much more selective in choosing my words, especially the jokes. I found that poking fun at the dinner chairman or the mayor of a community would bring laughs.

I know your mayor is one of the finest politicians money can buy.

I asked your chairman how long I should speak tonight, and he said, "Speak as long as you want. We're all going home at nine o'clock, no matter what you do."

I want to thank your mayor for arranging the police escort for my wife and myself all the way in from the city limits—although my wife did get a little tired running in between those two motorcycles. Especially in high heels.

It took some effort, but gradually I improved.

In New York one year—1944—coach Mike Keenan showed up—a surprise. And he was lugging the Stanley Cup—a bigger surprise. His Rangers had won it the day before, ending a 54-year drought, and there was a mob scene at the head table when members of the audience charged to have photos taken with it.

Looking back, I was booked for events from coast to coast and charged reasonable fees because I enjoyed the events and was flattered to be invited. Some banquet stories I remember—and some are even true. At a sports dinner in St. Catharines, Ontario, on October 8, 2002, I heard Scotty Bowman tell a story about his coaching days in St. Louis. His team was in a close contest with Detroit and trailed 1–0 after Gordie Howe scored the game's only goal. With five minutes to play, a young woman behind the Blues' bench screamed at Bowman, "You dummy. Pull the goalie!"

Bowman ignored her, but with four minutes to play she screamed again. "Hey, you dummy! Pull the goalie!" She issued the same order with three, then two, minutes to play.

Finally, with a minute left on the clock, Bowman waved his goaltender to the bench and sent an extra forward out. Just then, Gordie

Howe snared the puck and lofted it over everyone's head, and it landed in the empty net.

Red Wings 2. Blues 0.

The lady behind Bowman blasted him one more time. "You dummy coach. You should have pulled the other goalie."

"They didn't know a whole lot about hockey in St. Louis in those days," Bowman sighed.

At sports dinners, Red Storey often told the story behind his final game as an NHL referee. It was at the Chicago Stadium on April 4, 1959, and I watched it on TV. But this wasn't a funny story.

It was an emotional Game 6 of a semifinal series between Montreal and Chicago. With the score tied 3–3, the Hawks' Ed Litzenberger was tripped up by the Habs' Marcel Bonin. No whistle. Then Bobby Hull was sent sprawling by Junior Langlois, and again no penalty call. The Chicago fans screamed in dismay. Some of them wanted to murder referee Storey. On the next faceoff, one beefy fan leaped over the boards and chased after the ref, dousing him with beer. Montreal's Doug Harvey skated over and belted the fan. But another skidded along the ice and leaped on Storey's back. Harvey caressed him with his hockey stick when Storey flipped the interloper in the air. The Canadiens went on to win the game 5–4, but Red Storey was shaken.

"They wanted to tear me apart," he told me years later. "They hated my guts."

Storey's next assignment was on Tuesday in Boston. On Monday, Storey was told NHL president Clarence Campbell wanted to see him in his hotel room.

"Have you read anything in the papers about the Chicago game?" Campbell asked.

"No," Storey replied. "Why?"

"Well, there were some things said by me, and they weren't meant the way they came out. I thought I was speaking off the record." Later in the day, Storey met with his two linesmen and standby referee Eddie Powers. He had bought several newspapers.

"Storey Chokes," read one headline.

"Storey Chicken," said a second.

"Storey Gutless," blared a third.

Storey was shocked. He turned to Powers. "Don't drink too much tonight," he said. "You're refereeing tomorrow. I've refereed my last game."

"Come on," Powers said. "Don't talk stupid."

"Eddie," Storey said, "I was never more serious in my life."

Storey was as good as his word. He never regretted the move.

A long time later, he told me: "I read the papers, and the reporters described my character, nothing about my refereeing. I was a chicken. I was a choke artist. I was gutless. Hell, if they had said I was a bad official, I would have said: 'Yeah, at times I've stunk out the joint.'

"But don't call me gutless. Don't say things that aren't true."

Storey was voted into the Hockey Hall of Fame in 1967. Most people don't know that he was a great football player as well. In a Grey Cup game, he scored three touchdowns in 12 minutes for the Toronto Argonauts in a win over Winnipeg.

CHAPTER 40

CONVERSATIONS RECALLED

During the 1990–91 season, producer Jim Hough and I flew to Atlantic City to interview Canadian singer Anne Murray, who was performing there. Hough and I shared a hotel room, which became a problem for him because I have a nose and throat problem and I apparently snore—loudly.

In the morning he says, "Jesus, Brian, you snored a lot. Didn't you hear me tell you to stop snoring?"

I said, "No, all I heard you say was, 'Get off of me.'"

The interview with Murray was one of my best. After her sparkling onstage performance, she invited us back to her dressing room, kicked off her heels and put her feet up on the coffee table, popped the cap off a beer, and drank straight from the bottle. I liked that. We talked hockey and show business for an hour.

Here are some snippets of what she told me:

"I bought my doctor father a Guy Lafleur jersey once. And he wore it proudly around the house in Springhill, Nova Scotia, but not when he was seeing patients or on house calls.

"My five brothers and my father watched *Hockey Night in Canada* every Saturday night. My father was a Montreal fan, my brothers were Toronto fans, and I was a Red Wings fan. That's because I was a big

Gordie Howe fan. I also liked Toronto. I liked any team but Montreal. I'm not sure why, because I was a big fan of Jean Beliveau, who, as it turns out, is a distant cousin of mine."

"Some time ago we heard you were attempting to buy the Toronto Maple Leafs," I said. "How serious was that?"

"Very serious. I had some people who were backing me. A bid of 64 million was discussed. Of course, Harold Ballard was not interested in selling. His selling price was just out of this world."

"What would you have done if you'd owned the Leafs?" I asked.

"I wouldn't have traded all of the good players away. I remember the line of Darryl Sittler, Lanny McDonald, and Errol Thompson. It was the most productive line in the history of the Toronto franchise, and the next thing you know, they are all gone."

"Who would you hire to sing the national anthem at the Leafs games?"

"I would sing it myself every night. I wouldn't have to go on the road then."

"Let's talk about Wayne Gretzky. Did you get close to him?" I asked.

"I've met Wayne a few times. He and his parents were at my house for supper one night. We had lobster flown in from PEI, and that was nice. He is a great guy. I felt as shocked as anybody when the Oilers traded him away. But, in hindsight, it has been a great thing for hockey. At first, I thought that it was the worst thing that could ever happen, but it has turned out really well."

A New York Ranger confided in me one night after a game at Madison Square Garden:

> Patti LuPone, the Broadway star of *Evita*, came to see
> Barry Beck and the Rangers play one night. Beck got her a
> couple of tickets and after the match, they climbed into her
> little Volkswagen Rabbit and went to a night club. Some
> of the players were in the club, and when they were ready
> to leave it was pouring buckets outside. Beck called Nick
> Fotiu over and offered him a ride. "Nick, it'll save you from

getting soaked." When Fotiu ran half a block to the car, Patti and Barry scooted inside, slammed the door, and took off without him, leaving Nick to get drenched to the skin.

But the evening wasn't over. Beck and LuPone wound up at another club, and before long, Fotiu and some of his Ranger mates came strolling in. Fotiu appeared to have forgotten the joke Beck had played on him because he had a big grin on his face. Beck said, "Oh, oh, Patti. When he looks like that, there's something up."

They went to the window and looked out. There at the curb was Patti's Volkswagen—covered with a ton of garbage from the street. It was piled about six feet high over her car. Later, Beck had his lawyer write a letter to Fotiu stating there had been $800 damage to Miss LuPone's car, and Fotiu was being sued for damages. Fotiu opened the letter and exploded in anger. He shouted, "What is this bullshit. That woman will be singing 'Goodbye to You, Argentina' from the bottom of the East River, if she gets on my case."

Beck figured he'd won the battle until he turned on the hair dryer after the next morning's skate. A load of talcum powder came shooting out and filled the room, sending players scattering.

Decades ago I listened in as Leafs owner Harold Ballard was talking with reporters:

"If you were to undress me here, I'm sure that you would find a Maple Leaf tattooed right on my ass. The last 10 years have been depressing for me and depressing to all the Maple Leafs. It hurts me more than anyone, cause I'm paying the bills and taking all of the flack. I am quite willing to fight with anyone at the drop of a hat."

There's a joke about the tattoo. Somebody says, "I've got a tattoo on one side of my ass of Darryl Sittler. And on the other, I have a tattoo of Lanny McDonald." The other guy says, "Let me guess the one in the middle. Harold Ballard?"

Ballard hated Russians. One night during a Soviet-versus-Canada game at the Gardens, he put a message on the scoreboard: "Don't cheer the Russians, just boo." It was his unique way of objecting to the Soviet downing of Korean Air Lines flight 007. He was asked: "Is it true that you do these things just to get attention?"

"No, I do it because I say what I think. Anyone who doesn't is just two-faced. If I didn't like you, I would tell you to get the hell out of this place, that I didn't want you around."

(Actually, Ballard often avoided confrontation. He dismissed people by sending a flunky around to tell them he was "shutting down their department.")

He was then asked: "Have you ever said anything you regret?"

"I have never said anything that I regret. I'm Canadian enough not to let those Soviet rats get away with anything and put it ahead of our game. When their circus came to town, the day they came in, they downed the 007. It cost me $600,000 to cancel the show, but that didn't matter. It is sickening what they did."

And then: "You have been described as charming, mean-spirited, rude, boorish, outlandish, and thoughtful. Which is the real Ballard?"

"I will take credit for all of them. I don't make excuses. I tell anybody what I think about them. I don't stab a guy in the back, I tell him right to his kisser what I think of him."

Ballard unknowingly did me a big favour one day. He brought me down into the bowels of the Gardens and pointed out a huge collection of kinescopes of Leafs games played years earlier.

"Get rid of all this crap," he told me. "Throw it in a dumpster."

"Can I have it?" I asked.

"Sure you can have it. Why the hell would you want it?"

"I dunno. It might have some value someday."

"Fat chance. Just get it out of here."

I called a man I knew in the film business named Jack Taylor. He got excited when I told him the story.

"I'll take the kines and clean them and store them," he said. "We'll go 50/50 on any profit if I sell them."

"Sounds good," I said. "I'll draw up a letter of agreement."

In a few days, they were gone, cleaned, and stored safely at Taylor's. Where they remained for the next 30 years.

There were no buyers—at least none that I knew about.

Eventually, Taylor sickened and died. His assistant, Mary, took charge of Taylor's firm.

I phoned her. "Mary, we should try again to sell the kines I have stored with you. Remember, I own 50 percent of them."

"You do not," she replied hotly. "Besides, they are totally worthless. Nobody has ever shown any interest in them."

"Well, I'm showing interest. We should sell them. I have a letter from Jack stating I own half of them."

"Forget it," Mary said. "And stop harassing me." She hung up.

A couple of years later, I heard that Mary had died. Her brother had somehow inherited the business.

At about that time, I got a call from a young woman from Molson's. Could we meet for breakfast?

Over coffee, she broached the subject of the vintage kines. Would I sell them? And for how much?"

I told her whatever the price was, half of it would go to Mary's brother. I had a figure of $25,000 in mind.

"Why not make me an offer?" I suggested.

"All right," she said. "Our offer is $150,000."

I almost spilled my coffee. Six times the amount I had in mind. I was such a dumbbell. I should have declined her offer and said, "Oh, they're worth a lot more than that." Instead, I said, "Your offer sounds fair. I accept."

Even today, a couple of decades later, I still feel I'm a total klutz at business. But Mary's brother thought I was a genius for negotiating such a sum for a bunch of worthless kinescopes. And he happily pocketed $75,000.

My wife said recently, "How are you going to mention all the twists and turns in our life one book? In the first dozen years we were married, you went from out-of-work to overworked."

She's right. From five bucks in my pocket when CFRB called to stints with CBS, CFCF-TV, CFTO-TV, MacLaren, *Hockey Night in Canada*, and NBC. Producing intermission features, writing a couple of books per year, dean of the Hockey College, raising three kids, taking them from one end of Canada to the other, camping trips and cruises, flying around the world, playing in hundreds of hockey games, all those speaking engagements, buying world rights to and marketing Peter Puck, owning a pro lacrosse team, the Montreal Canadiens with John Ferguson as general manager, and building a log home on 37 acres purchased for a pittance and now worth a million or more (I'm guessing).

And always chronicling hockey stories, some of them you may have heard and seen before.

One night in the '70s, when Derek Sanderson was at his peak, I bumped into him in a restaurant in New York. He'd been my guest on a telecast and he greeted me like a long-lost brother. He looked at his watch. "I'm gonna go to two or three clubs. Why don't you come with me?" I hesitated, imagining what it might be like to go nightclubbing with Sanderson.

"Come on," he says, "I'll get you back to your hotel before dawn."

"Nah," I said, thinking of my early flight. "Maybe next time."

You'll like this anecdote as told by former Leaf Mike Walton:

"Brian, we're in Los Angeles at this fancy restaurant. People driving up to the door in Rolls-Royces and sitting down next to us. Now we had just brought one of those blow-up dolls down the street, and we blew her up and brought her along. We brought her in the restaurant with us, as a date, eh! There were six of us.

"We put the blow-up doll down in a chair and ordered a full-course meal for her. Expensive, eh? Put a napkin around her neck. I said to her, 'Like some wine, dear? What kind of wine? How does the wine taste?' By then the guys were absolutely mental—and other diners, too. You have no idea. I'd say, 'You don't like the salad? What do you mean you don't like the salad? Just eat your friggin' salad.'

"The waiters in their tuxedos went absolutely nuts, eh! The other diners staring at us and pointing. And we're laughing like hyenas. That was one of the best nights we ever had.

"Then I really put on a show for them. I got mad and said to her, 'I don't like your tone of voice. You talking back to me? How dare you talk to me like that.' And I'd give her a little tap, and she'd rattle around in her chair. A couple of guys fell off their chairs laughing.

"Then we'd make up, and I put my arm around her—all lovey-dovey. The music started up, and I took her out on the floor, eh! The music was great, and we danced real close—cheek to cheek. And this was in one of the top restaurants in L.A. It was unbelievable. I think she had a good time, even though she never said so. But we sure did."

Do modern-day players ever pull stunts like Walton's? I don't think so.

And this from Canada's favourite "Dad" and his less-than-famous son. On a May day in 2014, Walter Gretzky and son Brent attended a golf tournament in London, Ontario. I chatted with Walter, my tape recorder spinning, and he told me how Wayne wanted him to retire from his job with the telephone company. Walter took a leave of absence, but decided he'd always told his kids not to rely on anyone else to look out for them, why should he let Wayne take care of things? So he went back to work.

Brent Gretzky was listening to all this, and he ran up to me afterwards:

"I've got to tell you this. Yeah, my dad took six months' leave of absence from Bell Canada. The night before he was supposed to go back to work, he went into the bedroom where Mom was sleeping. He shook her awake and he said, 'I'm going back to work. How do I explain to the rest of the kids how they've got to make their own way in life if I'm sitting back and not working?' So he turned down Wayne's offer to help him out.

"I was listening just now as my dad told you that story, and a light went on. I jumped out of my seat to tell you I can add to it. You know what? Back in 2004–05, Mom had just passed away. I'd just blown my shoulder out, and my hockey career was finished. So Wayne was gracious enough to call and say, 'I can help you out, Brent. There's an opportunity here in Los Angeles that's ideal for you. Come on out.' So I fly out on a private jet to L.A. and stayed at Wayne's house. The next day I meet with these men I didn't know, well—Eddie Mio was one, the former goalie and Wayne's good friend—and I was told what was happening with the restaurant. They'd be using Wayne's name, and Wayne said to me, 'Brent, these are good people. And you'll be one of the partners. Sounds great.'

"Well, I flew home thinking about the offer, and I said to my wife, 'What am I teaching my children if I let Wayne look after me? It's not how real life is like, or should be, when things are just handed to you. Right? When things are just given. Even though Wayne was awesome to say, 'I can help you out.' So who knows where that might have gone. But it's not what you're supposed to be teaching your kids.

"Tonight, when I heard my dad telling you his story, I jumped out of my seat. I wanted to tell you that's why my dad is my hero. He worked when he didn't have to work. For 34 years. He was proud. He didn't want to rely on Wayne. So I called Wayne and turned down the L.A. offer.

"After that, I worked at the GM plant in Belleville making headlights for $16 per hour. Then there was a big strike—in 2007, I guess it was—and everything went south. So I went into the OPP and I love it. That was the kind of career I wanted in the first place, ever since I was six years old.

"I have no regrets. I love my job."

In my chat with Walter, he told me the name Gretzky was originally spelled "Gretsky." But his grandfather, when he came to Canada, spelled the letter *S* backwards, and the name became "Gretzky."

We miss you, Walter.

Don "Sockeye" Uren was a laugh-provoking hockey trainer who was then with Chicago. He told me a little-known fact about the great Hawk goalie Glenn Hall:

"That's no bull about Glenn getting sick before the games and often between periods. He'd bring everything up.

"The only remedy we ever found that helped him was straight from Sockeye's medical book. Believe it or not, we started wrestling each other an hour or two before game time.

"Glenn would be Sweet Daddy Siki, and I'd be Bulldog Brower, and we'd clear the dressing room and go at it hammer and tongs. Anybody who saw us in there thought we were nuts. We'd beat the heck out of each other, and after a while, Glenn would call a halt and say he felt better and was ready to suit up. It was the only way we discovered to release Glenn's pre-game tension. But it sure was rough on me because I'd often be battered and bruised after Sweet Daddy got through with me.

"I loved Glenn Hall's humor. He said to me, 'When I read somewhere you scored a goal on me in junior, are you sure you didn't make up that crap? I'll bet you shot the puck 20 feet wide.'

"And when Montreal journalist Dave Stubbs visited the Hall farm for a few days and pocketed an acorn he found on the property, he confessed at the dinner table. 'Glenn, I took this acorn without asking.'

"Glenn said, 'So that's where it went.'"

It was a big thrill to interview the immortal Cyclone Taylor on *HNIC* one night. Approaching 90, Taylor made his way high onto a girder above the ice. And he was lugging a bouquet of flowers—a gift to me. That was a first.

I was so impressed with Taylor, I asked him if he'd skate with me on a future telecast.

"Yes, I can skate," he told me. "You'll be surprised. Of course I'll skate with you."

But our skate wasn't on *Hockey Night in Canada*. The producers thought he might fall down and embarrass himself. They vetoed the skate.

It took place on one of our NBC telecasts in Vancouver—circa 1974.

We circled the ice at the old Pacific Coliseum, and Taylor, just a bit unsteady, held my arm as we skated and talked. Another first.

The late John Candy was my guest on an intermission in Edmonton one night, and I was surprised at how nervous he was. "Geez, Brian," he said, "this is *Hockey Night in Canada*. This is huge for me."

On camera, I asked him about his passion for the game.

"Yeah, like all Canadian boys, I was born with a blanket and a hockey stick waiting for me. In East York, I played minor hockey and all through high school."

"John, on SCTV, I hear you talk about a team you played for in some obscure league?"

"That would be the Melonville Mexicans. We had a goalie named Eddie Lumley. A wonderful fellow, but a rotten goalie. The team owner, Chief Stoner, was arrested and thrown in jail for a number of crimes. So he took this fourth-string goalie and made him club president and team captain and, of course, number one goaltender. But Eddie had a rough time of it. He had a win and two ties and 700 losses.

"Eddie never played with a mask or a cup, and I think he should have worn the cup because there was an incident involving jewels I'd better not discuss. In his book *The Lumley Years, The Lonely Years*, he mentions that. It was a good book—sold seven copies—all of them in Melonville."

In 1994, while on vacation in Durango City, Mexico, Candy called CFL commissioner Larry Smith, to tell him he was putting the Toronto Argos up for sale. He then went to sleep. Sometime after midnight, on March 4, 1994, he was found dead from a presumed myocardial infarction, even though this was not proven, as no autopsy was performed. He was 43 years old. There was a family history of heart attacks.

Another good man gone.

Everybody loved John Candy.

CHAPTER 41

COLE AND GALLIVAN

In Winnipeg, Don Wittman was a versatile, gifted announcer who became a friend when we worked games together on *Hockey Night in Canada*. He could announce a game of tiddlywinks or mud wrestling and hold your attention. But we lost him to cancer in 2008 at age 71. Always smiling, he loved whatever assignment the CBC had in mind for him.

Former NHL goaltender John Davidson, who worked a lot of games on TV with Witt and me and others before getting in to NHL management, said of Witt, "He was a world-class broadcaster. For four decades he was at the top of his field in curling, in track and field, in the CFL and NHL and the Olympics. I don't know anybody else in any country who has done that."

Over the years, others won my respect for assisting and befriending me: Dave Hodge, Jack Dennett, Fred Sgambati, Bob Goldham, Jim Robson, Howie Meeker, Harry Neale, Dan Kelly, Joe Bowen, Gary Dornhoefer, Scott Oake, Gilles Tremblay, Bobby Orr, Dick Beddoes, Tim Ryan, and Ted Lindsay (on NBC) were all good companions in the booth or in the studio. I was there to see Dave Hodge and Don Cherry and Ron MacLean break in and soar in popularity over the years. They were "fun to be with" guys, and Grapes has always been most supportive. And Dick Irvin, of course, who almost couldn't afford to get into the business it paid so little. I had to prod him. Doug Beeforth, Rick Briggs-Jude, Joel Darling and others on the production side—and the guys at CHCH-TV in Hamilton for midweek games—were all supportive and very professional.

Ron Harrison was born to be a great director, and I missed him when he was elevated to executive producer, where he was less effective, in my opinion. Producer Mark Askin won my approval and respect and became my friend, and while I always had mixed emotions about my boss, Ted Hough, I enjoyed working with his son Jim on many intermission features.

The men and women on the NBC crew were fabulous.

I enjoy the current broadcasters, Chris Cuthbert, Jim Hughson, and Craig Simpson. And I liked Craig's sister Chris Simpson, one of the first—and best—female hockey broadcasters. I admire Cassie Campbell-Pascall, but I was gone before she arrived. And I respect guys like David Amber, Kelly Hrudey, Nick Kypreos, and Kevin Bieksa, a fresh new face and voice. Brian Burke was a bonus but moved on. Of course, they all do it better than we did. Every time I see them, I tell them so. And I was a huge fan of Doc Emrick, a top American broadcaster with a unique voice and delivery—now retired.

When I see Ed Olczyk on TV, I think of a good-looking 16-year-old coming up to me in the Chicago Stadium in the late '70s and saying, "Mr. McFarlane, my name is Ed Olczyk, and I'm going to play in the NHL someday." He sounded so sure of it. I guess I wasn't surprised when he was drafted third overall by Chicago in 1984 and played 16 seasons and more than one thousand games. Now he's an extremely talented broadcaster and a cancer survivor.

Eddie Olczyk has won a couple of Emmys, a Stanley Cup, and is a commentator at major horse races like the Kentucky Derby and the Belmont Stakes each year.

This brings me to Bob Cole and Danny Gallivan. And a story that came to me via another good friend, Joe Bowen.

It was June 4, 2018, and I was at our monthly hockey luncheon of old-timers, and Joe Bowen made a surprise appearance. The voice of the

Leafs for more than 30 years, Bowen sat next to me through lunch and attracted a lot of attention. I hear one old-timer congratulate him and I say, "Hey, what's happening? Why the congratulations?"

Bowen says, "Well, come November, they're putting me in that place you're in. I just heard this week."

"The Hockey Hall of Fame? Why, that's wonderful, Joe. So, deserving. I'm thrilled for you.

"Joe, this is huge. You are going in ahead of a lot of deserving broadcasters. This is a tremendous honour for you."

"I thought this might be Grapes's year," he said. "I'm a very lucky man."

We agree that Grapes should have been inducted long ago. The guy with the largest weekly audience of any hockey broadcaster—and a faithful audience in the millions—can't find a berth in the Hall? Ridiculous. "They should put Cherry and Maclean in together," I said. "Then again, maybe not. They're obviously not as close as they once were."

A lot of guys in the broadcasting community—guys with votes—hesitate about casting a ballot for Grapes. Do they not consider him a legitimate broadcaster? He can be overlooked for various honours year after year and yet be named one of the top 10 Canadians. I don't get it.

"On another note," says Bowen, "have you ever heard of Newfie shin-kicking?"

"No. Never have."

"Well, early in the playoffs a couple of seasons ago, Bob Cole, Ron MacLean, and I were in a hotel room having some pops, and Cole, who does have an Order of Canada, brought it up. 'Come on, guys, let's indulge in a bit of Newfie shin-kicking.'

"I said, 'Bob, what exactly is that?'

"'It's a test of courage. Someone kicks you in the shins, and you get to kick him back.'

"I told Cole I wasn't exactly eager to find out more. But MacLean, who'd had a few more pops than I, said he'd be willing to try it.

"So, Cole says, 'Okay, you kick me first.'

"And MacLean takes aim and gives Cole a kick to the shins. But it was a harmless kick, no real force to it."

Bowen says, "Now Cole steps up and crashes a big foot into MacLean's shins. Jesus! Cole is over 80, and he almost broke MacLean's leg. MacLean is howling, and the rest of us are in shock. We'd all heard how Cole was a tough customer on the ice when he played hockey as a youth. But that was 60, 70 years ago.

"So be warned," says Bowen, "If anyone suggests a game of Newfie shin-kicking, take a pass. Coley is the unofficial world champion. And know this. Whoever gets the second kick wins the game."

But let's give Cole credit. He outlasted all of us. And he's earned the plaudits he's received. He once took time to send me a note complimenting me on an All-Star Game I hosted. A small gesture perhaps, but one I've not forgotten. And I enjoyed working with him when he took over from Bill Hewitt after Bill's sad breakdown.

Bob Cole established himself as one of the best hockey announcers in the game. He's the King of Newfoundland. And I'm guessing he wears a pair of shin guards under his pants at all times—in case anyone tougher challenges him to a game of shin-kicking.

This brings me to Danny Gallivan. When Bill Hewitt became ill one season, Gallivan filled in for midweek games on CHCH-TV in Hamilton. Gallivan was a joy to work with—a real hockey guy. And a baseball nut, too.

He was with me for a game in Minnesota one night. During the intermission, we were part of a panel (Dave Hodge and Dick Beddoes the others) discussing the fact that Darryl Sittler had opted out of the game and stayed home—a huge story at the time. I defended Sittler's decision to call in sick—he was under great mental and emotional stress—but Ballard was furious with my opinions and demanded that I be replaced.

I learned later that Sittler's stress level was elevated even higher back home when teammate Terry Martin's wife collapsed, and Darryl, thinking it might be a life-threatening situation, raced to the Martin home to offer what help he could.

I thought hard about what I would say about all this on TV. During our panel discussion, I wanted to support Sittler, but I was well aware that Imlach, coach Mike Nykoluk, and Ballard would be enraged if I did.

I thought I chose my words carefully, suggesting that Imlach and the Leafs might consider treating Sittler the way the Philadelphia Flyers treated their team captain, Bobby Clarke. Whatever I said, it caused Ballard to go ballistic—but only after his flunky, Stan Obodiac, happily told him of my comments. Ballard hadn't heard or seen the TV segment, but Obodiac made sure he got a full description the following day. Ballard told my bosses at *Hockey Night in Canada* that I'd never be allowed in his building ever again.

Flying back from that game, I began to realize my career might be over. Danny Gallivan, sitting next to me, was honest with me. He said he thought so, too.

"As soon as you started in to defend Sittler, I knew you were in trouble," he told me. "I tended to agree with you, but when my turn came, I mealy-mouthed something about a player's commitment to his team. Team owners and managers can get really nasty if you don't always agree with them. When you get back home, take the phone off the hook."

Before I could get it off the hook, it rang.

"Brian, its Frank Selke. You won't be working any more games as colour man for the Leafs. Ballard is furious and initially he wanted you gone. But Dick Beddoes and Dave Hodge have pleaded with him on your behalf, and he softened a bit. He'll allow you to do the post-game show, and that's about it. The good news is, now we can use you as host of the Winnipeg Jets telecasts. So, you'll still be involved."

Good news? Being banned from the Gardens was good news. I never worked another game in the famous gondola. Sadly, the rapport and bonding I felt with Gallivan was gone, too. A real loss. But I was the dummy. I screwed up. The only consolation I had was having Darryl Sittler express his sincere thanks for sticking up for him during those trying days.

I agreed to work the Winnipeg games and commuted there for four years. I enjoyed the relaxed atmosphere in Winnipeg and the words of welcome I received. Then followed four more seasons working games in

Montreal, where I reconnected with my pal Dick Irvin. There I got to work with Danny Gallivan once again—a bonus, even if my role was in the studio, not the broadcast booth. He would soon retire after calling Montreal games for 32 years.

Gallivan was a fascinating character with great charm and personality. He invited me to speak at his annual golf tournament in Halifax one year, and I watched in amazement at how he handled the crowd at the banquet that followed.

All the golfers present, beer and wine glasses in hand, were at their tables laughing and chattering loudly. Gallivan got up and moved to the microphone at the head table. At first, few noticed. He stood there. No tapping of the microphone, no motion of his hands calling for silence. He simply stood there. Seconds passed, and some attendees began to sense his presence. They glanced up, nudged others, whispered. Suddenly, a hush fell over the room.

It's the hush I remember. It was a total hush caused by utmost respect for the man behind the mic. Like nothing I'd seen before.

I mean total respect. And affection.

Gallivan smiled. "Gentlemen," he began.

You may have heard the story of how Gallivan insisted on working with a microphone he held in his hand. He rebelled when the new headset mics were in vogue. But he finally agreed to use them. Still, he wanted to hold a microphone even though it was not "live." A prop.

One night, Gallivan turned to statistician Ron Andrews, who sat nearby, thrust his hand mic in Andrews's face, and asked him to confirm a stat Gallivan had mentioned.

The answer could barely be heard. Andrews was talking into a dead mic.

We all chuckled over that. But nobody ever laughed at Danny Gallivan. Or mocked him. He was a legend and deserves a few more paragraphs in this book because he was such an icon and was so interesting.

Danny's first choice as a career was professional baseball.

Between 1932 and 1938 he was the best baseball pitcher in Nova Scotia. In 1938, he was invited to the New York Giants' tryout camp, where he rubbed shoulders with Giants greats Mel Ott and Carl Hubbell. Scouting reports indicated he had the "best fastball and best curve ball" in camp and was the "most consistent batter".

But somehow he injured his arm and shoulder. Giants trainers told him if he continued to throw hard he might "end up disabled" and that he'd "pitched too often when his body was still developing." He left baseball, went to college and found his place in broadcasting.

When he switched off his microphone, Gallivan had called more than 1,800 NHL games. He was the Ironman of broadcasters. Twenty-two years passed before he missed a game through illness in 1974.

When he retired, he became a goodwill ambassador for *Hockey Night in Canada*. Dick Irvin says that every time Gallivan appeared in person at an event—it didn't matter how many famous athletes were there—if Gallivan were at the head table, he was the number one attraction.

Gallivan died in his sleep in his Nuns' Island apartment in Montreal in 1993. He was 75.

CHAPTER 42

SCOTTY BOWMAN: BORN TO COACH

Before I worked with Scotty Bowman on numerous *Hockey Night in Canada* games, most of them in Montreal, I approached him at the Mount Royal Hotel one summer day. I was writing a hockey history book and I wanted his story in it, how he led the St. Louis Blues to three straight Stanley Cup Finals in the late 1960s. This was in June 1971, and we met in the hotel lobby. Before we began taping an interview, he cautioned me. "Brian, this is a very difficult time for me, and I won't be able to give you much of a story. I can tell you this. In all probability, I won't be back coaching the Blues next season."

That was a surprise. "How come?" I asked.

"Well, I don't want to tell you that. Or anyone else. Not right now."

"Are you moving to another club, Scotty?"

"Again, I can't talk about that, either. So, if you don't mind, let's postpone our interview until I know exactly what's going to happen."

I agreed, thinking it was good of him to meet with me and explain his feelings.

What impressed me was that he confided in me. He'd given me a little scoop. But I didn't work for a newspaper or a radio station. So, news that he might be leaving St. Louis was relatively safe with me. I didn't know Bowman well at the time, although we would become close years later when he worked as a regular analyst on *Hockey Night in Canada*.

Later, I would discover that a few harsh words in St. Louis with the owners of the Blues—the Salomon family—led to Bowman's departure and a second stint with the Montreal Canadiens. That was the season (1971) the Montreal Canadiens won the Stanley Cup under coach Al MacNeil. But MacNeil couldn't possibly survive in Montreal—not as coach and not with the French media—after Henri Richard had roasted him in the 1971 playoffs. "He's the worst coach I ever played for," Richard stated emphatically.

MacNeil was dispatched to Halifax to coach the Habs' AHL farm club, and before the door closed behind him, Sam Pollock was on the phone to Scotty Bowman, his first choice to replace MacNeil.

Bowman jumped at the opportunity to return to Montreal. He had begun his hockey career with the Canadiens organization in 1954, as an assistant to Sam Pollock, then manager of the Hull-Ottawa Junior Habs. Prior to the 1967–68 expansion season, with the NHL about to double in size, Bowman moved up to the Blues, where he soon replaced Lynn Patrick as coach and guided the Blues to the Stanley Cup Finals for the next three seasons.

His greatest coaching successes came after he donned his Montreal cap. In eight seasons the teams he coached captured the Stanley Cup five times. From 1975–76 through 1978–79, his teams were the class of the NHL, winning 229 games while losing a mere 46. During the 1976–77 season, Bowman's Habs won a record 60 games of 80 played and lost only eight. It was a mark that stood until the 1995–96 campaign, when Detroit, another Bowman-coached team, captured 62 wins in the 82-game schedule. In 2019, Tampa Bay tied the NHL record for wins, with 62, and amassed 128 points, fourth-best in NHL history.

Bowman is the winningest coach ever and has 14 Stanley Cup rings to prove it. Nine as a head coach and five as a team executive. He was inducted into the Hockey Hall of Fame in 1991. That early honour puzzled me. The Hall's selection committee usually waits until a builder, manager, or coach is fully retired before ushering him in. Perhaps someone said, "Hell, Scotty will never retire. Let's put him in now." He is the only coach to win the Cup with three different teams (Montreal, Pittsburgh, and Detroit).

When he was coach and GM of the Buffalo Sabres, we met one day in the lobby of the Westin Hotel in Winnipeg. We talked about several players he'd coached. I asked Bowman to name one or two who stood out above the rest for dedication and discipline—players he could always count on.

I thought he might begin with Guy Lafleur, or perhaps Gilbert Perreault. He thought for a few seconds. "Yeah, I think Bob Gainey in Montreal—and Doug Jarvis—were those kind of guys. And Jacques Lemaire. You could always count on Lemaire in a big game. And Serge Savard, of course. You see, those fellows knew how to play the game. You never had to tell them how to do this or that. They knew the game. On the Sabres, Craig Ramsay is that way. He's a hockey man. He knows how to win. The trouble we have in Buffalo is not having a natural leader. We don't have a Bobby Clarke type. Now, Gilbert Perreault is a wonderful hockey player—one of the best—but he's not a leader. Not the way Clarke is."

Bowman celebrated his 14th Stanley Cup championship with the Chicago Blackhawks as the team's senior advisor for hockey operations. Bowman's son, Stan, who is named after the Cup, is the Blackhawks' general manager and vice-president. "When Stan was born," Bowman told me years ago, "I called him Stanley Cup. But when I filled out some forms one day, he heard me tell a clerk my son's name was Stanley. Stan started to cry, 'Dad, you mean my name's not Stanley Cup anymore?' I said, 'Son, you'll always be Stanley Cup to me.' Now, he's won two of them in Chicago, and he's only 39. I only had one by that age."

Bowman learned the hockey business from former Canadiens GM Sam Pollock, a Hall of Famer who led the Canadiens to nine Stanley Cups during his 14 years as general manager of the Habs from 1964 to 1978.

"Sam wasn't interested in coaching," Bowman said. We had a good relationship. I really didn't want to be the manager, and he didn't want to be the coach. Sam always got good players for me. It's a big plus when your manager gets you good players."

When Pollock decided to move on after the 1978 Stanley Cup, the Canadiens hired Irving Grundman as his replacement, instead of Bowman. It was a surprise to me. I'd known Grundman from my days at CFCF-TV. Dick Irvin and I had done bowling shows from Grundman's Laurentian Lanes. He'd never talked hockey with us. He was a businessman, not a hockey man.

With Grundman as GM and Bowman as coach, the Canadiens won their fourth straight Stanley Cup in 1979. By then they were barely speaking.

On June 11, 1979, Bowman announced he was leaving the Canadiens to become coach and GM of the Buffalo Sabres.

"There was no room for Irving Grundman and me on the same team," Bowman said at his farewell press conference.

"I couldn't tolerate the way Grundman directed the club. I had no respect for him as a hockey man."

In 2007, I asked Bowman if he'd have taken the Canadiens GM job if it had been offered to him.

"The GM's job is always a better job than coach. But I got an opportunity to go to Buffalo as GM and coach, which was a much more lucrative position."

Bowmans parents came over from Scotland many decades ago and settled in Montreal. They knew nothing of hockey and were surprised when their son became immersed in it. Bowman told me they soon learned an old Canadian custom—ordering from the Eaton's catalogue. His mom bought a chair from the catalogue and had it delivered cash-on-delivery (COD). Bowman's dad was home alone when the big box arrived—labelled *COD*.

"What in hell did she order all that cod for?" he grumbled. "We'll never eat all that."

George Morrison, one of our NHL Oldtimers, told me his favourite Scotty Bowman stories one day. Bowman was his coach in St. Louis:

"Scotty suffered a serious head injury while playing junior hockey, and we all heard he had a plate in his head. So, one day I cut out a big cardboard horseshoe with a magnet on the end of it and I hung it over the dressing room door. That's where Scotty always stood when he made his pre-game speech. Well, Scotty came in this night and he was ticked off about something. You so-and-sos had better do this, you better do that, you know, giving everybody shit.

"And the guys kept looking up at this big horseshoe over his head—pasted up there. They just couldn't control themselves, couldn't stop laughing. Glenn Hall put his goal mask on to hide his laughter, and the players were just about falling on the floor laughing. And Scotty couldn't understand what everybody was laughing at. And nobody was about to tell him.

"You should have been there the night Scotty called me a dog. That's right. He said to me, 'Hey, Morrison, you are a dog!' And then he started barking at me. Ruf! Ruf! Ruf! I thought he was going to put a leash on me. Maybe pat me on the head—with a fist.

"We were on a road trip out west, and Scotty wasn't playing me at all. Against the Kings, I sat at the end of the bench when an usher whispered to me, 'George, can I have your stick after the game?' I said, 'Sure, if you'll get me a hot dog and a drink.' He was back in minutes, and I munched on the hot dog when Scotty wasn't looking. Then, uh-oh—we had a penalty, and I heard Scotty shout, 'Morrison, get out there! Kill that penalty!'

"Geez, I dumped the drink on the floor and stuffed the rest of the hot dog down the cuff of my hockey glove. But on the ice, a guy whacked my hand and the hot dog flew into the air. The Kings' goalie, Rogie Vachon, swept it into his net, and there was a line change. Scotty never did find out where that hot dog came from—but he knows now."

Morrison died young in 2008, while coaching women's hockey at Union College in Schenectady, New York.

I enjoyed working with Bowman when he joined us for a season or two on *Hockey Night in Canada*. He was totally focused on the game, as I soon found out. I flew from Toronto to Montreal on a flight that encountered extreme turbulence one day. Went straight to the Forum for the morning skate and ran into Bowman. "Geez, that was a nasty flight in, Scotty," I told him.

"Yeah, well the Montreal power play is lousy," he answered. I got it. Forget your lousy flight. Stick to hockey.

I once asked Bowman if he'd give me a blurb to put on the dust jacket of a hockey history book I was writing. He came back with a solid one-liner: "If it's not in this book, it didn't happen."

CHAPTER 43

SMALL WORLD STORIES

Here's a small world story.

I was at the beach in Naples, Florida, one Thursday having coffee with Joan and her fitness class friends—about 12 of us at the long table. I'd just been on my computer in the condo writing about the great Russian player Valeri Kharlamov, but I'd struggled with an ending to the story and decided to take a coffee break with the fitness people. At the beach, a woman we'd never seen before approached our table. She was younger than most of us, a good-looking stranger wearing a broad-brimmed hat and sunglasses. There was one seat left at the table—next to me—and she nodded hello and sat in it. She began talking to the man across from her, and I resumed a conversation I was having with the person to my right.

A few minutes later, I overheard the name "Kharlamov" and I reacted instantly. "Pardon me," I said to the newcomer. "Did you just mention the name 'Kharlamov'—the Russian hockey player?"

She smiled. "Yes, I did."

"But how on earth would you know him?" I asked.

"First, let me introduce myself. My name is Anna—Anna Berger—and I now live in Boston. But I come from Riga, in Latvia."

"And Kharlamov? You knew him?"

"Of course. Valeri left his wife for me. We were in love. We stayed together for five years—in Moscow. Then he told me it—our affair—was over. He missed his family, his children. So, he went back to them. And not long after, there was the tragic accident. He and his wife were killed. Do you know about that?"

"Yes, I do," I said. "A car accident. In Moscow."

"And did you know him, too?"

"No, not really. I saw him play with Team Russia in 1972. But I was just writing about him this morning for a hockey book. And I didn't have a good ending for my story, so I came here to the beach. And suddenly you came along and sat with us. If I'd been sitting anywhere else at this table, I'd never have heard you say 'Kharlamov.'"

She laughed and said, "He was such a wonderful man. And so popular. In Moscow, we could never go anywhere without his fans approaching him for autographs, for photos."

"Well, yes," I agreed. "He was one of the greatest players in the world. I'm from Canada, and Canadians put him on a huge pedestal after the big series in 1972. He was brilliant—until Bobby Clarke slashed him with a two-hander and put him out."

We talked hockey for a few minutes—and more about Kharlamov. We ignored the others at the table. Before she got up to leave, she scribbled her Boston phone number on a slip of paper.

"Call me if I can help you with your book," she said. "I'm pleased you are finding a place in it for Valeri."

Of course, I lost her number, never saw her again. The fitness ladies were puzzled.

"She seemed nice," they said. "But where did she come from? Why did she come sit with us—all strangers to her? Is she coming back?"

"I don't think so," I told them. "But she just gave me a good ending to a story I'm writing about a Russian hockey player."

Sometime later, I'm back again at the beach, having coffee with the same fitness people.

But I notice a new face in the gathering. She notices the hockey cap I'm wearing and comes over. "You must be Brian, the hockey guy" she says. "My name is Anna, and I'm a hockey mom." But she wasn't just any hockey mom. When she told me her full name was Anna Moore from Thornhill, Ontario, I was astonished. She was Steve Moore's mom—and Dominic's, who played for 10 NHL teams. Both Harvard grads. There was a third brother—Mark—also a Harvard grad, who did not turn pro. She told me how her family life was affected, and how the family business was all but destroyed after the brutal beating laid on son Steve by Todd Bertuzzi years ago. Moore's head injuries were so severe that his parents were too distraught to focus on business. Their son's NHL career was destroyed in a matter of seconds by a premeditated vengeful act of on-ice violence. He will never lead a normal life. And there was a multi-million-dollar lawsuit against Bertuzzi, the Vancouver Canucks, and the NHL that was settled out of court. For years after his attack, Bertuzzi continued to play in the NHL, earning millions. I asked Anna Moore if she'd talk into my tape recorder, but she declined because of the lawsuit. Steve's lawyer Tim Danson, was once my lawyer. Danson gained fame when he filed on behalf of the victims of murderers Paul Bernardo and Karla Homolka—the Mahaffy and French families. Danson represented me—very professionally, I might add—in a case involving a young lawyer with another firm who mangled a contract I had with a major Canadian bank.

I'm amazed at how many simpletons defended Bertuzzi's unpardonable actions. Moore made it clear he wanted his day in court. He wanted his story told. Since Bertuzzi almost killed him, he wanted it known that his attacker has earned more than $30 million in hockey salary.

Ten years after the attack Moore's lawsuit was amended, seeking $68 million in damages, up from $38 million. On August 19, 2014, it was announced that an out-of-court settlement had been reached, but terms of the settlement are confidential.

Perhaps someday, Anna Moore will tell me more about the tragedy that changed the course of her son's life. She did come to our condo to look at my pond hockey paintings. She bought three—one for each of her sons.

I'll close this chapter with a story even I found hard to believe.

As a Centennial project in 1967, my wife and I bought an Apache tent-top trailer and took a six-week trip with the kids across Canada. From Ontario to Tofino, B.C., on the west coast of Vancouver Island, stopping at trailer parks and campsites along the way.

"I want you to see our beautiful country," I told them. "Next summer we'll go east—to the Maritimes and Newfoundland."

One night, camping on the north shore of Lake Superior, we put the kids to bed and joined a couple camping not far from us. We went to their trailer for a beer—a single beer.

At about 10 p.m., we said goodnight and returned to our campsite. Joan had a flashlight and went down a path to a privy. I looked at the skyline and noticed a small light glowing far off in the distance—to the north.

"That's odd," I said to myself. "There's nothing up there. No roads, no campsites. Nothing."

Just then Joan came back, and I mentioned the strange light.

"Maybe it's a car light," she said. "Or kids waving a flashlight—like this."

She took her own flashlight and waved it in the air.

To our absolute amazement, the small glow near the horizon hurtled toward us at rocket speed.

"Put out the damn flashlight," I shouted.

And she did.

Now the small glowing light was a huge glowing mass hovering over us.

"Gotta be a UFO," I said.

Be a good reporter, I thought. I did a question-and-answer with myself.

Brian, can you describe it?

Well, it's dark in the middle and with most of the glow graduating to the circumference.

How high in the sky is it?

Don't know. Maybe three thousand feet. Maybe five thousand.

How big is it?

Can't tell. Maybe one hundred feet in diameter. Maybe two hundred. Or more.

Hear any sound from it? See any entrance to it?

No, neither.

How long has it hovered overhead?

About five minutes now.

Joan and I talked, almost in whispers. We agreed it was awesome. We were more astonished than frightened. Joan suggested it might be ready to scoop us up. "But it appears they've rejected us."

Then, as suddenly as it appeared, it silently flashed north at incredible speed and was lost to sight in a second. I mean a second.

It was obviously a UFO and I was thrilled to have seen it. I promised myself to write a report to the government agency in charge of such things.

And days later, I did.

We heard there were many sightings that year around the Great Lakes, both in the U.S. and Canada.

If I told goalie Glenn Hall this small world story he'd scoff and say, "Come on. You sure you're not making up this crap?"

Years ago, we spent a week in Barbados. Rented a car early one morning and toured the island. Coming back late in the day and still 40 miles away from our hotel, Joan suggested I turn the car lights on. I couldn't find the light switch on the foreign vehicle so, impulsively, I turned left onto the street of a small town and stopped by the curb. A man approached and we put our windows down.

"Can I help you, sir?" he asked.

"Perhaps," I said. "It's a rental car and I can't seem to find the light switch."

He grinned and said, "Well, I forgot to show you that."

He found it in five seconds

"You don't recognize me, sir?" he said.

Our mouths flew open. It was the man who rented us the car that morning—40 miles away.

What brought him to that place at that precise time to greet us as we made a random stop, remains a mystery. One even the Hardy Boys could not solve.

CHAPTER 44

COUNTRY LIVING

We bought some property in 1972. I felt the need to own something, I think, because my dad always rented the homes we lived in. He never owned a house or a car until his second marriage. Even then, he never drove.

We found a hundred acres north of Port Hope, Ontario, that we liked. We explored the land, found a spot where we could dig a pond, a place to build a log house, and were leaving when I encountered a man walking his dog. We got chatting, and I told him I was enthused about the property.

"It's just the kind of place we're looking for," I told him. "And the price seems fair."

We parted, and the bad news came the following day as we were preparing our offer.

The man with the dog bought the property and paid cash.

I was despondent. And my wife was, too.

She said, "There you go. Always talking to strangers."

Sometime later, we purchased 37 acres farther east of Toronto, but ideal for our needs. And for $14,000, less than half the price of the Port Hope property.

It had a pond site, a trout stream, a back pasture, a home site, and an abundance of trees.

We camped out on the property initially. A kind neighbour drove up in a pickup truck and dropped off an outhouse. "You'll need one of these, and we don't use it anymore." he said. And we had a pond dug the size of a football field, which soon filled with 16 feet of spring water.

I went up to Quebec and bought two tumbledown log homes, a small shed, and a much larger one that once belonged to the Hudson Bay Company, where they had stored the company's canoes.

The canoe shed, a beauty, cost me $300. "For another $300," the owner said, "I'll deliver the logs. And a bunch of other logs, too. I drive an 18-wheeler."

He delivered them all. A great deal.

In Quebec, I hired a local old-timer with a tractor to help me pull the log homes apart. His tractor had been stored in a shed all winter and spring.

"When I went in to get 'er started," he told me, "I found my false teeth in the tool box. For months I wondered where they'd been."

We love this property. We held our daughter's wedding reception—120 guests—in the canoe shed. But, of course, there were problems. My neighbour's son and six of his buddies broke into our house one night and vandalized the place. They took a chainsaw to our furniture and used my vintage axe to chop into walls and floors.

And the same axe to total a station wagon I parked in the driveway to let people know we were home. "I guess they don't like my hockey announcing," I said to Joan.

"Perhaps it's your writing," she said.

And the same axe and saw to savage another house belonging to an award-winning architect who lived about five hundred yards away.

"Well, it appears they don't like architects, either," Joan said.

In time they were all apprehended and charged. But most were young offenders and were given a slap on the wrist. The ringleader, 19, was given a two-year prison term. He'd been doing other naughty stuff. None of the parents called, and nobody ever apologized.

My neighbours to the south had sons, too. These were the folks who sold us the acreage. The teenagers cut down a bunch of cedars to make fence posts. But the trees were on my property. My cedars. I found them shooting a .22 into my pond one day and chased them through the woods, thinking this is a dumb idea. They could turn around and shoot me.

Luckily, both neighbours moved away.

I stocked the pond with trout, but people, aware that I was working a hockey game in Montreal, came around and augered holes in the ice and stole all my fish.

We had ducks on the pond and a feeding place for them. But hunters came along, surrounded the pond, and shot all the ducks—about 20 of them.

I bought a nice wooden sign and had the name *HONEYWELL* painted on it. The name of the former owners. I hung the sign on a roadside post, and the next morning it was gone. Stolen.

I was alone in the log house one night when a loud thumping on the door woke me up. It was dawn, and four husky guys were at my back door.

"Can we use your phone, mister?" one of them called through the door. "Our car broke down."

Their small car was in my driveway, next to my station wagon.

I let one of them in—after I grabbed a long knife from a drawer—but not the others. And it was bitterly cold out.

He called for help.

"Someone's coming to pick us up," I was told. He rejoined his pals, and I locked the door after him.

They waited outside, drinking beer.

I loaded my .22—just in case—and watched them.

Half an hour later, another car appeared and whisked them away.

I went outside and examined their car. Then my own. There were tools on the ground, and someone had tampered with my car's side window—driver's side.

Turns out they'd tried to take the drive shaft out of my car and somehow insert it in theirs. Is that even possible?

I called the Ontario Provincial Police (OPP), who appeared in minutes. They arranged for the small car to be towed away.

When the four husky guys returned, they shouted through the door. "Where's our car?"

I shouted back "Somebody broke into my car, so the OPP had it towed into town."

"It wasn't us."

"Tell it to the cops. They're on their way."

The OPP arrested them. Took them away.

I wondered if they might return one night and burn down my house. Or inflict some bodily harm. I kept my .22 close at hand. When they appeared before the judge, we were comforted when he said, "If anything happens at the McFarlane place, the OPP will know where to go to charge you guys, and you are ordered to pay for the damage you did to the McFarlane car."

Country living. It's such fun.

My wife was alone in the kitchen one day when she heard a car door slam. She looked out the window and saw a stranger hop over the cedar rail fence and stroll up to the front door. Did he knock? No, he tried the door, opened it, and walked in, right in to our living room area. My wife came around the corner from the kitchen and went on the attack.

"What are you doing in here?"

He was startled. "Oh, nothing. I didn't think anyone was home."

"Obviously," she shouted. "You get the hell out!" And he ran. Disappeared down the road. I'm surprised she didn't run after him and tackle him. And give him a good lecture.

I admonished her. Told her she should have called the OPP.

I bought Joan a new tiller for her garden. Used it once and put it in the unlocked shed. Closed the gate but left it unlocked. We went into town for a couple of hours and when we came back, the tiller was gone. So were some hanging flower baskets we'd just hung.

Other than these incidents, it's idyllic there.

The people who lived just a few hundred yards south of us were the Doigs. Nice folks who invited us to a family skating party one winter.

They'd rented the local indoor rink, and I was told to bring a hockey stick. During the party, sides were chosen, and a fast game of hockey played. The best player on the ice was Peter Doig, a son home from England, where he was studying.

Peter and I bonded briefly that day. I was impressed with his skating and playmaking. But I never saw him again.

About 30 years later, I read about him being involved in some court case where someone was trying to impersonate him and his paintings. I Googled Peter Doig and to my consternation found that he was a world-famous artist. In 2007, Peter Doig went from being a relatively unknown painter to an art-world sensation when his work *White Canoe*—created 16 years earlier—was auctioned for $11.3 million.

Come on. Nobody sells 16-year-old paintings in that price range. But Peter Doig does. I was also painting by then, but lacked his creative magic and have achieved much less acclaim, fame, and fortune—not even a million for one of my acrylics.

Well, not yet. And some of mine will soon be 16 years old.

Peter Doig and I have been exchanging emails. He lives in Trinidad. He's a Habs fan, and when he was back in Canada a few seasons ago, he was invited to visit the Montreal dressing room. P.K. Subban told him, "I always wanted to be an artist, Peter, but I got so good at hockey I couldn't afford to consider another career."

Doig painted a lovely painting of our log home. No, I don't have the original. But his father gave us a nice print. Peter says when he's ready to build an ice rink in Trinidad, he'll let me know. Maybe we can play shinny there. I'll put him in touch with Jet Ice, a company founded by my good friend Doug Moore, once the chief engineer at Maple Leaf Gardens. Moore died too soon to cancer. His daughter Debbie (Wilcock) stepped in and made Jet Ice world famous. She can advise Peter on how to make good ice in a Trinidad rink. Someday, perhaps I'll travel to Trinidad and visit Peter Doig. I'm sure he'd like to hear my tips on how to paint pond hockey scenes in acrylics. They should sell well in Trinidad.

CHAPTER 45

SUMMING UP

At speaking engagements, I often recite the following, a poem I wrote 10 years ago. One night a couple applauded wildly when I finished. Alas, I learned later they were both deaf.

GIVE ME OLD-TIME HOCKEY

Give me old-time hockey, the Original Six.
CCM Tacks and wooden sticks.
Give me three-dollar tickets for an NHL tilt
In those old-time arenas, the best ever built.
Parking on the street, a brisk walk to the rink.
Ten cents for a hot dog, 10 cents for a drink.
We knew all the players from the subs to the aces
No helmets, no visors hiding their faces.
There's Johnny Bower stopping pucks with his chin.
He just stopped the Rocket from putting one in.
The Rocket and Gordie were the best of the lot.
And Beliveau the classiest—at least, that's what I thought.
Bring back Dave Keon, Tim Horton, and Baun.

They were my heroes, where have they gone?
Boom Boom and Shackie and the Golden Jet
Providing thrills one can never forget.
Bring back the Hewitts—Danny Gallivan, too.
Hockey Night legends we all listened to.
Bring back games of shinny played on pond and street.
Hurly-burly action, frozen noses and feet.
Hand-me-down skates, sticks worn thin at the blade.
Pucks lost in snowbanks, memories that never fade.
Wind stinging our eyes, frost-bitten faces
Fingers so numb you can't tie your laces.
Endless games of shinny, played at 30 below.
Shovels at rinkside to scrape off the snow.
Tattered old sweaters, toques on our heads.
Picking sides, "You're blue, we're reds."
Dozens of kids on similar rinks all over town
Yelping and laughing and having fun
Whooping it up until the sun goes down.
That's when it all began for me, my love for the game.
Stompin' Tom immortalized it as "the best game you can name."
It's a lovely game of speed and skill and the crunch of body contact.
And while I long for old-time hockey, I know it won't come back.
So, raise your glasses in a toast as we gather here together
To the joy of old-time hockey, alas, it's gone forever.

So, here I am, my 90th birthday behind me, living in a world so unlike the one I was born into. And finishing another book in the middle of a pandemic.

I write my books and paint my pond hockey scenes that sell reasonably well because they take the buyer back to their beginnings. But I seldom see youngsters playing pond hockey today. There are fewer ponds to skate on, and often there are barriers. *No Trespassing* signs, sturdy metal fences, unpredictable ice conditions, fear of a kid drowning or being bowled over by an older, bigger kid with no referee to interfere. Perhaps the simple but genuine fear of letting a son or daughter leave the house for hours without knowing exactly where they are. Most parents prefer to put their kids in structured hockey, played indoors, in full equipment, in heated arenas, where they can watch in comfort, drink bad coffee, and mingle with other parents.

Wayne Gretzky said recently, "If you take a bunch of kids to a frozen pond today, they'll say, 'Okay, what do we do now?'"

And yet. There are dozens of pond hockey tournaments played each year in places far and wide. Organized tournaments. With hundreds of men and women and youngsters participating.

There was so much more I might have written about in this book. Little-known stories I seek and often find. Perhaps I should have mentioned some of the perks a broadcaster might receive, like riding in an open convertible in the Calgary Stampede parade, being named King of the Malone, N.Y, Winter Carnival, and King of Octoberfest in Kitchener, and that memorable weekend at Gander Days in Newfoundland, to mention a few.

I think of the birth of a pro lacrosse league in 1968 and how I raised my hand at the initial meeting in answer to the question, "Who wants the Montreal franchise?" No other hands were raised so I suddenly owned a team I would call—with permission—the Montreal Canadiens. Toronto, Detroit, and Peterborough were rival cities. I drafted well, mostly Ontario players because the Quebec League decided to ban for life any player who even tried out for my Canadiens. So, I hired hockey star John Ferguson as general manager and he made a big difference. When the Montreal Forum became unavailable because of major renovations, I booked Paul Sauve Arena for home games. Knowing it was risky to put an all-English team in a mostly French community, I lured one star away from the Quebec League and paid him top dollar. And I found two Indigenous players from the Kahnawake Reserve who fit right in. My team, thanks to Fergie and his assistant, ex-NHLer Bob Lemieux, made it to the finals but lost to Peterborough. I don't think either Fergie or Lemieux cashed a paycheque. The league soon folded but it triggered a lot of interest.

In recent days, my research revealed a professional hockey league in Florida in 1938–39—the Tropical Hockey League. One team was from Havana, Cuba, the other three from South Florida. Imagine Havana having a pro hockey team. A nation with no rinks and no players. No pucks and no skates or sticks. All games were played in an arena in Miami, and King Clancy, vacationing in the area, refereed a few games. All but three players were from Canada. The league folded after a single season of 14 games. Winnipeg's Mike Goodman—a former member of the Winnipeg Falcons, who won the gold medal in hockey for Canada in the 1920 Summer Olympics—starred for the league champion Coral Gables Seminoles as player-coach.

I love finding hockey stories like that.

On the lighter side, there was playing golf, with notables like Moe Norman, Lorie Kane, Bobby Orr, Mario Lemieux, Gordon Lightfoot, Johnny Bower, Ted Lindsay, the Good Brothers. With me always in the woods or the water. My wife's had a hole-in-one, and I've never come close. Well, once I did. I had a five.

My worst round ever? That's easy. I hadn't played in a few years, while we were building our log home in the country. Then came an invitation to play in a hockey players' tournament in Cobourg. I agreed to play, but insisted they put me in the worst grouping possible. As a joke, they placed me in the top foursome, with the famous pro Moe Norman and two of the club's champions. I looked around, and a gallery was forming—maybe 50 people, all there to see Norman.

"This isn't a scramble?" I asked.

"No, sir. It's keep your own score, and all these guys should break par."

I almost had a meltdown. Too late to back out. So I played and I was dreadful. The gallery members shook their heads in sympathy. The two club champs wanted to beat Moe Norman and they were deadly serious. Norman kept saying each time I emerged from the woods, "Come on, come on. Let's go. Let's pick it up."

I wanted to pick up my ball and go home. But often, I couldn't find my ball.

And guess who was in the foursome behind me? Eddie Shack. He roared with laughter as my golf balls bounced off trees and drowned in ponds.

For years after, I envisioned Moe Norman giving an interview, perhaps on TV. "Moe, you've played with many of golf's greatest names," he's asked. "But who was the absolute worst golfer you ever played with?"

"Well, there was this klutz in Cobourg I was stuck with one day."

There was never a shortage of hockey topics to chronicle, especially in the years after the '68 expansion. I've already begun a book titled *The Leafs of the Sixties: I Was There!* And another—*Hockey Ha Ha*—the funniest moments in the game. And a third—*Unsung Hockey Heroes.* Maybe a book on the joys of pond hockey. Perhaps I'll finish them, perhaps not. More likely such yarns will be written by others. It may be time (and there may not be a lot of time left) to take the easier road, painting over publishing. But then, my vision is also fading. Perhaps I'll soon be painting ponds that look like potholes or pancakes.

Finally, I'll mention one of the NHL coaches I most admired— Roger Neilson. He touched me deeply with a handwritten letter after a banquet we attended in Peterborough in 1986. It was a roast for Bob Gainey, and Neilson surprised us with some hilarious lines. He was the star. A week later, I received the following:

Dear Brian:

Just a note to let you know how proud I was to be part of your evening at the Kiwanis Centre. The event was far superior to most that I've attended.

You did a really masterful job as MC to round out the roast. There is little doubt that you are one of Canada's most respected hockey broadcasters—and a classy individual as well. Personally, I've always looked forward to seeing you— whether it be for an interview or just a chat.

While my career has been rather turbulent, associations with top people like yourself make it all seem worthwhile. Continued success in the future, Brian. You have made many friends in hockey. Sincerely,

Roger

Roger Neilson was more popular with more fans, more players, and more media types than he ever knew. On a spring night in 1982, he raised a white towel in a gesture of mock surrender, and Towel Power was born.

But our story begins in Quebec City, late in the season—Vancouver versus Quebec. The fans began heckling Canucks head coach Harry Neale. When Neale was peppered with debris, he and his players turned on the howling mob.

When the melee ended, Neale was suspended for the remaining six games of the season.

Neilson stepped in, and the Canucks went undefeated for the rest of the season.

Neale was smart enough to keep Neilson behind the bench for the playoffs. The Canucks swarmed all over Calgary in the first round. In the next round, they faced the L.A. Kings, who were coming off a stunning upset over the Edmonton Oilers.

The Kings were hot, but they couldn't cope with Neilson's magic.

The third round was memorable. The Canucks invaded the old Chicago Stadium and emerged with a double-overtime victory in Game 1.

I was there in the *Hockey Night in Canada* booth for Game 2 and watched the Canucks stumble, dinged with four straight penalties in the second period.

Tiger Williams would later accuse referee Bob Myers of making terrible decisions.

When Myers signalled a fifth penalty to the Canucks, Williams lost his cool. He was about to "throw every friggin' stick on the ice." But Neilson said, "Watch this." He grabbed a spare stick and threw a white towel around the blade. He lifted it high in Myers's face, in mock surrender.

The Chicago mob booed, then roared with laughter.

Neilson's perfect protest won huge support from Vancouver fans watching on television. The Canucks were unbeatable in the next three games as towel-waving fans were everywhere.

For Game 3 in Vancouver, it was a sea of white. More than 16 thousand rabid fans looked on gleefully as the Canucks edged ahead in the series.

The snowstorm was back when the Canucks rolled to another win.

In the deciding game, played in Chicago, the Hawks fell again. Late in the match, they tossed in the towel.

Richard Brodeur's fabulous goaltending and a million towels sent the Canucks into their first-ever Stanley Cup Finals.

But alas, the magic in Neilson's towels was running out. The Isles seized their third straight Stanley Cup and would come right back with a fourth, becoming the first American team to do so.

Neilson is no longer with us, but his impulsive stick wave, with white towel flapping, will forever be remembered.

This is Neilson's five-step plan for the player who wants to have a really solid season. It's the kind of sage advice every young player should heed.

1. Determination

You want to be the best player you can be? This means being the hardest-working player at practice and in the games. You should get to the arena early and be one of the first players ready to hit the ice. Everyone should know that you play hard every shift and never give up, no matter what the score.

2. Leadership

To be a good leader, you must be a good example, both on and off the ice. This means supporting your teammates, following the game plan, giving encouragement when necessary, communicating with your linemates on the ice, and respecting the officials. Good leaders are always alert to all that happens in a game.

3. Setting Goals

In pre-season tryouts, you should have a clear plan on what you must do to make the team. Play to your strengths. If you're a scorer, concentrate on scoring goals. If you're a skater, use your speed by driving wide or busting hard through the middle. If you're a checker, do a superb job of checking, whether it is by use of an alert stick or a solid bodycheck. As the season progresses, the time will come to work on improving your weaker areas.

4. Team First

Be a good team player. Pass the puck to the open player. Keep your shifts the proper length. Listen to your coaches. Help your teammates in battles along the boards. Try and encourage your goaltender. Avoid selfish penalties. Coaches love a good team player.

5. Have Fun

Many players who I coached in minor hockey years later have told me that those were the happiest years of their lives. There's nothing better than playing on a team where everyone works hard and has lots of fun. So, have fun this season!

Looking back on Neilson's advice and my own approach to the game, in junior and university, I took myself aside before each game and said, *You're going to be the best player on the ice tonight. So be ready to give 100 percent.* Sometimes I was the best player, more often I wasn't. But I aspired to be.

And looking over Neilson's five-step plan, I felt I followed all of them. I never had a big-league coach like Neilson to provide a simple common-sense approach. It was easy to reach the same conclusions. And the game was always fun—more fun than any other sport. And remember, skating is the paramount skill. The better you can skate, the more success you will have. And the more fun the game will be.

Perhaps you'll pass Neilson's message along to the young players in your life. (But don't show them any of the naughty words that appeared in this book.)

Perhaps one day soon I'll write something like this:

GOODBYE

Goodbye my friends, it's time to go
To a distant place I do not know
An afterlife perhaps, although I doubt
But what the heck, I'll soon find out
I love you all, family and friends
I know not what Dear God intends
But he knows me well and I truly think
He'll place me beside a hockey rink.

ACKNOWLEDGEMENTS

Somewhere in this book, I reminded editor Michael Holmes that I liked writing other people's stories, not my own. He came to my home and asked me a hundred questions about my life in hockey and that was the starting point for *A Helluva Life in Hockey*. Thank you, Michael. Take a bow.